FIR, OAK AND FERN

ROSS RICHDALE

From Canadian fir forests, oaks of England and onto the fern bush in New Zealand, this family saga centres around four forthright, liberal women, spans five generations, three continents, two world wars, and one hundred years.

The story begins in present day New Zealand when Nicole receives an ancient diary from her Canadian grandmother, Cindy that she begins to read. It begins in 1898 with Amanda's elopement with her beloved Jack and her struggle to survive and prosper away from her domineering father in Washington State. The two begin a new life in Vancouver, Canada where, over the years, she develops a publishing empire.

Her daughter, Dorothy becomes a nurse serving in England. She falls in love with a soldier about to be charged for desertion from the trenches in the Western Front in World War 1. Will he be court-martialled and shot?

In World War 11, Cindy becomes a Land Girl in war torn England and tragedy strikes their family.

Each period in time is filled with drama, joy and sometimes tragedy, but vividly illustrates the determination of each woman to enrich her life through love of partners and families and a liberal outlook on life.

National Library of New Zealand Cataloguing-in-Publication Data

Richdale, Ross, 1941-
Liberty & opportunity
Fir, oak and fern / Ross Richdale.
Originally published 2000 as an E-book under the title: Liberty & opportunity.
ISBN-13: 978-1-877438-02-8
ISBN-10: 1-877438-02-2
1. Richdale, Ross, 1941- Liberty & opportunity. II. Title.
NZ823.3—dc 22

Cover design by Ross Richdale

Published by
Purrbooks
Palmerston North
New Zealand

PROLOGUE

January in the Waikato district of New Zealand was usually hot and dry but the latest summer was about to become the hottest on record as the ongoing drought scorched the rural landscape. Even the trees in the bush looked dull and lifeless with their dust-covered leaves shading the parched grass where even thistles found it hard to grow. A slim, blonde haired woman in brief shorts, loose red blouse and large floppy sun hat ambled along the drive with her sandals squelching in the melting tar. At the gateway of *The Blue Mist Motel* she pulled down the letterbox door and reached for the daily mail that the rural delivery van had just dropped off.

Nicole Tucker sighed as she sorted through the pile of letters. There were three bills, inquiries by the look of them or perhaps cancellations and the usual junk mail. She recognised the writing on a small parcel the letters had been held to by a large rubber band. Grandma had written again. Dear Grandma seemed to quite lonely and enjoyed the letters she wrote. A parcel, though, was unusual.

Nicole grimaced, glanced around at the bush-clad hills, poked the parcel and letters in a plastic bag she had with her and walked back to the motel.

For two years, her partner, Simon McDoyle and herself had been running *The Blue Mist Motel* and camping ground but attempts to build it up as a tourist centre had been only mediocre. She frowned. The scorching weather had driven guests away rather than attracted them. The waterfall, one of the main attractions in the area was now a mere trickle and the stream so shallow visitors could jump across from rock to rock without getting their feet wet.

Of the twelve motel units, only five were in use that night. Three families had cancelled bookings and no casuals had arrived, whereas usually the motel was full and visitors turned away at this time of the year. Also, the campsite was almost empty and only three caravans and two motor homes remained plugged into power sockets. The games room had an empty eerie look usually associated with the winter off-season.

Simon's theory that they fell between the upmarket hotels that catered for overseas tourists and the massive camping grounds and backpackers' places catering for younger people was probably correct. Throughout the country, too, overseas tourist traffic was hit by recent terrorist activities. The busloads, who visited in 2005, the year they bought the property, were a luxury of the past. Nicole sighed again and hoped some rain would arrive soon to settle the dust and replenish the stream.

She walked into the administration block and through the office to the living quarters. Simon should be back from work soon. He'd been doing seasonal farm work for local farmers to supplement their income but all it had really done was make him tired and moody.

*

When the bearded man walked in the door without even taking off his work boots Nicole knew he was in one of his moods. All summer there seemed to be something wrong with the man.

'We need to talk,' he grunted, grabbed a beer out of the refrigerator, sat down at the kitchen table, ripped the tab open and gulped a quarter of the contents down before wiping the froth off his moustache. He burped and Nicole shuddered. He only displayed these shocking manners when he was angry or nervous.

'I guessed that.' She sighed and waited for the outburst. 'Look, this is only a slack period. Once the cooler weather returns and the stream level rises, I am sure the campers will return.'

Simon gulped another mouthful of beer before he fixed his eyes on her. 'It's not the business, Nicole. It is us.' He drank the rest of the can as if he needed sustenance to build up his nerve.

'Well, for God's sake out with it,' retorted Nicole. She considered herself an easygoing, tolerant person but there were limits to her resilience.

The man's eyes turned away. 'There's no way easy of saying this, Nicole. The truth is things have fizzled out between us and I'm leaving.'

Nicole stared at him. 'Just like that,' she whispered. 'After everything we've done together you've decided it is too much of a commitment and you're leaving.'

'It isn't like that. I've just...err...Well, you know.'

'No,' Nicole felt burning anger in her throat. 'I don't bloody know. Pray, tell me.'

'I'm shifting away with Madison Greaves. She's going back to 'varsity in Auckland and invited me along.'

Nicole stood up from the chair where she had been sitting and stared in utter disbelief. She knew Simon and herself had been having a rough patch lately but never suspected there was more to her partner's moods. Madison Greaves, a bubbly girl three or four years younger than herself, was one of the students employed over the summer to help out at the motel.

'You bastard!' she hissed as she thought back over the last month. Of course, in hindsight that could explain a lot. Those late nights home, hay making he said then other feeble excuses over the last week. That was the trouble; she was too trusting and had even blamed herself for not doing enough for their partnership. 'I suppose you've been fooling around with her for weeks.' She glared at her partner and saw he had the grace to flush red. 'No wonder you haven't been so keen with me.'

Simon nodded. 'Well, our relations haven't been much fun lately.'

'Fun!' Nicole screamed. 'That's all you can think about. Fun! Grow up, Simon. Take a few responsibilities in your life.' She stood and walked over to the window so he would not see the tears welling in her eyes. 'Well, I stuck by you, Simon but God knows why. I don't sleep around; I worked hard to try to get this little venture going and invested all my money in it.'

'So have I but...'

Nicole swung around with the embarrassment forgotten. 'Just go, you bastard. Go to Auckland with your young bit of fluff and see how long you last. Don't expect to come crawling back here when she decides the boys there are more fun.' She leaned on the table and fixed her tear filled eyes on him. 'I'll speak to my lawyer and bank manager and arrange finance so I can buy you out of your share of the motel.'

'There's no need,' Simon replied.

Nicole stood back and continued to glare at him before she swallowed and sat down. 'I thought it would work out, the business would pick up and perhaps we'd even get married and have a family,' she whispered, jumped up again in frustration and headed for the door. 'Just bloody go!' she stormed, stomped outside and slammed the door behind her.

*

It wasn't until later that evening after Simon had packed his old station wagon with his belongings and Madison Greaves had discretely left, that Nicole returned to her living room. She sat down and stared around with that numb feeling inside. Part of her felt like crying while her more practical side realised that, in the long run, she would be better off without Simon. His public relations had never been good and on more than one occasion he'd driven irate customers away with his surely attitude.

It didn't look as if anyone would arrive now so Nicole decided she'd get the evening chores around the camp completed, shut the office and have a hot both. As she walked back through the room she spied the mail still sitting on the bench and reached for it. In a half-hearted manner she sliced the motel letters open and filed the bookings; tomorrow would do for any replies. Finally she came to her grandmother's parcel.

She cut the binding, undid the brown wrapping and was about to open the cardboard box inside when a photograph fell out and landed on the counter. Nicole frowned. It was an old black and white photo, quite tatty around the edges and yellowing with age.

She picked it up and studied the image. The photo was of a woman about her own age, dressed in white clothes from the beginning of the last century and standing in front of a suspension bridge. Nicole peered at the woman. The profile of the face looked familiar with a long nose and gentle smile. My God, if it wasn't for the clothes and hair style it could be a photograph of herself.

With shaking hands, she turned the old photograph over. A whiff of the musty paper tickled her nose as she noticed faded writing on the back. It was barely legible but by holding it up to the light at the end of the counter she could just make out the words.

*

Wednesday 8 August 1906
Dearest Diary: With Samuel being a photographer, I can now include a few of his photos with my writings. This is one taken at the Capilano Suspension Bridge in North Vancouver, British Columbia. Yours sincerely Amanda

*

Filled with curiosity, Nicole continued to open the box and found two cloth bound books inside, one with a faded blue cloth cover and the other just as old and but with what would have once been red cloth for its cover. They looked ancient and had the same musty smell of age as the photograph. Her grandmother had included a brief one-page note clipped to the cover of the topmost book. This was unusual as the elderly lady usually wrote heaps.

"Dear Nicole," read the note. "*I haven't been too well lately and decided it was time to pass these diaries onto you. If you take time to read them, they are really self-explanatory. Thanks for your last letter. I hope your motel is coming on okay. Will write a longer letter when I get over this persistent flu virus. Love Grandma.*"

Nicole frowned and opened the top book, the blue one, and realised that it was not printed but filled with handwriting. The faded black ink was flowing, beautifully styled and still quite legible. In spite of the bath she had planned a few moments earlier, she sat down and began to read.

An hour later with the chores and her cheating partner forgotten, she was still engrossed in the writing. It was a diary of the woman in the photograph, her grandmother's grandmother. The words seemed to spring out at her as if they were only written a week earlier.

PART 1 AMANDA 1898

CHAPTER ONE

Monday 19 September 1898
Dear Diary,
The decision is made. Tonight, I am leaving my home of the last twenty years.
Father will not compromise and has banned any association with Jack Williams. Why,
you might ask? Is it only, as he says, because Jack is a Presbyterian and our family is
Irish Catholic? No, I believe it is also because we are the landed gentry and he is but a
poor worker in Father's lumber mill.

We are leaving for Canada and a new life away from this autocratic atmosphere
where women are expected to obey without question. I shall miss Mother but dare not
tell her of my plans because she is sure to pass the information onto Father and he will
carry out his threat.

I attended Mass for the last time ever yesterday and hope God forgives me for
forsaking the Church. Jack is doing the same as we do not believe God only looks down
on one religion; Catholic or Presbyterian. We shall be neither but shall pick a third
faith to follow. I will take my money and the shares given to me for my eighteenth
birthday so Father cannot withdraw them.

As I stare in the mirror I see my auburn hair and freckled nose. Even though I
wish them gone Jack loves my freckles and my curves but I must not be vain.

Have I made the right decision? I only know I love Jack with all my heart and
he loves me in return. Only you, Dear Diary, will unfold the truth as Jack and I move
forward into the new century together. The 1900s are only a little over a year away.
What do they behold?
Sincerely,
Amanda O'Donnell.

*

Amanda blotted the entry and tucked the cloth bound notebook in her cane pouch; it was a bag really that held her clothes and other necessities. She glanced around the bedroom for the last time. Wasn't it strange that to do something for love, one had to become so sad?

She brushed her hair, rolled it up high and put her Sunday frock on. It was probably entirely inappropriate for the horse ride they were about to make but she could think of nothing else to wear. She pulled the especially made bag over her head and tied the strings around her waist, wiggled into her coat, bonnet and gloves and, except for her riding boots, was dressed to leave.

'Honey, are you still awake?' Her mother's voice came up the corridor.

Amanda jumped in fright at the sound and swung back from the dressing table. Her face drained of colour as she stared at the door. If Mother walked in now their plans would be ruined.

'Just reading, Mother,' she called and tried to disguise the quiver in her voice. 'I'll have the light off soon.'

'Don't be long, Honey. Father says you should not let the electric light burn too long or it will overheat.'

'No, Mother,' Amanda replied and pulled the cord so the light went off. 'I've decided to sleep now. See you in the morning.'

'Night, My Love.'

She shivered and stared at the silhouette of the window in the darkened room. The only other light in the house, the one in the main bedroom along the corridor, clicked off and she heard her mother's cough. It was like any other night. Father was at a meeting and would not be back before midnight and by then she'd be long gone. Amanda could just make out the hands of the clock on the mantelpiece. Nine thirty-five! Jack would arrive at ten but promised to wait if there were any delays.

It was a three-hour journey north from their Washington State home to the border into British Columbia. Afterwards they'd continue onto Vancouver. If discovered here in United States she would be brought back home but Canada was a new country beyond Father's influence. She would be safe. Just three hours away! Amanda waited with a pounding heart for almost five minutes before she adjusted the strings of her pouch and grabbed her boots.

She tiptoed to the landing and glanced along the corridor. The door to her three brothers' room was shut. She was the eldest and would miss them, especially five-year-old Jamie. A touch of sadness crossed her mind as she thought back to her only sister, Georgina who would have been nineteen now but had died three years earlier from diphtheria.

Mother's door was open but all was silent. Using her left hand to run fingers along the wall, Amanda made her way to the banister and felt, rather than saw her way down the stairs. Her eyes were open but could see nothing except pitch-blackness.

Suddenly her foot hit something soft and a cat screamed.

Amanda froze!

Shed forgotten Patches slept on the stairs. She reached down, patted the animal and hoped the noise didn't disturb her mother.

Luckily, all remained quiet and Patches seemed content once he realised who it was. He gave a more pleasant meow and followed her to the kitchen. She could feel him by her leg as she crept forward. The kitchen stood silent and eerie in the white reflected light from the window but now, at least, the outline of the bench could be seen. Amanda moved forward and opened the veranda door. Cold air puffed into her face. It was only autumn but already the night temperatures had dropped and snow was close.

'Bye, Patches,' Amanda whispered and patted her pet for one last time. The door squeaked when she pushed it but everything remained still. The barn was across the cobblestone yard and beyond, the lane where Jack would be waiting with Stargo, her horse, already saddled. Everything was going to plan.

She squeezed into her boots and moved across to the barn.

*

'Amanda! Here,' whispered a hoarse voice.

Jack was there, as loyal as ever. Amanda wanted to smile but tears were in the way. She felt his hand, a brief kiss on the cheek and a helping hand up onto Stargo. She hitched her frock and petticoats up and straddled the horse the proper way, not side-saddle as she'd been taught at finishing school.

Even in the comparative safety of Jack's company, she dared not talk but allowed him to lead Stargo away up the lane to the road where a left turn headed north to Canada. There was no going back, not now or ever. She knew that if they were caught, Jack would be horse whipped and herself, banished to a convent. Her father had threatened to do this only two days before. Perhaps the threat was an unexpected benefit for it helped to make their decision to leave a necessity. Amanda moved her one free hand to her breast. The straw pouch was safe and fingers touched her diary. Somehow the book gave her security, more so than any other possession.

At the road Jack turned in the opposite direction from where she expected.

'Jack?' she asked.

'We have to take a back road,' he replied. There's a group of riders on the road and they're heading this way.' He grimaced in the darkness. 'I recognised some of them. They're your father's friends.'

'Oh, my God!' Amanda said. 'You mean they know?'

Jack shrugged. 'Probably not but it would he foolish to ride right past them, wouldn't it? We'll take the fork road around the lumber mill. It's not much further.'

'Jack,' whispered Amanda and stared across at her companion. 'I'm scared. There is no reason for those men to be on the road at this time unless they're looking for something. Are you sure you never told anyone?'

Jack looked tall and the same as ever, clean shaven with a floppy black hat, jacket, trousers and boots. His white teeth smiled in the dull moonlight.

'My Dear,' he said as the two horses increased their pace to a canter. 'It's okay. By breakfast we'll be in Vancouver and free. Now, just relax and let Stargo do the work.'

'I will,' she replied but a nagging doubt filled her mind. Her father was an astute man. Perhaps her willingness to go to church the day before wasn't a good thing. In hindsight, she realised she should have made her usual grumbles. By trying to make everything normal, perhaps she'd made things worse.

'You'll be fine,' Jack encouraged as if he could sense her misgivings. 'Come on. The turn's just ahead.'

Amanda enjoyed riding Stargo and relaxed a little as they turned into the skinny road through the firs. Without Jack, the desolate scene would have been frightening with the towering trees and dark ground beside them. It was cold and already her cheeks felt numb.

Time ticked by. After two more turns they were back on the deserted main highway north of the village. Nobody should be around now, not even the occasional automobile with chugging motors and powerful lights. It was close to midnight when Jack called a halt. In the whole two hours they'd passed nobody and had only seen lights from half a dozen ranch houses.

'Listen!' he hissed.

Amanda strained her ears and heard the clip clop of at least three horses coming up behind them. Her heart raced. It could only mean one thing. They were being followed.

'Come on,' Jack called. 'They're probably following our tracks in the dust. We can't be more than five miles from the border.'

Amanda clicked her heels into Stargo's side and her horse responded. They raced forward at a gallop but Amanda knew the pace was too difficult to maintain. Stargo was already tired. She could not expect him to continue this way. They came to a hilly section where the road curved around through the forest when Amanda called a stop.

'The horses,' she gasped. 'We can't keep this pace up. The poor creatures are exhausted. As if to support her, Stargo whinnied and Amanda bent forward to pat him. In spite of the cold temperatures he was covered in perspiration.

'Right,' said Jack. 'We'll turn back a few yards and go into the trees. With luck, they won't notice. If we can get behind them....' His sentence trailed off into doubt and Amanda could sense his fear.

'There's something you never told me, isn't there?' she asked as they halted, turned and walked the horses back into the trees.

'Your father knew,' Jack gulped. 'He laid a trap. I just avoided it getting to your place.'

'But how?' Amanda gasped.

'I don't know. Perhaps he just guessed...'

For the first time Amanda saw that Jack looked scared. 'Look,' she added. 'Let's get further back in the trees. There's room for us. Whoa Stargo!' She patted the horse again and slid off the saddle. Her bottom felt stiff and the insides of her legs were chaffed. She sniffed back a tear but it was for Jack. If they caught them out here there was no telling what the men would do.

Jack had also dismounted and, without another word, led their horses back down a small slope into a dry creek bed. The moonlight was a mixed blessing. It helped their vision but also lit up the trail for their pursuers.

'Quiet Stargo,' Amanda whispered. She listened. Horses were approaching at a slower speed than earlier but still at a more rapid pace than they could have maintained themselves.

The noise came closer and closer until at least half a dozen horses thundered by immediately above them. Amanda felt a hand in hers and glanced up at Jack. She squeezed his hand and moved back a fraction so her hair brushed against his chin. It wasn't fair. Why was her father such a pig of a man?

'Let's follow this creek bed a bit,' Jack suggested. 'I heard no dogs so that's a good sign.'

Amanda bit on her lip and nodded. It seemed hopeless. "Jack it won't take Father long to realise we're in the trees off the road.. Our only hope is to take the horses to the road and turn them loose. Stargo will return home and your horse will follow.'

Jack grunted and it seemed as if he was about to argue. After all, five miles was a long way to walk. The border could be even further and, if their direction was out, they might never reach it. In this remote countryside the border wasn't even marked. Locals wandered back and forth between the two countries all the time.

'You're right,' he finally conceded and followed Amanda back to the road.

They removed the bits and saddles from the horses and Amanda gave Stargo a small slap on the rump. 'Go home, Stargo,' she commanded. 'Go back to Mother.'

The horse gazed at her, gave a reluctant snort as a final protest and headed back. Jack's horse seemed more enthusiastic and bounded away as soon as it was out of the saddle. The two humans carried the saddles into the foliage and hid them as well as they could behind a rocky outcrop before returning to the creek bed.

The following hour was almost an anticlimax as they made their way forward to a small forest track. Jack slipped a tiny compass from his pocket and watched the needle spin. It could barely be seen in the darkness but he confidently pointed to the left.

'This way,' he whispered and took Amanda's hand.

Hours slipped by and the sky reddened. Amanda was exhausted but refused to stop. Her frock brushed the ground and hair dropped over her shoulders from under her dishevelled bonnet. She envied Jack's more logical clothes that allowed freedom of movement.

'Apple?' asked Jack and pressed one in her hand.

'Thanks,' Amanda smiled at him. 'I'm sorry, My Love. If it wasn't for me...'

Jack stopped, turned and glared at her. 'Cut that out, Amanda,' he said. 'We're in this together. We planned to go to Canada and are still going to do it. Okay?'

'Okay?' she replied and bit into the apple.

*

A crunch of footsteps made Amanda turn. Six men stood up behind them. Sean O'Donnell glared at his daughter and signalled to the others. Amanda recognised the burly men from the lumber mill.

'Well, Amanda,' O'Donnell snarled. In one brief step he was in front of her and slapped her so hard across the cheek, the apple in her hand went flying and she crashed back on the ground.

She screamed and wiped her hand across a bleeding mouth. Jack couldn't help. The furious man was struggling to free himself from two men but his efforts were futile.

'You cowardly bastard!' Jack yelled as Amanda struggled to her feet.

'Your turn will come,' O'Donnell said in a quiet voice and very slowly pulled a long thin cane out from a leather bag attached to his saddle. 'Strip her top off,' he ordered.

Two leering men moved forward and grabbed Amanda. With one tug her frock was yanked down to her waist, her remaining petticoat suffered the same fate and the cane pouch was cut off and tossed away.

'For modesty's sake she can leave the rest on,' O'Donnell hissed. 'Turn the little harlot around.'

Rough hands thrust her, none too gently, over a round rock while Jack screamed and struggled to be free of his captors. With one almighty crash Sean O'Donnell lashed her across the bare back. Excruciating pain, worse than she had ever felt in her life made her scream. Her whole body jerked up and tears rolled down her face. She banged down on the stone and jarred her chin so hard it felt as if her teeth would fall out.

'I shall report you to Father McNeil for this,' she shouted defiantly through her teeth and spat out some blood. 'You may have the town wrapped around your fingers but not Father McNeil.'

O'Donnell had his hand up ready for another lash. He hesitated. The one person in the county not under his control was the local priest. 'Let her go,' he grunted and Amanda felt herself released.

She fell to the ground, stopped and pulled her frock up before turning again towards her father. 'You will never touch me again, Father,' she said. 'Now let Jack go and we'll be on our way.'

'Oh yes, the young man' said O'Donnell. 'You can have him when we've finished, Amanda. He's not even Catholic so Father McNeil won't worry about him. You can watch and see what happens to heathens who go around raping my daughter. No court in the United States will convict me for a right and just punishment.'

He turned and was about to give an order when Amanda heard another voice, a calm clear voice that everyone else also heard.

'Not yours, maybe, but ours will. In the name of Her Majesty's Government, you will stop and drop all your arms.'

Amanda stared in the direction of the voice. In the pale dawn light, a man dressed in a red jacket, lemon squeezer hat, brown riding trousers and knee high black boots, stood with a rifle in his hand.

'The name is Dutton, Sergeant Anthony Dutton of the Northwest Mounted Police. You men are illegal immigrants into Canada.'

O'Donnell leaped around and his hand went for a gun but stopped half way there. There was a click of a bolt and the Canadian moved his rifle up ever so slightly.

'I wouldn't,' he said. 'I don't know about The United States but in Canada it is against the law to assault women.' He grimaced. 'If you want to try anything...' He added no more but two more red-coated men, with rifles aimed and ready, stepped out from the trees, both.

'You have no authority here,' O'Donnell snarled but made sure his hands were free and away from his gun. 'This is the State of Washington.'

A rifle cracked. Amanda screamed but her voice was obliterated by the sound. One of O'Donnell's henchmen stumbled. The man groaned and stared at his blood stained arm where a bullet had hit him.

'You're half a mile within Canadian territory,' Sergeant Dutton said softly as clicked back the bolt and expelled the expired cartridge from his rifle. He turned. 'Constable, if you'd be kind enough to give the lady a hand.'

Amanda found a hand grab hers and a Mountie, hardly her age, assisted her up. 'You're safe now, Ma'am,' he said. 'Welcome to Canada.'

She glanced across and saw Jack had been released and her father's men were backing up with their hands behind their heads. It was only when her eyes met Jack's and she saw the compassion that she allow the tears to flow.

Jack stared at O'Donnell. 'You are not even a man,' he spoke quietly but with venom in his voice. 'No man would treat his daughter in the manner you have just done. My God, it is almost 1900, not the 1830s. You are even too gutless to do anything on your own but had to use six great oaths to hold us down. Six!' Jack repeated and spat on the ground.

O'Donnell's face was black. He almost stepped forward towards the pair but hesitated when a Mountie click a rifle bolt.

Jack gave Amanda a tiny kiss on the forehead and turned her around so her back was exposed. She couldn't see it, of course, but could feel the throbbing ugly welt crossed across her back Blood dripped onto her clothes.

Jack turned to O'Donnell. 'My advice is to never come near Amanda or myself again. If you do, then, I promise God I shall repay this brutal punishment with interest.'

He took a handkerchief out of his pocket; quietly dabbed the punctured skin before doing the buttons of Amanda's frock up. Three were missing and the front was torn but she was now covered. When he had finished she spun around and buried her face in his chest.

'I'm okay,' she whispered and stepped back. Her eyes bore into her father. 'I always found you a strict but honourable man, Father. Until now, that is. I want nothing to do with you again and hereby renounce my association with the O'Donnell family. My only regret is for that of my mother.'

'If you ever come across the border, my girl...' threatened O'Donnell. 'You are under age and I have the legal right to discipline you any way I see fit.'

He was about to say more when Jack stepped forward. With one almighty swing, his closed fist connected with O'Donnell's chin. The man sprawled to the ground. He gave a howl of rage and dived at Jack but was stopped by a Mountie who stepped forward and pointed a rifle at the man's chest.

'I wouldn't,' he hissed.

'Hold it, Son,' Sergeant Dutton said at the same time to Jack who stood with bleeding knuckles ready for the fight. 'He's not worth it.' He turned to O'Donnell and his men. 'Your rifles stay here but I will give you fifteen minutes to retreat back across the border. If any of you show your face in British Columbia again, you'll be arrested for assault on a woman.'

O'Donnell stared with his face flush with anger. However, the three Mounties stood firm ready to fire, if necessary.

'It is now thirteen minutes,' Dutton said.

'Come on, boys,' O'Donnell said. His eyes stared at Amanda but she avoided the dark look. The rifles dropped on the ground and the men walked away.

'Oh Father,' Amanda called out just before the group disappeared.

The man glared back.

'Not that you care but I am still a virgin. You may wish to tell Mother that.' She swung around so his reaction could not be seen.

'Now go,' Dutton instructed.

*

After O'Donnell had vanished, Dutton turned to Amanda and Jack. 'I am afraid your horses have gone but if you don't mind riding together you can have one of ours.'

'Thank you, Anthony. Can I call you that?' Amanda replied.

'No,' answered the sergeant with a grin. 'My friends call me Tony.'

'Tony it is,' Amanda said and slipped her hand into Jack's.

As the morning sun began to rise in the east, the Mountie police and two rescued Americans turned into a wider path. Amanda noticed a tiny red and white post on the roadside.

'The border,' grunted Tom.

'You mean!' gasped Amanda.

'Yes,' replied one of the other Mounties. 'That's why we let your father go. We were at least two miles inside Washington State.'

'Oh my God!' Amanda said. 'You did this all for us. How did you know where we were?'

Jack grinned and continued the story. 'Last Wednesday, I came up to BC and arranged for Tony to meet us at the border. I knew that if your father chased us he wouldn't be stopped by any little post in the ground.

'We realised you were late and decided to investigate,' Tony continued. 'The chance of anyone else being in this part of the forest was extremely remote.

'And you risked this all for us,' she whispered. 'How can I thank you?'

'Just don't tell anyone,' Tony replied.

'About what?' In spite of her painful back, Amanda felt relief flow through her body. 'As a loyal Canadian citizen I wouldn't dream of breaking any of Her Majesty's laws.'

*

Since the arrival of the Canadian Pacific Railway a few years previously, Vancouver had mushroomed. Everywhere, new buildings were rising. Carriages, horseback riders and even some automobiles crowded the wide streets. Amanda was impressed. It was now morning and the city was waking up. The only differences from home were the Mounties and the flagpoles where the Union Jack fluttered instead of the Stars and Stripes.

After a few formalities, Amanda was taken to a doctor who bathed her wound and declared her a brave young lady. Afterwards she was booked into the *Prince Albert Hostelry for Young Ladies* while Jack had to be contented with less pretentious accommodation closer to the waterfront.

'I'll be fine,' she said to Jack by the hostelry's entrance. She reached into her cane bag and took out some money. 'If they take American dollars I could do with a new blouse, though. Can you buy me one, My Dear?'

Jack flushed bright red but nodded. 'Having a beautiful young lady to look after is an awesome responsibility,' he said in a solemn voice.

'Don't worry,' Amanda replied just as seriously. 'I can look after myself. If you'd rather not...'

'No,' Jack retorted and squeezed her hand. 'One new blouse coming up.' He turned and disappeared down the sidewalk.

'Your fiancée?' asked the proprietress who had overheard the conversation.

'Almost!' Amanda grinned and walked inside.

*

CHAPTER TWO

Thursday 20 October 1898:
Dear Diary,

I must apologise for neglecting my entries but it is silly to write every day when nothing really happens. I notice I now tend to make several long entries well spread out. But so be it.

It is over a month now since our arrival in Vancouver and life has settled into a routine. Jack has been a perfect gentleman, so much so I could almost scream. I swear I'll have to do something about the situation.

The Prince Albert allows no men indoors but the cellar is fitted out for these men to become gratified as Suzanne (one of the girls) calls it. It seems the cellar isn't counted as indoors.

Poor Jack is depressed lately as he can only get casual labourer's job working ten hours a day for a dollar fifty. I must admit my money is going too but I won't tell Jack.

One good arrangement. I sold my shares in Father's firm and made a wee profit when, on my broker's advice, bought into Canadian Pacific Railway. It's safer than money in the bank Mr. Houghton, that's the broker, told me. Strange man he is, but once he swallowed his pride and agreed to take a woman on as a client, was very helpful. One would think our different shape changes our ability to use our brains or is it that men don't want to lose their control?

Once again, Dear Diary, this is our secret. I haven't told Jack about the shares, as it would only make him feel inadequate, which, I assure you, he isn't.

Sincerely,
Amanda O'Donnell

*

Amanda smiled as she reread her entry and glanced out the bedroom window. It was upstairs and provided a view over the veranda and along the busy street where horse drawn carriages and an occasional automobile competed with pedestrians who seemed to wander everywhere. She grinned. Jack was bustling along the street with an envelope in his hand. He stopped, spied her in the window and waved wildly.

'Amanda,' he shouted after she'd opened the window and waved back in a most unladylike fashion, 'I've something to show you!' He acted excited.

'Be right down,' she replied and again, without considering how a lady should behave, gathered up her skirt and dashed downstairs.

Jack took her two hands and almost kissed her on the public street in front of everyone he was so elated. 'I got a job,' he said. 'A proper job! You said my steam certificate would help and it did.'

'Well, tell me,' she answered and guided her friend over to one of the cane chairs on the veranda.

'It's as a trainee locomotive driver on the Canadian Pacific Railway.' He grinned and handed her the envelope.

Amanda pulled the letter out, saw the Canadian Pacific Shield with the picture of a beaver and smelt a whiff of new paper. Underneath was the usual introduction but Amanda skipped her eyes down to the important part.

'We hereby appoint you as Trainee Locomotive Driver, 2nd Class, to be employed the Canadian Pacific Railway. After a period of training, you will assist in the running of locomotives within British Columbia and Alberta.' She read the page orally before gazing up with a look of surprise and continued to read the next sentence. *'The wages shall be at the rate of 60 cents an hour rising to 90 cents on the completion of training.'*

'Not too bad is it?'

'Jack,' said Amanda. 'That's wonderful! It's even more than your pay at Father's mill. You're going to accept, aren't you?'

'There's one tiny problem,' Jack coughed as if he was embarrassed. 'Read the next paragraph, Amanda.'

Amanda nodded and read on. 'It says a house is provided for your wife and yourself.' She glanced up at her companion. 'So what? '

Jack flushed. 'Only married men were allowed to apply,' he muttered.

'But you aren't.' An impudent look appeared on her face. She was beginning to enjoy the direction the conversation was leading.

'No,' muttered Jack. 'I'm not but I really want to be.' He looked at his feet that didn't seem to know where to be placed.

'Well, damn well ask then,' she retorted and went crimson herself. This was the first time she'd sworn in front of Jack though the girls often did it when they were alone together.

'But you're Catholic.' The man looked thoroughly miserable.

'Was!' Amanda flung back her auburn hair and glared at Jack. 'We can get married with a Justice of the Peace. I turn twenty-one next month so need nobody's approval.'

Jack glanced up and their eyes met. Suddenly he smiled. 'You don't mind?'

'No,' said Amanda. She laughed and touched his lips with her fingers. 'Well?'

'What?'

'Are you going to ask me?'

'Oh yes, ' he said. 'Amanda will you marry me?'

'There is a condition,' she answered in a sombre voice.

Jack nodded but looked apprehensive.

'Our marriage is to be a partnership,' Amanda stated with her eyes intense. 'I am not going to give away my rights to be free and to think for myself. I will not become your property like poor Mother, who is scared to move without Father's permission. It is almost 1900 and I believe women should be equal in all ways. We should be able to vote, to run a business or do whatever we wish.' She grabbed Jack's jacket sleeve. 'If you don't agree to that, well...' Her voice trailed off.

Jack fixed her with an equally intense stare. 'Have I ever stopped you doing anything, Amanda?'

'No, My Love, you haven't but I just want to be sure. That's all.' She smiled. Until now she had made most of the decisions, anyway, not that Jack was a wimp...

'I agree, Amanda,' Jack continued but hesitated again. 'They need a reply within ten days so...'

'Straight after my birthday, then,' Amanda directed. She swung her arms around his neck, kissed him and made sure her bosom rubbed against his chest. Too bad if it was not the thing a young lady did on a public street. 'If you walk along the fire escape tonight about eleven I'll let you in my room.'

Jack stared. 'Men aren't allowed?'

'Why worry,' Amanda retorted. 'I'm sick of being a goody good.'

*

On Friday, November the fourth 1898, Amanda turned twenty-one and was awakened by a knock on her bedroom door. She tumbled out of bed, shivered in the chilly air and opened the door.

'Jack,' she gasped. 'What are you doing here?'

He stood grinning with a large box in his hand. 'Yeah, I know I usually come in the window but I have a birthday present for you.' He held the box forward and kissed her cheek.

'Come in,' Amanda said. 'Half the hostelry knows of your nocturnal visits, anyway.'

She almost skipped across to the bed and pulled the large red ribbon apart to discover inside a beautiful gown, all cream and full of lace.

'Jack!' cried Amanda and held it against herself. 'It's simply wonderful.' She swung around. 'Where did you get it? There's nothing in Vancouver this fabulous. How could you afford it?' She laid the garment on the bed and flung her arms around her lover. 'Oh, Jack,' she wept and buried her head in his chest.

'It's your wedding dress, Amanda,' he said. 'I bought it from New York through a mail catalogue. I hope it fits and as for the cost that's for me to know isn't it?'

'Jack!' Amanda said. 'I'm sure it will fit just right.' She stopped. 'However, you are not going to see until our wedding.'

'It's tomorrow, Saturday,' gulped Jack.

'What?' Amanda retorted.

'Our wedding. I've booked in at the courthouse at ten. You're twenty-one now, so...' He seemed all flustered again. 'I know we agreed to share all our decisions but...'

Amanda tried to look serious. 'My God you've got the cheek, Mr. Williams.... but I'll forgive you this time.' Her mouth broke into a smile as she picked up the gown and held it to her body again. 'Thank you, My Darling. Thank you.'

*

The next day, a small group of friends gathered in an anteroom of the courthouse for Amanda's and Jack's wedding. He looked dashing in his hired black suit but all eyes were on the bride as she stepped from the carriage in the cream frock with full skirt and high-laced collar. She never told Jack but it took the girls at the hostelry and herself most of the day to get the frock fitting just right.

After the very brief ceremony the new Mrs. Williams turned and saw someone familiar in the small crowd.

'Mother!' she screamed.

Amanda rushed down and grabbed her mother in her arms.

'Jack wrote and invited me,' Dorothy O'Donnell cried. 'Sean banned me from coming but I told him to go to hell.' The older woman held her daughter out in her two arms. 'How could I not come to my own daughter's wedding? You look so beautiful, My Dearest.'

'Oh Mom,' Amanda cried and held her mother close. 'I never wanted to leave you but I couldn't stay.'

'I understand,' Dorothy O'Donnell smiled through her own tears. 'You know, I heard you leave that night. I cried but knew you had your own life to lead.' She glanced back at Jack waiting patiently a step behind. 'I couldn't have picked a finer man.'

'Thank you, Mrs. O'Donnell,' Jack replied in a gruff voice.

He reached his arm around Amanda's waist and guided her on, through the well-wishers to the waiting carriage. Their wedding may have lacked the pomp and glandular of a church but in their eyes it was everything they wanted.

'Thank you for asking Mother, Dear,' Amanda whispered to her husband as the horses pulled the carriage away.

Jack grinned at her and, without a word, reached across and placed an arm around her. The proud look in his eyes portrayed all that was needed on that, their wedding day.

*

Their honeymoon was on Vancouver Island. They caught the ferry to Victoria, a beautiful town that was now the capital of British Columbia. Three days were spent in a delightful little hotel doing all the things newly weds did. Jack was due to start work in a week and their new railway home was waiting for them to shift into.

When they stepped off the ferry back in Vancouver, a carriage was waiting for them. Dorothy O'Donnell stood beside it with a tiny smile on her face.

'I have a wedding present for you, Dear,' she said after she had hugged them both and their bags were all placed in the carriage. 'Well, it's more for you than Jack but I'm sure he will not mind.'

'What is it, Mother?' Amanda asked. The air of mystery intrigued her.

'Oh you just wait,' Dorothy replied. 'Driver, to the shop if you please.'

'Shop! What shop, Mother?' Amanda sensed it had something to do with the present. Probably there was a gift to pick up.

'Oh, my impatient daughter, you just wait and see.' Her mother chuckled and turned to Jack. 'She is so brazen isn't she, Jack?'

'Yes,' he replied and grinned when Amanda slapped his arm.

The coach travelled through the crowded streets to the downtown area and turned into Cordova Street. Amanda stared at the three and four storied buildings towering above each side of the road. Electric power poles strung wires above the pavement and in the centre of the road, ran the rails of the brand new street railway.

'They're killing our business,' shorted their cab driver as a BCER electric rail car hissed by with a clack, clack of the steel wheels on the rails.' Passengers could be seen gripping on the open interior. 'Damn things are allowed to travel twelve miles an hour.' He glanced back and saw Amanda's excited face. 'Sorry about the bad language, Ma'am.'

'I've heard worse,' she replied.

'Well, at least the horses are used to them now. You should have seen the fuss when they first arrived. Terrified horses everywhere.'

'We need to have progress,' Jack added.

'Yes, I suppose so,' the cabby replied and pulled in next to an ornate building towering above them.

The ground floor consisted of a line of shops opening directly onto the pavement, barbershops, emporiums, fashion shops and banks. When Amanda alighted she saw two workmen erecting a brand new sign above the front windows of one slim shop with the two large display windows filled with books.

"O'Donnell and Williams, Stationers and Booksellers" it stated in curly brown letters painted against a green background.

'What's this, Mom?' Amanda asked with a puzzled expression.

Dorothy smiled. 'I am quite a rich old lady, Amanda,' she said. 'That lumber mill of your father's is really mine. It belonged to your grandfather, my father. You were only five when he died and, since I had no brothers, everything came to me. Sean was only a foreman at the lumber mill in those days.' She sighed. 'I foolishly let him take control and you know what happened?'

Amanda glanced at Jack, saw his look of support and nodded for her mother to continue.

'I wasn't a complete fool though, Amanda. I kept some investments back. Those shares we gave you were really mine, not Sean's, and I sold others to buy this shop.'

'Yours!' gasped Amanda and looked at her mother in a new light.

'You're half right, My Darling,' said Dorothy. 'Only one third is mine.'

'And the rest?' Amanda felt a little buzz inside and clasped Jack's hand.

Dorothy turned and stared at her. 'My lawyers have drawn up the papers, Amanda. One-third share is for you and one third for Jack. I've made them clearly separate, just in case.' She coughed and glanced at Jack, 'Also, if you agree, you are appointed Managing Director. This book shop is for you Amanda; your little business to run how you please. I am merely a silent partner.' She turned to the young man listening. 'I hope you understand and approve, Jack.'

Jack let Amanda's hand go and stepped forward to place his hands on Dorothy's waist. 'I think this is a wonderful thing to do, Mom; I hope I can call you that.'

Dorothy nodded.

'The last thing I want is for Amanda to sit at home washing dishes and sweeping floors.'

Jack bent forward and gave his mother-in-law a kiss on the cheek.

Amanda just stared, flabbergasted, at the sign. She blinked tears from her eyes and turned to her mother. 'Mom, this is the most wonderful thing you've done. Thank you.' She moved in beside Jack and flung her arms around them both. 'And I thought I'd never see you again. I thought you'd tell Father all my plans. I treated you so badly, Mom, and you do this for me.'

'Well,' said her mother. 'I'm still part owner; you know and will want progress reports. Let's go in. The previous owner told me she'll stay on for two weeks to help you settle in. It's a lovely little shop in a good commercial area.'

Amanda was almost in a trance as she walked through; met Mrs. Hoffman, the elderly lady proprietress and present owner, and stared at the neat rows of books along the walls, the tiny stationery section and the long varnished counter. In the middle of the highly polished floor, a pop bellied stove radiating warmth throughout the shop. It was like a dream. She loved books and reading. Her mother knew that.

'You take over next week', Mrs. Hoffman said. 'It's a good time of the year with Christmas coming up. December is my busiest month.'

'Well Amanda?' her mother said after they left the shop. 'Do you want to staff it yourself or shall we employ a manager?'

'Mom.' Amanda said. 'What do you think?' She turned to Jack. 'Oh My Dear, you don't mind, do you?'

Jack grinned. 'We have a partnership, My Love,' he replied and gave her a hug. 'I can think of nothing better than having a shop proprietor for my wife.' Amanda beamed and kissed her husband fully on the lips. 'I love you,' she whispered before she turned back to her mother.

Dorothy coughed and pretended she didn't see the display of emotion.

'One other thing,' she said. 'Your father doesn't know about this. In fact, he doesn't even know I'm in Canada and has banned mention of your name at home.'

'He would,' retorted Amanda with anger appearing in her eyes.

'Anyhow, I have a mail box in Bellingham so you can write to me there.'

Bellingham was the small town just across the border in Washington State and the closest centre of population to the lumber mill where Amanda's old home was.

'Oh Mom, you've thought of everything.'

'I hope so but please Amanda, and you too Jack.' Dorothy's eyes grew tight. 'Don't go back across the border, even for a visit. Your father is a dangerous man. If either of you step into Washington State...' She stopped and swallowed. 'Don't come home at all. I'll keep in touch by mail and I'll try to visit when I can. If there are any emergencies, don't phone me. Telephone Mrs. Beattie, our neighbour, and she'll come to me. I'll leave her number with you.'

'I will,' Amanda replied and felt the scar across her back give a twitch. She knew what her father was like.

'Right,' replied Dorothy. 'Now let me see your new home. You're lucky to have a railway house. I've heard they're very comfortable.' She smiled at Jack. 'I'll call another cab.'

'No,' said Amanda. 'Let's ride the street railway. Our new house is only a block away from the line.'

*

'I'm beginning to like your mother,' Jack whispered a few moments later as they rode in the swaying rail car towards New Westminster and their suburb.

'Me too,' Amanda replied. 'She has more spunk than I thought.'

'Yes, I wondered where you got your determination from, My Love,' He laughed at Amanda's look of disdain. 'Come on; tell your mom we get off at the next stop.'

Arm in arm, the two newly weds climbed off the electric rail car and headed towards their new home with Mrs. Dorothy O'Donnell walking up the rear with a proud look on her face.

The house was quite tiny but provided everything they needed. There was electricity, gas and running hot water; something even their house in Washington never had. The narrow downstairs had a parlour at the front, kitchen and living room behind and a laundry out the back in the tiny yard. Up the narrow stairs were two bedrooms and a bathroom with a proper tin bath. Everything in the brand new building smelt of fresh wood.

Amanda walked through the rooms and sighed. 'My God, what a day,' she whispered. 'It's like a dream. I keep thinking I'll pinch myself and find myself back in my little room in Washington with Father growling outside.' She caught her mother's eye and stuttered. 'I'm sorry, Mom, I really loved it at home but just I grew up, I guess.'

'I know what you mean,' Dorothy replied. 'Your father was always a hard man. Still is,' she added in a sad voice.

'Then why go back to him?'

'For your brothers, Amanda. They need me like you did. Until they grow up, I need to be there for them.'

'Of course you do,' Amanda replied and felt annoyed with herself for the outburst. 'Remember we can help if you want us. We may be in a different country but it isn't really far away.'

'Thank you, My Darling,' Dorothy replied. 'You've grown into a young woman to be proud of.' She laughed. 'But I already told you that didn't I?'

The two women's eyes met for a moment. Amanda, however noticed that her mother's eyes looked so sad and even lonely. She nudged Jack.

'Yes,' he said with empathy in his tone. 'If you ever need our help, just contact us. Any time.'

*

CHAPTER THREE

Monday 1 January 1900
Dear Diary,
Yes, it is here. The new century has arrived. Jack and I mixed with the thousands of citizens last night to welcome it in at Stanley Park. The fireworks were so spectacular I'm sure our Chinese citizens provided the expertise.

I have a contribution to make to the new century, Dear Diary, as I am with child and have been so since the middle of the year. I was afraid my growing anatomy would make me unattractive for Jack but he just laughs and feels my tummy before telling me I am the most beautiful woman on Earth. That's what Jack is like. It is evening and he is now asleep on the couch.

I have been married for over a year now and love Jack with all my heart. I must admit, though, in the earlier days of our marriage he was often in too much of a hurry to bed me. He'll do anything for me before we consummate our marriage, yet again.

Onto other matters. Jack loves his job and now drives the Imperial Limited once a week to Calgary. He is away over night and brings the westbound express back to Vancouver. Each trip is a long two days but afterwards he has a day at home.

My little shop keeps me occupied. I now have an assistant called Sally McCorkindale, a sweet young woman who is very keen. I write to Mother on a regular basis and receive mail from her in return. My younger brothers are well and Father is the same. I don't know why she puts up with him.

Our big excursion to Toronto is almost here. Next month Mother and the boys are travelling on the Imperial Limited with me to visit publishers there. (Yes, it is the one Jack drives as far as Calgary). We hope to restock the shop with the latest books from the East, New York and even London. We'll be away two weeks so I hope poor Jack can tend to his own needs. Men can be so helpless at times.

Sincerely,
Amanda Williams.

*

It was just before seven in the morning and the pride of the Canadian Pacific Railway, The Imperial Limited, stood waiting at the station ready to commence its journey east to Montreal a hundred hours and a continent away. Jack waved out the cab of the massive steam 4-4-0 locomotive, as Amanda's four brothers dashed along the platform and joined him. Peter, Jeffrey and Jamie were enthralled at the privilege of being able to visit the cab and even cynical seventeen year old Abraham was impressed by the massive coal burning engine with roaring fire, brass levers and dials everywhere. However, it was soon time for them to take their seats in the third carriage for the journey east.

'Are you sure you'll be strong enough for the trip, Dear?' Dorothy O'Donnell asked her daughter yet again as Amanda sat down in the comfortable padded seat.

'I'm fine, Mom,' she said. 'The worst is over.' She switched her eyes to her eldest brother and gave him a glare as if she dared him to make a remark about her size. Abraham grinned but it was Jamie who spoke up.

'I don't like you fat, Amanda,' he said in a mournful voice. 'When will you be all beautiful and slim again?'

'Not long Jamie,' Amanda laughed and rubbed her youngest brother's hair. 'In a little over a month you'll be Uncle Jamie. Won't that be grand?'

'I guess,' the youngster shrugged but his attention turned to other matters. 'We're moving,' he yelled and almost tumbled over his sister to get to the window.

There was a hiss of steam; a jerk and the mighty train chugged forward. Slowly at first as the platform disappeared, the Imperial Limited moved through the railway yards, past dozens of carriages and wagons of every size; huge freight cars with opened doors, completely sealed grain cars, lumber wagons piled high with logs and tiny shunter locomotives belching smoke into the freezing morning air.

The O'Donnell boys sat glued to the windows as the city unfolded beside the tracks while the two women took a more genteel interest in the world outside.

'How did you persuade Father to let the boys come?' Amanda asked.

'I guess I took a page out of my daughter's book of methods and simply told him we needed to go to the east to purchase new books and I was taking the family with me.' She gave a tiny smile. 'I think he was quite relieved he wasn't left to look after them. You know now how he hates to do anything in the house.'

'But with me?' Amanda continued.

'Oh, he's okay. In fact, I think he was quite proud to know he'll become a grandfather soon.' Dorothy gave a little frown. 'He did count back the months from baby's arrival time, though.'

'He would and I bet he didn't wait until your wedding night.'

Dorothy stared at her daughter, 'Amanda,' she snapped. 'The boys will hear.'

'Well,' said the younger woman. 'It's true isn't it?'

Dorothy frowned for a moment and stared out the window before her eyes caught Amanda's and a crimson flush ran through her cheeks.

'I know,' Amanda laughed and squeezed her mother's arm. 'Don't tell Father but Jack and I didn't wait.'

'Amanda!' Dorothy gasped. 'Ladies shouldn't talk about these things.'

'I know Mom but it's a pity, isn't it?'

Her mother smiled and nodded. In the last few months the two had become quite close and had discussed things like two adults rather than the earlier situation of an austere woman lecturing a naive teenager.

Dorothy grinned again but changed the topic. 'The shop's doing well, isn't it?'

Amanda laughed. 'Oh Mom,' she added and stood up. 'I've got the call of nature, again. In my condition it's always happening,' she added and walked through the carriage to find the women's toilet at the end far of the carriage.

*

By the time Locomotive 1073 pulled out of Revelstoke Station, huge snowflakes had begun to drop onto the snow-covered forest. Ahead was the notorious Roger's Pass with its miles of zigzag tracks covered in snow sheds with huge sloping roofs above the lines. The snow at the moment had piled onto them and sections were already sliding off down the mountainside. However, under the structure, the line was free of snow and the Imperial Limited rumbled on.

Inside Carriage 3, the O'Donnell boys stared fascinated out the open side of the snow shed at the world of white below. Drifts were now so high it was almost like a tunnel as the mighty express rumbled on. Black smoke from the coal-burning engine swirled down and, even with all windows closed; the sooty smell filled the carriage and made passengers cough.

In the cab, Jack watched the pressure gauge and eased the throttle back slightly. Traction and power were more important than speed. Ahead, the powerful front light bathed the track in white light and steam hissed through the massive pistons driving them forward.

'These big wheels are all very well on the plains and give you speed,' he shouted to his stoker, Andy Carmichael, 'but in these mountains I prefer the older locomotives. Sure, they're slower but have more traction on these steep sections.'

'Sure!' grunted Andy. He scooped another shovel of coal into the fiery furnace and stood up. Perspiration rolled off his glistening muscles as he wiped a sooty hand over his brow. He leaned on the shovel for a few moments rest before starting again.

The locomotive slowed to almost a walking pace as they entered Snow Shed 8. Light faded into semi-darkness and smoke bellowed in around the two men in the cab. Jack coached more power into the slapping pistons and checked the stream pressure gauge that hovered on the edge of the red danger section.

He smiled and glanced back across the wide curve of carriages behind them. Smoke shot away through the freezing weather and the air in the cab became breathable again. Andy opened the fire door and shovelled in half a dozen loads of coal, shut it again and poked his head out the window into the freezing air.

'Roger's Pass Station coming up,' he yelled.

The tiny wooden station was largely abandoned now the snow sheds had been completed but a maintenance gang still used the building for gear and as a staff canteen.

Jack grunted and prepared to open the throttle. The worse of Roger's Pass was now through. Suddenly he saw that the signal beyond the station was down. The express had to stop! He shut the throttle and applied the brakes throughout the train. Wheels screamed and excess steam, not needed now, vented out while the whole train slowed to a crawl. The locomotive driver hoped the signal would change but it didn't. Damn, he would have to bring the train to a complete halt.

The locomotive came to a hissing stop in front of the down signal. Jack placed his head out the window into the frigid air and waited impatiently for the signal to change but it remained down. A man came bustling out of the station and rushed over to the locomotive.

'I've had a telegraph message from Lake Louise,' he yelled up at the cab. 'The last train through reported a huge build up of snow. The conditions are bad.'

'But is the line open?' Jack screamed back. His voice was almost lost in the howling storm and hissing engine noises.

'Just!' screamed back the man. 'I'd only give it an hour.'

'That should be enough,' Jack grumbled. He didn't want a trainload of passengers stranded in these conditions.

*

In Carriage 3, the O'Donnell boys rushed to the window while Amanda stood up and stretched her rotund body. She felt stiff from lack of movement, her back ached and baby was kicking like crazy.

She grinned at her mother. 'I'm off back to the toilet, Mom,' she said. 'See you soon.'

'Right Dear,' Dorothy replied and switched her attention back to the novel she was reading.

The tiny cubical that held the toilet was so small Amanda had to manipulate her body in sideways and, once there, she could barely close the door.

*

Jack heard a roar like thunder and saw thousands of tons of accumulated snow in the misty mountainside topple and slide downwards. Within seconds it became a mammoth avalanche heading directly towards them. Even though the signal was still down he made the instantaneous decision to start the train moving.

'Hang on!' he screamed to Andy who stared, opened mouthed out the inside window.

Jack opened the throttle, increased steam pressure and released the brakes. The wheels spun on the icy rails, gripped and the mighty express edged forward.

'Come on! Come on!' Jack cursed as the screaming thunder of the avalanche could be heard above the roar of their engine..

Smoke bellowed out the chimney and hissing pistons did their job. The locomotive was past the signal box as were the first two carriages.

'Keep her going!' screamed Andy who watched behind while Jack concentrated on the line ahead.

The heavily laden train, though, had no chance. Jack watched the wall of snow sweep the wooden station building aside. The walls and roof just snapped and crumbled, buried in the deluge. Jack knew it was too late and pulled on the emergency brakes. Wheels screamed and steam hissed but it was to no avail.

The avalanche struck the express two carriages back from the cab.

In a scream of timber, voices, ice and snow, the second carriage was flung off the tracks by the avalanche, tossed upside down and buried in a mountain of snow. Jack stared in numb horror. Everything behind Carriage 1 was gone. In seconds the raw power of nature had buried the carriages under in a thousand tons of snow. Clouds of airborne ice and snow hit the locomotive cab, glass shattered and the last thing Jack remembered was being flung to the steel floor and searing pain as his head hit a lever.

*

Carriage 3 crumbled under the pressure and movement of the avalanche. Voices of terror screamed out unheard as the roof and walls collapsed. Those not killed beneath the timber superstructure were engulfed in snow. It was complete and utter annihilation! Over thirty humans, including the O'Donnell family, had their lives snuffed out in those few terrible seconds. What thoughts entered their minds, indeed if they even had time to form them, nobody would ever know.

When the avalanche hit, the end of Carriage 3 was flung up, ripped away from the following carriages and propelled down the mountainside, along with the splintered wood from the station and snapping fir trees. However, one massive tree caught the carriage, three quarters of the way back and sliced through it like a lumber saw. The motion sent the remaining section off on a tangent into another tree, down a gully and finally into a gigantic snow bank where it stopped.

*

Amanda screamed hysterically throughout the ordeal as she was flung around the tiny toilet cubical. Her head hit the ceiling; she was upside down; a steel pipe slammed into her stomach and her body whiplashed back.

Purple clouds floated through her mind. Her eyes did not want to open but she forced them to. Her head pounded and she felt another pain. Her lower body was in agony and she felt wet from the inside, not out.

'My God!' she screamed. 'My baby!'

The distraught young woman realised three things in that instant; she was alive, the cubicle had stopped moving and her water had burst. Wanted or not at that time, her baby was coming into the world. Another spasm shot through her body, so sever Amanda bit on her lip and blood filled her mouth.

'Help me!' she cried but she was alone in that tiny toilet thirty feet below the locomotive and what was left of the railway track.

*

Time was meaningless. All Amanda's thoughts were on the birth, the contractions and the realisation that her baby was coming. It was cold stuffy and dark but, all alone in that confined space, the young mother removed her underwear so the baby would have room. Perspiration poured off her body as she grabbed a door handle, the only thing available and pushed...

The agony continued on and on. Her screams turned to sobs until after an eternity, she realised her baby was there in the cubical crying.

Amanda reached down and tried to remember what do. Her eyes felt heavy. Nothing seemed real. Everything was a dream, a terrible nightmare.

She woke and realised she had passed out. The infant was in her arms with her coat around it and the knotted umbilical cord down its side.

She had no recollection of having wrapped up the baby but she must have done it. There was nobody else there. The cubicle was splattered in blood but baby was alive and still crying.

'Oh your poor little darling,' Amanda cried and hugged her infant close. She didn't even know if it was a girl or boy.

She heard a noise; scrapping sounds and screamed hysterically. Now that help had arrived, reality returned and with it fears of the situation. Without warning a pick axe blade hit the wall near her head. She stared in horror and screamed again.

A hand appeared. A woollen glove reached in and pulled back the splintered wooden wall. Cold air rushed in and a face appeared.

That nose! She knew the nose and the concerned eyes!

'Amanda. You're alive' sobbed a voice. It was Jack.

*

Amanda woke up again to find herself lying on the floor of a railway carriage. It looked like the dining car but she wasn't sure. She felt sore, stiff but warm. A man was looking at her.

'Hello, Mrs. Williams,' he said in a soothing voice, 'I'm Doctor Steinhov. Just lie back. You are safe in one of the undamaged carriages.'

'My baby! Jack!' Amanda cried and attempted to sit up but the carriage began to spin before her eyes and she collapsed back against a pillow.

'I'm here My Darling,' Jack's voice was right beside her. He was kissing her. 'Our baby daughter is fine.'

'Oh Jack!' sobbed Amanda. She felt Jack embracing and rubbing his stubby chin against her. 'Oh Jack!

Her eyes swung up to focus on his face she smiled. He was holding a tiny bundle still wrapped in her coat. A wee head stuck out with long eyelashes. Her baby was asleep.

'Everything will be fine,' the doctor said. 'You are a brave woman, Amanda. When we dug you out your baby was already born and wrapped up like a cocoon. Your forethought saved her life for I believe the infant would have frozen otherwise.'

Amanda nodded but the relief was shattered by a terrible thought. 'Mom! Where is my mother; and brothers?'

Jack took his hand in hers. 'They never made it, My Love.' His voice quivered with emotion. 'Everyone in your carriage was killed. When that tiny toilet was flung away from the avalanche, you and our baby were saved. Over thirty people are missing.'

'Oh my God! 'Amanda sobbed. 'Not the whole family?'

'I'm afraid so,' Jack replied in a sombre tone. 'I thought you had gone too.'

'But he never gave up,' said another voice. It was Andy the stoker. 'I'd say Jack saved six lives today, four from Carriage 1 and you two.' He shook his head in wonder. 'I guess he even saved more. If we hadn't moved that locomotive forward, the whole express would have gone. There's no station there. Nothing's left.'

Jack, though, only frowned. 'But two minutes later we would have been completely clear. If only that signal wasn't down.'

Amanda looked up and saw tears roll down her husband's cheeks.' 'Perhaps God wanted us to survive,' she whispered. 'My little girl, you and me, My Darling.' She reached up and pulled Jack down into in her arms.

*

CHAPTER FOUR

Friday, February 9 1900
Dear Diary,
The week since the accident has been a conflict of heart rendering sadness at the loss of my dearest mother and four brothers and relief at the survival of Dearest Jack and my beautiful little daughter.

We have agreed to name her Dorothy Amanda Williams, the first forename after Mother. She is tiny, a little over five pounds, having arrived in this world a month early but is rapidly putting on weight. I have little recollection of the journey back to Vancouver but Jack said a relief locomotive pulled the end carriages the avalanche missed back to Revelstoke and from there we returned home.

Unfortunately, I was not as well as the doctor on the train stated and it is the sad truth that wee Dorothy will be my only infant. I was told something went wrong inside and an operation back in Vancouver to stem a flow of blood left me barren. I hope Poor Jack forgives me.

Tomorrow will be the worst day of my life, I believe. Jack and I will be travelling south over the border to Mother's and the boys' funeral. Even though my doctor advised against it, I have insisted on taking the journey. It will be on a train that is warm and comfortable so I told Jack my baby and myself will manage.

Sincerely,
Amanda Williams

*

A cold wind carried dark clouds and drizzle over Bellingham, Washington State almost as if the elements had gone into mourning with most of the townspeople. Jack and Amanda had taken the Great Northern Railroad express south over the border. They had been met at the station by a horse carriage and transported to the Catholic Church in the main street. The pale young women clasped her husband's hand as she stepped out onto the muddy pavement and walked slowly forward towards the building. It was the first time since their elopement she had been in a Catholic Church.

'It is all right, Amanda,' Jack whispered as they stepped towards the door. 'Nobody will hurt you, today. We have come south of the border to honour the memory of your dear mother and brothers. All personal vendettas have been pushed aside out of mutual respect for your family.'

'I know,' Amanda replied with quivering lips. 'That sounded so easy back home but now I am here...'

When she walked through the main door into the dull interior her reserve broke at the sight of five coffins lined in front of the altar. Even Jack's supporting arm could not stop the shuddering tears that raked her slim body.

'Here, hand Dorothy to me My Love,' Jack whispered and took the tiny week old infant from her arms.

They were about to step forward up the aisle when Amanda turned and noticed a man dressed in white robes standing beside her.

'Father McNeil,' she gasped and wiped her tears away with a handkerchief.

The tall parish priest put out his arms. 'I know this is not the time but welcome back to Saint Mary's Church, Amanda,' he said in his deep voice.

'Am I welcome?' Anna's eyes turned to the man.

'We are all God's children, Amanda. If He forgives those of the flock who have strayed who am I, a mere mortal, to interfere.' The priest turned to Jack and placed a hand on his shoulder. 'You, too, are welcome Jack.' His eyes switched to the bundle in Jack's arms. 'Can I have a tiny glance at your daughter?'

'Certainly...err... Father,' Jack stumbled. In more pleasant times, Amanda would have grinned at his attempts to follow the etiquette of the Catholic Church. He handed the pink bundle with the minute head poking out to the priest. Dorothy opened her eyes and almost appeared to focus them on the priest and a tiny hand hardly larger than Jack's thumb poked out of the blanket.

'Blue eyes like her mother,' Father McNeil said and cuddled the baby for a moment before handing her back to Jack. 'I don't suppose she will be raised a Catholic.'

'No Father,' Amanda replied in a resolute voice, 'and I don't want...'

The priest, though, raised his hand and smiled. 'I don't necessarily agree with your decision, My Child, but I respect your decision. We have known each other for many years Amanda and I had hoped you would return, even as a friend. However, if it took this tragedy to bring us together, so be it.' His brown compassionate eyes gazed fondly at her. 'Could I ask you but one small favour?'

'What is that, Father?' Amanda replied. She wiped her eyes yet again and stood in the foyer of the packed church waiting for the priest to answer.

'After the ceremony could you all visit me at the Pastoral Centre? There is a small matter I wish to discuss.'

Amanda glanced at Jack who nodded. 'I shall, Father,' she whispered and put her arm through her husband's.

Together they walked through the mourners to the front pew and sat to the right. Amanda avoided looking at her father just across the aisle. It was a heart rendering experience at the church and the procession behind horse drawn carriages to the cemetery was almost more than Amanda could cope with. Twice it was only Jack's strong arm that saved her from collapsing to the ground as the five coffins were lowered into the ground and she led the mourners to drop a pinch of soil into each of the graves. Even then with careful manipulation, she avoided eye contact with her father.

Finally it was over; the last hands were shaken and condolences were heard. Old friends of the family, Amanda's and Jack's, said a few awkward words, invited them back in happier times and departed to continue their lives.

*

'I guess we'll see Father McNeil now,' Jack said as he held the door of the carriage open and handed Dorothy onto Amanda after she was inside.

'Soon,' she replied. 'Dorothy needs her feed.'

Jack grimaced. As far as he knew the baby's feed time wasn't for an hour and the tiny girl was fast asleep. He looked at his wife's eyes and saw the fear.

'We've come this far, My Dear,' he said. 'Within an hour well be on the train heading north back to British Columbia. Father McNeil will not harm you. He struck me as a very compassionate and honest man.'

He is, gulped Amanda. 'That is why it is so hard.' She swallowed and gave Jack a thin smile. 'You knew I was procrastinating didn't you, My Love?'

'I suspected,' Jack replied. 'Come on. Let's get it over with.' With one arm around his daughter and another around his wife he signalled for the driver to start the journey. 'No matter what happens, remember, I love you Amanda and nobody in this world can take that love away.'

'It's not this world I'm worried about,' she replied.

*

'Welcome to my home as a friend, Frank McNeil said and ushered them into the parlour where a hot coffee percolator and tray of scones stood waiting. 'I know you've had plenty to eat but perhaps a little refreshment before you go back on the train.'

'Thank you,' Amanda replied and sat nervously on the edge of a chair. She sipped the coffee handed to her and waited.

'I wish to speak about your father,' Frank McNeil started leaned forward and to look at her. 'He is a hard man set in his ways, Amanda, perhaps even a ruthless man but...' He stopped and glanced over at Jack. 'I am saying this as a friend of the family, not a priest. Understood?'

Amanda nodded.

'I know what happened that night. I know of the beating and the possibility that it could have been worse. I even know the Northwest Mounties were on our side of the border...'

'Father confessed,' Amanda whispered.

'What your father said was between him and God. It cannot be repeated.'

'Okay,' Amanda replied in an indignant tone. 'So you know?'

'God has forgiven your father, Amanda. Sean has withdrawn any threats against Jack and yourself. He even recognises your civilian marriage so can you, in your heart forgive him, especially after this terrible tragedy? Jack and you are his sole surviving family now. He has no one else.'

'There's Dorothy,' Amanda whispered.

'Yes and Baby Dorothy.' Father McNeil said. 'Your father is in the other parlour. I invited him here. All I ask is for you to have a few brief words with him. That is all.'

'I see,' Amanda answered and looked over to Jack.

'I think we should, My Love,' Jack said. "I'll come in with you."

'I promise nothing,' Amanda whispered.

Frank McNeil nodded, opened a connecting door and stood back for her to enter. She squeezed Jack's arm, took the baby from him, raised her chin and entered the room.

Her father stood at the bay window with his back to her.

'Father,' Amanda said in a firm voice and walked forward. 'Would you like to hold your granddaughter?'

Sean O'Donnell turned and stared at her holding the infant. For the first time all day, Dorothy let her mother down. The tiny girl started to cry; a quiet sound that newly born babies make. Sean stood tall but the eyes gave the man away. They could not hide the grief of the day.

'What is the child's name, Amanda?' he asked.

'Dorothy after Mother,' Amanda replied. 'I wanted her name to live on. I hope you approve.'

Sean O'Donnell reached out and took the crying child in his arms. He cuddled the tiny infant and held his rough hands under the minute head. Amanda had never seen the gruff and undemonstrative man seem so tender.

'I approve, Amanda,' he replied. 'And God bless Jack and yourself. Dorothy has gone and the boys...' He looked up and tears rolled down his eyes. 'You are the only family I have now, Amanda, and I almost lost you. Please forgive a stern uncompromising old man.'

Amanda stared. She had never, ever, seen her father cry. 'We are not returning to The Church, Father.'

'I guessed you wouldn't but you are still my daughter. That is enough.'

Amanda wanted to hug her father but stood her ground and replied with caution in her voice. 'If you take me as I am and accept Jack as my husband, I believe we can be friends. Those are my only terms. Understand?'

'I do,' Sean O'Donnell replied. He blew his nose. 'I'm so glad you escaped the avalanche and never lost the child, Amanda. I heard that if it wasn't for Jack you would not be here.'

Jack reached out his hand to the older man. 'My only regret is that I could not reach the rest of the family in time. I tried but they never stood a chance. If it is any comfort, I doubt if they suffered at all.'

Sean O'Donnell grabbed Jack's hand in a tight grip. 'I know. I had a full report,' he said. Their eyes met and Amanda felt a new understanding was begun, still not trust but a beginning.

*

'Perhaps Baby Dorothy is a good judge of character,' Amanda said.

They had just cleared customs, the train was chugging towards Vancouver and she relaxed for the first time.

'How's that?' Jack said. He also looked relieved they were north of the border.

'Well, as soon as she saw Father she bawled her eyes out,' Amanda laughed for a moment before her eyes turned serious. 'You know, I think Father was genuine today but will he stay that way?'

'It's hard to say,' Jack replied. 'Perhaps we can invite him up here one day. It would be in our territory so he could spring no surprises.'

'That's a good idea,' Amanda replied. 'I thought this would be the worst day of my life but it ended up not too bad.'

'Thanks to Father McNeil,' Jack replied. 'He is one astute gentleman and not the indoctrinated priest I expected.'

Amanda smiled. 'He is,' she whispered. 'A rare man, indeed.'

She leaned back on the seat and undid her blouse. It was Dorothy's feeding time; this was the twentieth century so she was not about to retreat to the women's room to feed her child. Jack flushed and said nothing but discretely placed his jacket over an arm to hide her from view. After all, not everyone was as liberal as they were.

'Oh Jack,' Amanda said when she realised what he did and leaned forward to kiss his lips. 'I do love you, you silly man but there's no need.'

Jack grinned at the two females in his life "Queen Victoria would not be amused,' he said smugly.

*

Three months slipped by and Amanda spent most of her time looking after Dot, as Baby Dorothy became known, and maintaining the household. She did, however, try to spend a few hours a week down at *"O'Donnell and Williams"* that was becoming one of the more upmarket and desirable book shops in the city.

'Mrs. Williams,' asked Sally McCorkindale, now shop manager, one morning. 'What do I do with these crates of books that arrived in yesterday's train from New York? There's no space on the shelves?'

Amanda grinned. Even with a large turnover of books, their small display area was filled to capacity. She gazed around and her eyes settled on the long counter running down one whole side of the narrow shop.

'Why don't we take out the counter and replace it with a smaller one near the door? At least two shelves can be added above the existing one. They will almost double our display space.'

'But won't we have trouble with shop lifting?' Sally was a hard working girl but tended to be conservative in her ideas.

'Possibly but our clients are generally from good families. The magazine stores closer to the waterfront cater for the riffraff. I'll phone for a carpenter. In the meantime, pick the best of our new books and display them in the window.'

'I shall do that, Mrs. Williams,' Sally replied. Even though she'd been told it wasn't necessary, the manager still used Amanda's surname when they were in the store.

'I'll be off then,' Amanda said. 'My baby sitter gets grumpy if I arrive home after noon.'

Dot had grown from a tiny premature baby into a chubby little girl with a fuzz of blonde hair and gorgeous blue eyes. Except for the odd rash and upset tummy she was a healthy contented child adored by and perhaps spoiled by both her parents.

Amanda gathered up her jacket and purse. She was about to dash out to the street railcar when the doorbell tingled and an immaculately dressed gentleman walked in.

'Mrs. Amanda Williams?' he inquired as he removed his hat.

'Why yes,' she replied. 'Can I be of assistance to you?' She would have referred the man onto Sally but he seemed to be more than a customer.

'Allow me to introduce myself,' the man continued and held out his hand. This was unusual as most business people only shook hands with male customers and colleagues. 'My name is Richard Smith from *"Smith, Smith and Golding"*. We are the Bellingham lawyers handling your late mother's estate. I was in Vancouver on unrelated business and thought I'd approach you personally rather than just send a letter. Can we speak?'

Amanda removed her glove, shook Richard Smiths hand and showed him through to the tiny office at the rear of the store.

'I have a copy of the last will and testament of Dorothy Mary O'Donnell in my procession.' Richard Smith placed a small suitcase on the desk and extracted a document. 'It is somewhat unusual, Mrs. Williams.'

Amanda frowned and sat across from the lawyer. 'Go on.'

'Due to the tragedy of the accident where your brothers were also killed, parts of the will are redundant but I'll summarise the parts that affect yourself.'

'Please do,' Amanda replied with impatience creeping into her voice.

'In regards to this business, your mother left her third share to her children that, as you are sole surviving child, is yourself. The shares she held in the North West Lumber Company; not that there were many, go to your father.' He stopped and lifted his eyebrows.

'That sounds fair,' Amanda answered and waited. By the man's body language and tone she knew there was more to come.

Mr. Smith coughed. 'Now the unusual part.' He flipped over three pages of the document and read a section silently before continuing. 'Two months after you left Washington and moved into exile, your mother approached us to rewrite her will. We tried to dissuade her from the following actions but she was adamant we write this will as she directed.'

Amanda frowned again but said nothing.

'At that time, your mother owned a quarter of North West Lumber, having turned over the remaining three quarters to your father on their marriage in June 1878...'

Amanda jumped at the words. She'd always thought her parents had been married in June 1887 but June 1878 was only five months before her birth. My God, no wonder her mother was embarrassed when she'd mentioned having been bedded by Jack before their marriage. She mentally grinned and switched back to the lawyer's voice.

'... Her shares were sold and reinvested in a group of companies; mainly banking and transport interests.' His voice droned on. 'Your mother has left her entire investments to her adult female descendant over the age of twenty-one a century and seven years in the future; January 1, Year 2007 to be precise.'

'What?'

'It can be appealed.'

'No, but please continue,' Amanda's mind was in a whirl.

'The inheritance is to go through the female line,' the lawyer continued. 'This is most unusual. I'll read her exact words.

"This inheritance shall be bequeathed to my daughter's eldest daughter's great great grand daughter; that being the eldest adult female descendant to the fifth generation (being the age of twenty one or over) on 1 January in the year of 2007.

The exceptions are as follows:- If there is no direct female descendent, the eldest male of the generation before eldest female child shall continue the line.

If the family line dies out and there are no fifth generation female members in the year 2007, the inheritance shall go to the eldest fourth generation female or if there is none or she is deceased; it shall be bequeathed to charities concerned with women's welfare and family life. Smith, Smith and Golding, or any such firm succeeding them shall nominate these charities. Smith, Smith and Golding, or succeeding legal firm, shall also administer the trust until it matures in the Year 2007."

Richard Smith glanced up. 'So you see, Mrs. Williams, it is an interesting and somewhat eccentric legacy, to say the least. I must add, your father has decided not to contest the will's contents but added that he would do so, if you wish.'

'Why the seven? 'Amanda asked.

Smith raised his eyebrows.

"It's a funny date, that is all. Why didn't she just make it the new millennium, the year 2000?

"I asked her that, too and she replied the number seven was significant to her, being married in 1877 and not a year later as her family had been told."

"It sounds like Mom," Amanda replied. "She hated half-truths."

"So do you wish to proceed with a challenge?"

'I am happy to let it stay as it is. If those were Mother's wishes, who am I to try to stop them?'

The lawyer frowned. 'Very well, Mrs. Williams,' he said. 'Your husband has to sign this document on your behalf and the legal probate can be drawn up.'

Amanda was about to ask why she couldn't sign for herself but shrugged. Jack would do it, of course, but she wondered what life would be like for women in 2007. She hoped women could sign for themselves at that time.

*

The inquiry into the tragedy at Rogers Pass was four months coming and before its release, Amanda knew Jack was apprehensive with the thought that, no matter what he'd done in those few seconds, it wasn't enough. Thirty-four people died as a result of the avalanche, thirty-one at the site and another three, though rescued, died later of their wounds.

The fact that he'd moved the express when the signal was still down was his chief concern. The signal operator was one of those killed in the accident but Jack's worry was that, in the hundreds of interviews held by the police and railroad itself, some of the passengers or crew would have seen the signal's position and reported it.

Amanda thought back. It was only on her insistence that Jack did not mention the signal in his own report.

'If you say anything and stab yourself in the back, Jack Williams,' she had stated in what almost became an argument, two weeks after the tragedy. 'I shall...' Her threat was never revealed but she knew Jack got the message. He said nothing. Andy, the stoker, also had a convenient lapse of memory on the topic.

The dark high ceiling room with oaken panels and equally dark stained furniture, thick curtains made the sombre atmosphere seem even more ominous. Amanda, dressed in ar new light blue frock with high lace collar and matching bonnet, sat beside a nervous Jack who fidgeted in his uncomfortable chair and tight formal clothes. She caught his eye, gave him an encouraging smile and squeezed his hand.

A hush settled over the small number of invited guests and handful of newspaper reporters when a Northwest Mountie stood up. 'Gentlemen,' he began and Amanda glanced around. She was the only woman in the room. 'Sir Cornelius Mansfeild, chairman of the Independent Board of Inquiry set up by the Province of British Columbia to investigate the...'

Amanda stopped listening and watched the chairman being introduced. The heavily bearded man dressed in a black suit, white starched shirt with black bow tie, sat with a cigar in his mouth and stared around the room with watery eyes. They rested on her for a moment, glanced down at her anatomy and moved on. Amanda shuddered. This man and the pomposity of the situation did not impress her.

Sir Cornelius stood and, after a brief introductory speech, began to read. His voice reflected his personality and was devoid of emotion as his voice droned on, and on and still on. For twenty minutes, the man continued but it wasn't until the mention of Jack's name jogged Amanda's thoughts that she listened again.

'It is the conclusion of this report then, Gentlemen.' The man's eyes found Amanda's again, 'and Lady, that if Mr. Jack Williams had not had the forethought to move the Imperial Limited, the avalanche would have carried away the locomotive and at lease four carriages in its path of devastation. Given a few more moments' grace, he would have succeeded in moving the express out of harm's way.' Sir Cornelius coughed as if it was difficult for him to say anything positive. 'Without this action by Mr. Williams, it is estimated the number of deaths would have been doubled.

This Board, therefore, cannot praise Mr. Williams more highly for his efforts and subsequent actions in rescuing eight passengers, including, I might add, his wife and prematurely born daughter.' He stopped. 'We are fortunate in having Mrs. Amanda Williams present with us today.'

Amanda found all eyes in the room turned towards her and the room erupted into polite applause.

'Jolly good show,' one gentleman rumbled and slapped Jack on the back.

'Hear! Hear!' added another.

Sir Cornelius again undressed Amanda with his eyes while he waited. She glared back at him and held his eyes, so long the man flushed and looked away.

'We must,' he continued, 'express our deep regret to Mr. and Mrs. Williams for the loss of five family members in the tragedy and also, of course, to the families of the other twenty-nine victims...'

Amanda squeezed Jack's hand again and their eyes met. 'Told you it would be all right,' she whispered.

Jack grinned for the first time and slipped an arm around her shoulders. In the whole report not one mention was made of the signal. Either nobody had mentioned it or the fact was not deemed important enough to be included in the report.

*

Three weeks later a long envelope with the Canadian Pacific Railway shield on the cover arrived at the Williams house. Amanda stared at it and her hand shook. For the first time she felt nervous. Why would the railway be writing to Jack?

She rushed inside grabbed the telephone, turned the handle and asked the operator for the Canadian Pacific Railway Station.

'He's here in the station, Mrs. Williams,' replied the receptionist. 'Hold the line and I'll get him.'

'Well open it, My Dear,' Jack said a few moments later.

Amanda slit open the envelope, nervously unfolded the paper inside and read the contents to herself. Her frown turned to a smile and she turned to speak in the mouthpiece of the phone.

'Jack,' she spluttered. 'They've offered you a position as Senior Train Dispatcher for the whole Southern British Columbia area. Oh my God.' she gasped.

'Yes, My Love,'

'You have a salary offered, Jack. Night hundred dollars a year.'

'Sounds good,' Jack said.

'Good!' Amanda shouted. 'You only get about six hundred now. Oh Jack, it also means you'll be in Vancouver all the time and not have those nights away all the time.'

'Yeah,' rumbled Jack. 'I wonder what I can do with all that spare time. With my beautiful wife waiting for me...'

'You naughty man.' Amanda said. 'Now Dot is on the bottle you can help feed and change her diapers in the middle of the night.'

*

'Your Daddy's going to be an important man,' Amanda said and picked the toddler up from her playpen. 'Come on, Mommy will find you something to eat then well take the railcar down to the shop.'

Dot gave a big chuckle. Amanda was sure her daughter understood what the word "Shop" meant and loved the attention she received there.

The shop improvements had been completed and the last month's turnover was up thirty per cent; so good that Amanda was considering opening a branch of "O'Donnell and Williams" in New Westminster or even Victoria on Vancouver Island.

She kissed Dot and grabbed their coats. Now Jack was promoted and things were working out so well for them all, perhaps they could even buy their own house.

*

CHAPTER FIVE

Tuesday 8 May 1900

Dear Diary,
With the exception of Jack whom, as you know, I love dearly, I've come to the conclusion I hate the hypocritical behaviour of men. This evening was the most humiliating experience of my life. I am so embarrassed, not to mention sore, I do not even know if I can put pen to paper...

*

It was raining and Amanda was running late when she left the shop. Her baby-sitter didn't like waiting too long as there was a husband returning home for supper and Jack was not due home from work until late. She had just missed the railcar when a hansom cab pulled in beside her.

'Mrs. Williams, do you require a lift home?' the driver called down.

This was not a cab for hire but an up-market one use by the more prosperous people of the city. The rain was now a steady downpour and Amanda was becoming quite wet, the next railcar was ten minutes away but she still hesitated.

'Sir Cornelius will be honoured to have your company,' the man continued and Amanda saw the cab door open.

'Why thank you,' she finally replied and climbed in beside the man.

'You are wet, Mrs. Williams,' Sir Cornelius said. 'Why don't you remove your coat? '

Those piercing eyes from the inquiry were staring at her again. Perhaps it had been a mistake to accept the ride.

'I shall be all right, thank you,' Amanda replied with caution in her voice.

'I see,' replied the man and pulled the dark velvet curtains on the two side windows. 'You are a business lady, Mrs. Williams and I have a proposition I wish to discuss.'

Amanda frowned. 'I'm only accepting your kind offer of a ride home, Sir Cornelius. Nothing more,' she replied.

'Oh, but there is more, young lady. Hear me out, if you please.'

Amanda's heart gave a lurch. The man's words were pleasant enough but his eyes and body language sent a shiver of caution through Amanda's body. What could this man possibly want from her? She was certain it would be nothing positive.

The man turned to her. 'You are a lady of very high principles, I can see that, Mrs. Williams but also, no doubt you have desires within you all young women have.'

Amanda bit on her lip and just stared at those watery eyes.

'To put it bluntly,' said the man. 'I find you a most attractive woman and would like you to be my mistress.'

'What!' Amanda retorted angrily. 'You...' She could not even get the words out to express her disgust.

'Come now, Mrs. Williams, think of the benefits. For only one appointment, say for two hours every Wednesday night, I am prepared to deposit one hundred dollars in any bank account of your choice. We can even make it seem you are visiting a Ladies Guild meeting. Your husband need not know.'

'You contemptuous bastard,' Amanda spluttered. 'I am not a prostitute, Sir Cornelius nor are you a gentleman. Stop this vehicle straight away. I wish to get out.'

The man gave a small laugh. 'Aye Amanda,' he replied with all culture removed from his voice. 'I thought it might come to this, so I'll be even more frank. If you are prepared to offer me a little comfort in my bed, shall we say, I am prepared to ignore the section of the Roger's Pass report that noted your husband moved the Imperial Express when the signal was down.'

Amanda gasped and pulled her coat around herself. The man was staring straight at her bosom without even attempting to be discrete.

'A business arrangement,' the man leered and, without warning, grabbed Amanda and around the shoulders and pushed her back on the seat.

'My apartment!' he called to the driver. 'The lady is cold.'

This was obviously a prearranged signal for the cabby cracked his whip and the horse broke into a canter. Amanda though, had other worries. A hand was already squeezing a breast and three buttons were undone down the front of her gown. Smelly smoke covered breath and black beard rubbed her face. Amanda's scream was stopped by another hand over her mouth and she heard a chuckle.

'Fight all you like, young lady, but I am about to have my way with you. It would be advisable to co-operate.'

A hand reached inside her dress and began fondling her breast. All pretence had gone. The man was about to rape her.

With one massive yank, Amanda's corset was cut loose at the back. Amanda screamed as she felt the small but sharp knife do its work. A hand grabbed the front and pulled downward so her breasts were fully exposed. Amanda bit the man's hand and screamed again but was merely slapped across the cheek in return.

'Co-operate and you won't be hurt,' the man retorted in an angry voice. For a second he pulled himself back and leered at her heaving bare breasts and his hand went down to undo his own fly buttons. No doubt, this vile creature had had his way with women on many occasions and they were too terrified to hinder his advances..

Amanda, though, was not terrified; she was disgusted and furious. How dare the man blackmail and strip her naked. The worse was about to come. His eyes were glued to her breasts and he was about to grab them with both hands when she lashed out. One massive kick was aimed straight between his trousers.

'You bitch!' he screamed but bent over in agony and raised a hand to slap her for a second time.

But Amanda wasn't there. She ducked, kicked out again and reached for the door. With another deft movement, she grabbed her underwear lying on the floor, turned the handle and without hesitating, leaped into the teeming rain.

She was a fit woman. In those vital seconds she let herself relax and probably saved herself from serious injury. Her body hit the road like an express train but she managed a sort of roll before sliding to an abrasive stop in a puddle. Her left leg and arms were grazed raw and bleeding but no other injuries were evident.

Amanda staggered to her feet, took one terrified glance at the cab that had pulled to a halt and ran. For several moments she sped up the darkening suburban street. Rain poured down on her flapping clothes that she held across her body with one hand to cover the nakedness. Her long skirt splashed through a curb puddle and her hair became loose and tumbled across the eyes. But she only stopped one second to kick off her shoes and continue in her stocking feet.

'Quick in here, My Lady!' hissed a voice and Amanda's desperate eyes saw a young woman holding a door open. Behind her, an electric light bulb glowed like a beacon of hope.

She surged in to crumble, sobbing, onto a wooden floor.

*

The woman, dressed in the clothes of a maid or waitress, clicked a bolt across the door, switched off the light and pulled back some curtains to cover a window beside the door so only pale light from an outside gas lamp filtered in.

'The driver chasing you is just up the road,' she whispered, 'He was around the corner when I opened the door so I doubt if he saw you come in.'

'Thank you,' sobbed Amanda. She climbed to her feet and stood in the tiny foyer with her whole body shaking. 'I was about to be raped.'

'I thought that might be the case. This is not a good part of town for a lady to be in now that it is getting dark,' the girl said. 'Molly's my name and this is my tiny apartment. You are safe here. Come on up and we'll get you tidied up.'

Amanda followed Molly up a narrow staircase and along a narrow corridor to a bedroom.

'Can I get you something dry, My Lady?' Molly asked and handed Amanda a towel. 'I am afraid I share my bathroom and it is in the cellar.'

'This is fine and I'm not a lady.' Amanda grinned and introduced herself. 'You have done enough for me. If I could phone for a cab?'

'I'm sorry but I have no phone. Costs too much, you see,' The young woman looked up at the sound of a baby's cry. 'That's my Peter. If you'll excuse me.'

When Molly left the room Amanda tried to stop shaking as she redressed. It was difficult squeezing into the clinging wet material. Her arm oozed blood from the sever graze but she didn't care about the minor discomfort. The thought at what could be happening to her at this very moment was enough to make her forget the wet soggy clothes and smarting arm. After drying her hair the best she could, she walked out to a tiny kitchen to see Molly

'Oh what a lovely baby,' she said. 'My daughter is not much younger. Can I hold him?'

'Certainly err..'

'Amanda Williams but call me Amanda, Molly.'

'There's only Peter and myself, Amanda,' Molly replied in a sad tone. 'Your husband?'

'I have none.' The girl seemed embarrassed. 'Peter just sort of came. The father was my employer, a banker. He wants nothing to do with us.'

'How do you manage?'

Molly looked at her feet. 'Peter's father pays for this apartment but does nothing else. I earn a little selling things.'

'Selling what,' Amanda pushed.

'My body, Amanda. Men pay to use my body.' She grimaced. 'Gentlemen like that one in the cab you jumped out from, pay me for sex. It's the only way.'

'I see, and how old are you Molly?'

'Eighteen. It didn't start like this.' The girl bit on her lip. 'Me getting a child, you know and now it's too late.'

Amanda stared. 'Tell me, do you enjoy these men?'

'Occasionally,' Molly admitted. Her eyes looked haunted, 'Usually not. They are crude and rough so I just lie there and let them have their way, a few dollars are left on the dresser and they leave. Most don't bother to come back.' She coughed. 'But that's enough about me. We need to get you to the railcar. I'll walk you to the stop. It's only two blocks away.'

Amanda gulped and suddenly made a decision. 'Listen Molly, if you'd give this life up I can give you a job.'

The girl stared. 'With Peter?'

'Why not? You can bring him with you. I own "*O'Donnell and Williams*" bookshop. Do you know it?'

'Why, yes,' Molly replied and her eyes lit up a little. 'I used to visit it when I was at high school but now...' She shrugged.

'You went to high school?' Girls from the servant class rarely went beyond elementary school and some even dropped out earlier.

'Yes,' Molly answered. 'Until my father disowned me for having Peter, I lived in a good family.' She swallowed. 'They won't speak to me now.'

Amanda nodded. She knew this happened and, in some ways her own situation wasn't a great deal different. 'The job would be only part time, pay a dollar an hour and only on the promise you give up prostitution.'

'But you don't know me,' Molly protested.

'Let's make it a month's trial.' Amanda said and cuddled Peter close. 'If, after that time either of us is not satisfied, we can pull out of the arrangement.'

'Yes.' Molly smiled and took her son back. 'Come on. I'll walk you to the railcar stop. I'm sure Sir Cornelius has gone now.'

'You know him?' Amanda frowned.

'Yeah. Thursday morning 10:30,' Molly replied with a snicker. 'The old fart stinks like a factory and is as rough as hell. I've heard he's already paid two gentlemen's wives off after they threatened to go to the Mounties. We call his carriage The Pillage Wagon. Often he let's his driver rape the woman when he is finished.'

Amanda's face drained of the little colour it had and she felt physically ill. 'The bastard,' she whispered. 'We'll have to put a stop to this, won't we?'

'Don't!' warned Molly. 'Just forget it. He is a politician and powerful man, Amanda.'

'Oh, I'm sure he is but no man is above the law.' She smiled. 'Look, gather up Peter's things and come home with me for the evening and we will finalise our agreement.'

*

It was a month before Amanda, with quite an amount of help from Molly had a case against Sir Cornelius Mansfeild. She had found eight women who had either been raped or coerced by blackmail or bribes into having sexual favours with the man. Of the eight, four were too terrified to participate in any court case, two more were only partly persuaded and two definitely ready to stand as witnesses.

One woman, Gertrude Somerville had had an episode almost like Amanda's except she had not succeeded in getting away. The second woman, Annette Mitchell was older, being in her late thirties. Her experience happened in the rear room of Sir Cornelius's home where a ball was taking place. During supper, Anton Pickett, the cab driver, dragged her out the back where she was stripped and raped by him and Sir Cornelius. Once again, a minor blackmail stopped her reporting the incident.

Amanda still never told Jack of the incident; mainly because she was afraid he would be too direct and attack the man. This would, Amanda surmised, only lead to Jack being thrown into prison for assault or even worse.

But now was the day. Sergeant Tony Dutton, the Mountie who had rescued Amanda in their flight across the border had been approached two weeks earlier and had persuaded his superiors the matter was serious.

*

At eight in the evening, three police carriages pulled up beside a mansion in one of the more desirable suburbs and Tony knocked on the front door.

A butler answered.

'Sir Cornelius is indisposed at the moment, Sergeant, and will not be available until tomorrow,' he said in an arrogant tone.

'Oh is he?' Tony retorted and held out a search warrant. 'We are coming in and if you attempt to stop us or give warning of our presence you'll be arrested for obstructing the police.' He turned. 'Search the house, men. Everyone in the building will be brought to the front parlour.' Already over a dozen other Northwest Mounties had the property completely encircled.

Within fifteen minutes, nine people were assembled in the parlour. Sir Cornelius was red with fury and threatened to have anyone's and everyone's badge.

'Come now, Sir Cornelius, you know we are employed by the Federal Government of Canada not the province of British Columbia,' Sergeant Dutton replied.

'You will not hear the end of this, Sergeant. I insist you explain this outrage immediately,' Mansfeild roared and turned to the butler. 'Get Superintendent Roy Mallory at the police headquarters on the phone. We'll see about this.'

Dutton, though, turned to the man. 'You do not move,' he ordered.

The butler frowned but remained still while Sergeant Dutton nodded to a constable. 'Show the ladies in, Constable,' continued.

The policeman nodded and moved silently out of the room; Lady Mansfeild stood with her face like ice while her husband still blustered. He stopped, though, when the three women walked into the room.

Amanda stared at the man with icy eyes while Gertrude and Annette appeared more nervous.

'Every male of the household will line up,' snapped the sergeant. 'Failure to do so will mean immediate arrest for obstruction of police in their line of duty.'

A faint hiss of protest went through the room but within two minutes, the scowling men were assembled in a line along a wall. Tony turned to Gertrude.

'Could you Mrs. Somerville, identify the two men about whom you filed your complaint.'

Though pale, Gertrude Somerville held her head high. She took a glove off and pointed at Anton Pickett. 'This man raped me, Sergeant Dutton,' she whispered, coughed and continued. 'This was in between the two rapes by Sir Cornelius Mansfeild.' Her face turned ashen and tears appeared in her eyes. 'He also blackmailed me and said if I reported the rape, my husband would be arrested for thief as a servant.'

'No,' interrupted a screaming hysterical voice. 'It can't be true!' Lady Mansfeild clutched at her bosom and stared, shaking, at her husband.

Annette Mitchell also identified the pair and one other servant as those who violated her in the very house they were standing.

'No!' sobbed Lady Mansfeild again. 'It's not true. You're only jealous. It can't be true.' She sat sobbing on a sofa and stared back at the women. 'Annette, you're my friend. Why are you saying these terrible things?'

'Because they're true,' whispered the other woman. 'I was too afraid to complain.'

'Sir Cornelius Mansfeild, Anton Pickett and Christopher Westbourne; you are all under arrest for multiple rape, kidnapping and blackmail. You have the right to remain silent... '

The men were seized by Mounties, handcuffed and led out of the room. Mansfeild said nothing but his eyes bore into Amanda who held them and stared back.

'Nobody is above the law, Sir Cornelius,' she said in a tense voice. 'Nobody. Not even you.' She swung around so her back was to him but not before saying. 'And I hope you rot in hell, you contemptuous little bastard.'

Amanda grinned when Gertrude whispered to Annette. "Thank The Lord this American woman is not intimidated by the British aristocracy."

*

'Look at this, My Love.' Jack looked up from the "*Vancouver Sun*" he was reading. 'Sir Cornelius Mansfeild, that politician who was arrested a while back and released on bail is dead. Wasn't he the chairman of the Avalanche Inquiry?'

'What!' Amanda swung around from where she was feeding Dot in a high chair. 'Dead, you say?"

'Yes,' said Jack. 'According to the paper he shot himself in the stables on his property last night.' He folded the paper, stood behind Amanda and tucked his arms around her waist and kissed her neck. 'Saves you giving evidence, doesn't it, My Love?'

Amanda swung around. 'You knew?' she spluttered.

'When one's wife comes home one night covered in scratches and bruises, one does get curious. Then when, almost straight away, a young lady is employed at the shop, one with an infant, I might add...'

'Okay,' Amanda interrupted. 'I didn't want you hurt. How did you find out about that horrible man, anyway?'

'Molly is a pleasant young girl but she does talk. Did you know she was a prostitute?'

'I did,' Amanda retorted. 'As long as you weren't a client.' Suddenly her bluster turned to a grin then a pout. 'Oh Jack,' she whispered. 'I know I should have told you but I was so ashamed.'

'Why? Anyway, from what Molly told me, if it wasn't for you, he'd never have been arrested.'

He grabbed her and deposited a kiss on her lips. 'I'm proud of you, My Darling.'

Amanda responded with tears as she described what happened that night. Jack listened and comforted his wife but underneath he was angry.

Amanda was correct; he would have tackled the bastard and could very well be languishing in jail as a result of his actions.

'You know me too well, My Love,' he said when she had finished, 'but, next time, tell me, please.'

'I will,' Amanda replied and kissed him again. 'I only hope there is no next time.'

*

Amanda's sudden decision to give Molly a job proved to be one of her more enlightened moves. Molly proved to be a highly educated girl with an excellent knowledge of books. Also, she worked well with Sally McCorkindale, the store manager, and tried so hard to make Peter's presence in the tiny back room so unobtrusive it was almost an embarrassment.

However, trouble came one morning when Amanda had arranged to meet a particularly irksome individual call Mr. O'Hagan. This was his second visit after Sally had been reduced to tears after the man's his first confrontation. He had arrived at the shop that day, stating he was from the *Brotherhood of Trades People and Shop Workers*, one of the new unions that were beginning to establish its hold in the young province.

'It has come to our notice that you are exploiting the labour force by employing undesirable employees, Mrs. Williams,' he said with a sniff.

'I see,' retorted Amanda, 'Tell me how this is so, Mr. O'Hagan?'

The man extracted a scruffy notebook from his pocket and turned over the pages with nicotine stained fingers. 'Here it is,' he mumbled. 'There are several matters, actually.'

'Are there indeed, Amanda replied coldly. 'You had better elaborate, hadn't you?' Unlike her manager, the man did not intimidate Amanda. She turned to Sally and nodded. 'Go back in the shop, Miss McCorkindale,' she said. 'I can look after this gentleman's inquiry.'

'Certainly, Ma'am', Sally replied and disappeared through the door. Whenever Amanda called her by her surname something serious was about to happen.

'You have in your employment, I believe, a Miss Molly Pegler, a woman of dubious background and lady of the night.' He flushed slightly and blinked behind dark eyebrows and a jutting beard.

'No,' Amanda replied in a tone so blunt that the man almost cringed.

'I saw the young woman serving customers when I walked in,' he snapped. 'I did not believe a lady of your standing would lie.'

Amanda glared. 'I employ a Miss Molly Pegler, yes, Mr. O'Hagan but she is not the woman of dubious background and lady of the night you speak of. You obviously muddled her with someone with a similar name.'

'Very well,' the man replied with renewed confidence, 'and that is not her infant I can hear crying in the anteroom, right now?'

'That Sir, is none of your business. Now if you will please leave...' Her eyes reflected anger.

'Oh, but it is,' O'Hagan answered. 'Our complaint is that this young woman is holding a position at the expense of a person of sound body and needs.'

'A male belonging to the brotherhood, no doubt,' retorted Amanda.

The man nodded. 'That is correct. If you continue to employ this sort of person in your store we shall have no recourse but to blacklist *"O'Donnell and Williams"* and picket the premises.'

Amanda frowned. She knew of other shops where this had happened and, on at least one occasion a small shop had been forced to close. She agreed that many workers were exploited but this was carrying the rights of workers too far.

'So we'll enrol Miss Pegler in the brotherhood,' she said. 'I'm sure she will not mind paying the fees and reaping the benefits of the organization.'

'We do not accept females in our union, Mrs. Williams. We advise you to replace this girl forthwith and hire a gentleman in her place.'

'So,' Amanda retorted with her eyes blazing. 'What about Miss McCorkindale? Shall I replace her too?'

'That is not necessary. Miss McCorkindale is of high moral standing and is management, not a worker.'

'I see,' Amanda glowered but her expression turned to a smile. 'Why didn't you say earlier and we would have not had the unpleasantness we have had to endure.'

The man hesitated. 'What do you mean?'

'You don't represent managers? Am I correct in saying that?'

'That is correct but...' The man frowned.

Amanda reached across her desk and rang a tiny bell. Immediately Sally poked her head in. 'Yes, Mrs. Williams?' she asked.

'Please send Molly in, Miss McCorkindale.'

'Certainly, Mrs. Williams.'

A very nervous Molly appeared with wide eyes and wringing hands. 'You wish to speak to me, Ma'am, she inquired in a timid voice.

'Why yes, Molly,' Amanda replied and gave her a gushy smile. 'I have been thinking of this for a week now but since Mr. O'Hagan has graced our premises with his presence he can hear of my offer.' Both the other people in the room frowned as Amanda waited for her words to sink in before continuing. 'You know we are opening a branch store in New Westminster next month?'

Molly nodded. This was common knowledge and had been discussed a lot over the last few days. Already books were being packaged ready to fill the shelves of the new shop.

'Good,' replied Amanda. 'I would therefore like to offer you the position as manageress of the "*O'Donnell and Williams*" New Westminster branch starting as soon as the store opens at the beginning of next month'

There were two quite different reactions in the room.

'Me,' spluttered Molly.

'You can't!' glowered the man.

'But I can, Mr. O'Hagan.' Amanda beamed. 'You yourself only told me a few moments ago you are not concerned with managers; only exploited workers, I believe.' She turned back to Molly. 'Would you like the position, Molly?'

'Why, yes, of course,' Molly spluttered.

'Good,' Amanda replied. 'We'll discuss the details later. Thank you, Molly. You may go.'

After the young woman had left O'Hagan stared at Amanda with a sullen expression. 'I must warn you....' he began.

'No,' Amanda interrupted. 'I shall warn you, Mr. O'Hagan. You are not welcome here. In fact, you will have no need to be concerned in our affairs as I intend to increase my hours at the shop and, with Miss McCorkindale as manager, we will not need to replace Miss Pegler when she moves into the managerial position. There will, therefore, be no workers on the premises, only a manager and owner.' She glowered at the man. 'Now, if you will excuse me, I have work to do.'

'But!'

'Go!' Amanda said quietly.

The man stared at the woman standing beside the opened door. Without another word he grabbed his hat and left in such a hurry he almost knocked Molly and a customer over on the way.

Molly laughed and dashed in. 'Thanks, Amanda,' she said. 'Sally told me what it was all about. That trick worked well.'

'It was no trick, Molly. I am, indeed offering you the position as manageress at our new branch.'

'You aren't?' gasped Molly.

'Why not?' Amanda said. 'In the few weeks you've been here you have more than proved your ability.'

'But I'm only eighteen and have a babe in arms.'

'Never say "only" Molly,' Amanda added. 'You are a well-educated young woman who deserves this position. If you don't want it, of course.'

Molly stood for a moment just staring at Amanda before she rushed forward and flung her arms around her. Tears appeared in her eyes.

'My parents disowned me,' she sobbed. 'Everyone treated me like dirt but now you do this. Oh Amanda, of course I want the job and I promise, it will be the best little bookshop in the city.'

'At the very least.' Amanda said. 'Come on; its your lunchtime isn't it? Let me take you to a cafe for a cup of coffee. Bring Peter with you.'

*

CHAPTER SIX

Saturday 24 November 1900
Dear Diary,
Goodness, hasn't the first year of the twentieth century gone quickly? Dot is no longer an infant but a smiling little girl with growing hair and beautiful blue eyes. Jack says they are like mine.

Our new shop at New Westminster is now open and, I must say Molly has exceeded our expectations for our turnover there exceeds the Vancouver store. We are still having few problems with Mr. O'Hagan and the brotherhood but are trying to ignore this obnoxious little man.

Jack is doing well, enjoys his position but does become tired and, at times I must say, quite worried about the responsibilities he carries.

We are, Dear Diary, a very happy family and I would trade places with nobody in the city or, indeed, the world.

Sincerely,
Amanda Williams.

*

It was close to midnight and two men slunk down an alleyway through the darkness until they reached the service lane behind the New Westminster main shopping street, right behind *"O'Donnell and Williams"* and adjacent stores.

'Right, this is the place,' O'Hagan retorted in a harsh whisper. 'But be careful with the stuff. It burns like hell.'

'Sure, Wesley,' the other man grunted.

He made his way to up the wooden fire escape, unscrewed the top of a tin container and watched as the petrol gulped out, ran along the unpainted wood and seeped down through the cracks.

'God the stuff stinks,' he muttered and proceeded to dose the small platform and steps with a line of the fluid.

'Ready!' O'Hagan grunted when his companion reached the ground. 'Get back.'

After a match flared, Wesley tossed it onto the small stain of liquid in the dust. The whoosh of flames caught him by surprise and he hardly had time to step back before the whole back steps were engulfed in flames. Mere seconds later, the line of fire to reach the upper landing and the whole back of the building was aflame. The original blue flames turned to orange and yellow with black wood smoke bellowing up into the frosty night air. Loud cracks of burning wood filled the air.

'Now, Mrs. High and Mighty Williams, well see how your new manager likes this. Come on Marcus. Let's go before were missed at the club.'

The two arsonists disappeared. Their aim to destroy Amanda's shop was to be achieved with interest. Within five minutes the whole building was ablaze, flames lit up the area while torrid heat and choking smoke kept witnesses away. The alarm went out quickly and two new fire trucks only recently changed from horse drawn appliances howled their way through the city.

*

The telephone rang. Amanda awoke from a deep sleep, heard Jack's light snores and slid out the side of their bed. Even with the coal furnace in the cellar warming the house, the floor was cold beneath her feet as she felt her way up the corridor to where the phone was attached to the wall. Night calls from the railway were not unusual for Jack was on call if signalmen needed advice.

'Amanda Williams,' she spoke in the mouthpiece but her sleepiness disappeared as he heard the voice at the other end. 'Thank you Officer. We'll get right there.'

'What is it, My Dear?' Jack stood in the corridor looking bleary eyed and shivering in the cool air.

'The shopping centre in New Westminster is ablaze; the whole block where our shop is.'

'Oh no!' Jack gasped.

For a second their eyes met before Amanda snapped into action. By the time Jack, carrying Dot, and she arrived in New Westminster, the street had been cordoned off. Behind, towering flames lit up the night sky and clouds of black smoke drove spectators back from the rope stretched across the road. Even as they arrived, there was a thunder of explosion and a sheet of roofing iron roared into the night sky.

'This block can't be saved,' a policeman commented grimly in reply to a question from Amanda. 'We are trying to create a fire break so the whole central town doesn't burn.'

'Oh my God!' Amanda gasped.

Jack placed an arm around her and nodded. The "O'Donnell and Williams" store was a massive ball of flames reaching hundreds of feet into the air. Firemen, dark silhouettes in front of the light of the flames, were retreating from the intense heat and hoses were now concentrating on the end buildings in an attempt to stop the spread of the all devouring flames. There was a massive explosion and a building four along from Amanda's store blew up.

'They're blowing up buildings to create a fire-break,' the policeman Amanda had talked to earlier, explained.

It seemed to work, too. The flames at that end flicked out while firemen turned the arching streams of water onto them to prevent any recovery.

An hour later the fire was under control but it was too late for *"O'Donnell and Williams Bookshop and Stationers"*. All that remained of four shops were a row of blackened timbers still smouldering in the early morning air.

Amanda cuddled Dot and walked forward to inspect the damage. Her eyes smarted from the smoke and expression, daunted. 'How could it happen so quickly, Jack?' she gasped.

'Everything's lumber,' he replied. 'Once it got going it was like kindling wood. That paint shop two up from yours didn't help either.

'I know,' Amanda said and kicked at a blackened smouldering tin lying on the road, 'but how would it have started?'

'Anything,' replied Jack. 'A furnace door left open, a chimney catching fire, a dropped cigarette butt...'

'Or it could have been lit!' Amanda added and her eyes turned to her husband.

Jack shrugged. 'Come on, My Dear. We can do no more now. Let's go home before Dot gets cold.'

Amanda stared at the ruined hulk of her shop, then her little girl and husband. 'At least nobody was inside,' she whispered.

*

The information about the fire came back quite early and from an unexpected direction, Jack's work place. He was in the main dispatch room of Canadian Pacific and ready for a break after five hours of work. A minor derailment in the shunting yards had caused several trains to be diverted. The *Imperial Express* had been delayed in the Fraser Canyon by snow and a controller from the Great Northern Railroad had rung, wanting to divert one of his expresses through a section of the Canadian railway line.

'Has your wife had trouble with the brotherhood?' muttered Henry Shotton, Jack's assistant as the two men watched the next shift take over.

'The union?' Jack replied, 'They're an offshoot of your railway union, aren't they?'

'Yeah,' Henry answered. 'Run by the same men.'

Jack nodded. 'I see. You railway employees are doing okay, I'd say. The union seems to be doing quite well trying to get wages boosted by twenty cents a day.'

'I know,' Henry continued, 'but there's something else. I've heard a rumour that may interest you.'

Jack studied the man. Henry was into the union movement and, as an employee was in a different one than Jack, who was classified as management.

'Go on,' Jack replied. He sensed Henry knew something important.

Henry glanced around the room. 'Come into the break room,' he muttered and continued when they were inside. 'Don't say where you heard it, okay?'

'Heard what?' Jack replied as he poured two cups of coffee and handed one to his companion.

'That fire over at New Westminster was deliberately set to burn your wife's shop down. '

'But why?' Jack retorted.

'Your wife told O'Hagan to piss off when he tried to get that young lassie fired. He didn't like it and then when the girl was given a manager's job at your new store, the bastard was incensed.'

'I see.' Jack grimaced and ran a hand over his chin. 'He's quite capable of doing that. Nasty customer, he is; more interested in power than helping the workers.'

'There's more,' continued Shotton.

Jack raised an eyebrow.

'He's planning to do the same with your wife's Vancouver store tomorrow night.'

Jack stood perfectly still and said nothing for a moment. Then he very deliberately cracked his knuckles and stared coldly at his assistant. 'And you know the time?'

Shotton nodded. 'Just before midnight. They're larger buildings there so I think they're planning to use more than a can of petrol. I would advise you to be there early.'

'The local police?'

'They can't help. If we tell them, O'Hagan will just pull back, deny everything and come back later.'

'I see,' Jack muttered. 'Can you help?'

Henry Shotton paled a little and shook his head. 'I'd like to but with my misses at home and...'

'Okay,' Jack answered. 'You've already stuck your head out for me, Henry. I owe you one.' He stood, squeezed his companion's shoulder and walked out of the room with a determined feeling in his throat.

At eleven thirty the next evening, an indiscreet horse and wagon pulled in beside *"O'Donnell and Williams"*. Two men jumped out the back, hauled a wooden crate off the tray and slipped into the narrow alleyway.

'Gid up, there!' the driver called, the two horses continued the journey and the street returned to quietness.

'Up the back and under the fire escape is the cellar door. I've already unlocked it,' said O'Hagan. 'Once we're inside, no one will see us.'

'Right, Wesley,' said the other man. He still had a blistered arm and singed eyebrows from the earlier expedition but was more at home with explosive, anyhow.

The men lugged the wooden crate through the darkness and were about to set it down by the steps leading down to the cellar door when two shapes loomed in front of them. O'Hagan swung around. In the thin strip of moonlight filtering down from the gap between the buildings, two more shapes materialised out of the darkness.

'What that...' he gasped but it was too late.

He was seized in a wresting hold and, before he could move, found his arm twisted up the back of his back, which was bent over like a staple.

'Not planning another little fire?' a voice hissed in his ear and Jack's eyes stared into O'Hagan's. They were not the gentle friendly ones Amanda gazed into every night, but deadly fierce and uncompromising.

O'Hagan was a bully and manipulator of men but he also knew human personality. Those eyes staring at him in the feeble light made him tremble. His mind tried to think of a way out of this latest situation but there was none.

The arm went further up his back.. 'Cut it out!' he screamed as perspiration ran off his forehead.

'Certainly, Mr. O'Hagan,' Jack replied and relaxed the pressure.

Suddenly a closed fist caught him in the pit of his stomach. This was followed by another under the chin, another full in the nose that broke with a clunk and the man found himself on his knees with blood flowing out of his nose and his lungs screaming for breath. He gasped and attempted to fling himself sideways but a boot connected with his ribs and he was slammed, whimpering into the wooden wall.

Meanwhile, O'Hagan's companion was pinned down by two of Jack's men.

'There is a change of plan,' Jack hissed.

He nodded; two men grabbed the wooden crate and carried it on to the service lane where another horse and wagon was waiting.

Jack hauled O'Hagan up and frog marched him forward. 'One false move, My Man and I'll break your arm.' he hissed as his victim staggered forward.

'What are you going to do?' O'Hagan managed to spit out between the blood and missing teeth.

'A tiny journey.' Jack said.

Two more men appeared so Jack's party now consisted of six, all burly railway employees. O'Hagan, the crate and O'Hagan's assistant were flung onto the wagon.

'One squeak and I'll break your damn neck,' Jack said.

He took the reins and the horse ambled forward, out of the service lane and along the deserted street. Twenty minutes later it pulled in beside another building, one of two stories and ornate carvings at the front that looked like a bank but wasn't. It was the local crime syndicate headquarters.

'Now,' Jack retorted. 'Well borrow your explosive.'

'You wouldn't dare!' O'Hagan replied with a small portion of his bravery restored.

'Oh, no,' Jack replied.

'They'll hunt you down and... .'

'I don't think so,' Jack replied and his sarcastic grin wasn't missed by O'Hagan. 'A small rumour, My Man. Ten minutes ago a Major vonCardosso was phoned and told of two malcontents who resented his authority in the city.'

O'Hagan paled. Major vonCardosso was no major at all but leader of the rising crime underworld in Vancouver and one of the most ruthless individuals around. He controlled most of the city's crime and the brotherhood was rapidly spreading its tentacles under his organization's control.

'You wouldn't...'

'Come now My Dear O'Hagan,' Jack replied with his voice like steel. 'You are repeating yourself.'

By now the wagon had stopped and the crate unloaded. Cardboard cylinders were soon set out beneath the building and the fuse wire played out.

'You can light it,' Jack hissed.

'I will not,' O'Hagan retorted but his voice turned to a scream as, again his arm bent back the way it shouldn't go.

'Take the wagon', Jack ordered to one of his men. 'I don't want the poor horse frightened.' He turned back to O'Hagan. 'You were about to blow our shop up. You light the fuse or, by God, we'll tie you up and leave you here.' He paused ... 'Right by this stick of dynamite.'

O'Hagan trembled but knew Jack Williams was not joking.

'There's a ten minute fuse,' he muttered.

'Good,' answered Jack. 'Lot's of time. Now, light it!'

The man's hands were shaking so much the first match went out. The second burst into flame and O'Hagan held it to the fuse. There was a faint cackle and the object began to hiss.

'Thank you,' Jack muttered. 'You may go.'

O'Hagan took one terrified look at the smouldering fuse, back at Jack and left.

Jack hardly glanced back as the explosion ripped through the night air behind him.

*

'Jack, you naughty man!' Amanda exclaimed the next evening when her husband explained what had happened. The whole city was talking about the crime headquarters being blown up. 'I'm angry with you.'

'Why?' Jack replied. 'You didn't want your main store destroyed, did you?'

'No,' Amanda said and swung her arms around him, 'but you promised; no secrets, remember?'

'Oh yes,' he replied. 'Sorry, My Dear. I forgot.'

'No you didn't,' scolded his wife. 'You knew I'd be worried.' She stopped as Jack's kiss interrupted her flow of words...

*

With the help from the insurance company and volunteers, it took only two weeks before the bookshop in New Westminster was ready to reopen in temporary premises. Molly again proved her worth as she telephoned warehouses, opposition bookshops and across the country to Toronto for replacement books. The new opening day was a tremendous success as the free publicity of the fire brought customers into the building from far and wide.

'You know, Amanda,' Molly said after they closed the doors that evening. 'When I was down in Seattle trying to buy books I came across the "*Lexington Card Company*". Have you heard of them?'

'No,' admitted Amanda, 'but I can see from the look in your eyes they are important to us so go on.'

Mary grinned. 'Well, they've gone bankrupt and their assets are for sale. What interested me was the small printing press there. Its one of the latest, you know. They printed their own cards and stationery and were on to a good idea.'

Amanda frowned. 'Then why did they go broke?'

'That's it. They were profitable but the firm that owned them went bankrupt. Tenders are being called for the plant and equipment right now. I'd say it would be half the price of a new press.'

'But still expensive,' Amanda added.

'Probably but if we could print our own postcards and even letterheads for local firms, I'm sure it will pay its own way. At the moment there are hardly any British Colombian post cards around. The few we have sell out almost as soon as they are displayed, especially those with pictures of the mountains and that.'

Amanda nodded at Mary's enthusiasm. On top of getting the shop going again, the rebuilding and so forth there was a great deal of money going out but.... She bit on her lip. This was a chance that mightn't come their way again and there was one backer she could ask.

'I'll see,' she said, 'When do the tenders close?'

Mary grinned and produced a clipping from a Seattle newspaper and handed it to Amanda. 'In two weeks,' she replied.

*

After the accident, Amanda's relations with her father had slowly improved. Sean O'Donnell had visited them on a few occasions and only a month previously had invited Jack, Dot and herself back to his home. The visit was not without apprehension but turned out well; Sean made a fuss of Dot and welcomed Jack as if the elopement never happened.

'How would you like to visit Dad over the weekend,' Amanda asked Jack that night.

Jack glanced up from the newspaper and grinned. Very methodically he stopped reading, folded the paper and placed it on the table. 'What scheming little thoughts are going through your mind, Amanda?' he asked.

Amanda grinned. 'Why should there be any?' she responded.

'My dear wife, you do nothing without a reason. Now out with it.'

'We need some capital so why not ask Dad?' She continued on to explain Molly's thoughts.

Jack frowned. 'Do you want him to be in on our affairs? Sure, he's okay now but he's still your father; the ruthless business man and autocrat.'

'That's the point, I guess,' Amanda answered. 'If the idea was no good he'd tell us but if it had merit.' She frowned. 'I know it's a risk but we could not do it ourselves. We already stretched ourselves getting the second store running then the fire and...'

'Amanda.' Jack said. 'You're trying to manipulate me again.'

'Me!' Amanda replied innocently.

*

'Wouldn't it be better to contest your mother's will?' Sean O'Donnell replied when he'd heard of Amanda's proposal. 'There's thousands of dollars of shares there that will do none of us any good.'

'They'll help Dot's children,' Amanda replied.

'Hardly even then,' O'Donnell retorted. 'I would imagine the whole family will die out and charity will benefit.'

'Okay, Father,' Amanda replied and shrugged. 'Forget about it.' Jack caught her eye. She was trying the same reverse psychology on her father.

Sean O'Donnell retorted. 'I didn't say I wasn't interested, Amanda.'

'Then you'll help?'

'I'll look into it and if it seems worth the risk I'll make a loan to your company. There'll be conditions, of course.'

Amanda glowered. This was business and her father was one tough businessman. Sean grinned. 'If it's a good investment and I stress the "if", I'll buy the machine for you but as a loan to be paid back by a certain date at a nominal rate of interest.'

'What date, Father?'

'The same as your mother's, Amanda. Your descendant can pay it back in Year 2007.'

Amanda smiled, '...and the interest?'

'Well how about two per cent per annum to be paid with the capital on maturity?'

'Only on the loan, not compounding, Father,' Amanda slipped in.

Sean O'Donnell sighed. 'You are a businesswoman, Amanda. I hope your descendants will appreciate it.'

'They're your descendants, too, Father,' Amanda replied. 'Also Jack's and Dots...'

'Okay,' her father grunted. 'I'll get my accountant to work out a reasonable tender next week. If we succeed, my lawyer can draw up the agreement and it can be filed with your mother's will.' He shrugged, 'Mother of God! By year 2007 the Germans will probably control the world and we'll all be Bolsheviks.'

Amanda frowned. 'Who are they?' she asked.

O'Donnell grinned. 'Just a far out group in Russia who have taken up the ideas of an English man called Carl Marx. Heard of him?'

'Vaguely,' Amanda replied without any real interest.

O'Donnell coughed, stared at his daughter and looked slightly uncomfortable. 'I'm glad you both visited. There's something else I wanted to discuss.'

Amanda caught Jack's eye and he gave her a "be careful" look.

'What is it, Father?'

'I'm getting married, Amanda and hope you'll give me your blessing.'

Amanda's expression was completely neutral. 'And who is the good lady?'

'Mrs. Cuthberg. You may remember her, Amanda.'

'Oh I do. Your mistress before Mother died, I believe, Father.'

Sean O'Donnell's face darkened.

'Come now, Father,' Amanda continued. 'This is not the time for hypocrisy, is it? It doesn't matter now, anyhow?'

'I suppose not,' O'Donnell grunted. 'None of us is perfect.'

Suddenly Amanda grinned. 'No, Father.' She laughed and lightened the atmosphere. 'And who am I to judge you any more than you are to force your values on me? I hardly know Mrs. Cuthberg but I'm sure you are making the right decision. Nobody should be alone in this world. We all need companions and partners.'

'Thank you, Amanda,' her father replied and gave a smile of relief. 'I thought you'd disapprove, that is all.'

'And would it have made any difference?'

Sean O'Donnell gave a sad smile. 'I think it may have,' he replied. 'You are, and always will be my daughter, Amanda. After that sad accident, I look on you in a new light and realised your life and opinions are important to me.' He glanced at his grandchild asleep in her baby carriage, 'Also, Dorothy is my step to immortality.'

Amanda stared at her father. 'That's a strange way of putting it, Father but thank you.'

This visit had twisted a little from its original purpose but had gone well.

*

'Well, it is the 1900s,' Jack said later when, on the train home, Amanda discussed her father's affair with this Amelia Cuthberg. It had been going on for years. 'Perhaps men will have two or three wives by 2007.'

'Don't be disgusting,' Amanda retorted then a twinkle came in her eyes. 'Of course the opposite could be true, too. Think of it, three husbands at my beckoned call.'

Jack grinned and squeezed her arm as the train slowed. The border was coming up. 'Funny how British Columbia is home now,' he added. 'It's pleasant to be able to return to Washington but even better to return home.'

'That's because you have a Canadian daughter, My Dear,' Amanda replied with a laugh.

*

Six weeks later when the printing press was assembled at the back of their New Westminster store, Amanda wondered if her descendant would mind getting the bill. Her father's tender was not high but Amanda was certain he had inside information. She had discretely said nothing. There were also plates for cards and two huge crates of paper and other supplementary gear. Amanda was certain some of it was brand new and not part of the original tender.

'Well, Mary,' she said, ' I'll give you six months to ring in a profit.'

'A bonus if I do,' her manager replied.

'Why not?' Amanda smiled and reached in her handbag. 'I have a gift for you.' She handed Mary a folder.

Mary opened it. 'Amanda, I can't afford these,' she chortled.

'They're a gift, Molly and will cost you nothing. Let's call them your bonus.'

The folder contained a hundred, one dollar shares in *"O'Donnell and Williams, Booksellers and Publishers"*.

'Like the new bit added?' Amanda asked.

'Yes, I do,' Molly replied and couldn't help smiling. 'When are you going to buy out *The Vancouver Sun?*

Oh, next year, I guess.' Amanda shrugged. 'Anyhow, you're a partner now so we sink or swim together.'

'We'll swim,' Molly promised. 'I guarantee it.'

*

The years rolled by and Baby Dot grew into abright little girl. She was the favourite of everyone and loved but not spoiled by her parents. The shop in New Westminster was rebuilt and a third *"O'Donnell and Williams"* branch opened in Victoria.

There were quiet times, busy times and prosperous times and that may have remained that way for years to come if another twist of fate had entered Amanda's life.

Just before midnight on Sunday 26 November 1905 was a cold wet night and railway traffic was at an all time high. Jack was on nightshift, tired and ready for home when a railway trackman rushed into the control room.

'There's trouble, Mr. Williams?' he announced. Jack looked up and the man continued. 'The one a.m. freight train was crossing from Track North Two to South One and the third to last freight car skipped a rail.'

'Where?' retorted Jack. This was potentially serious. The incoming Imperial Limited, already four hours late was due in Line North One in fifteen minutes.

'Right across the main line,' the man reported.

Jack grabbed his coat and walked out into the rail yards. The freight train had already been unhitched from the derailed carriage and had moved on. There were now only the last three carriages and the caboose sitting diagonally across three lines.

'If I remember, Shunter 186 should be fired up and in the yards. If we can pull the freight cars back.'

He walked over and examined the offending freight car. One wheel had become jammed where the cross switch section had not quite joined. A pull backwards would, with a little luck, bring the wheel back on the line. He told the men to get Shunter 186 up to the caboose and link it up.

'Meanwhile, shut the signal down and keep the express out of the yards,' he directed.

Another worker nodded and moved to the signal box while Jack walked to the caboose. He glanced up. The shunter was puffing up the track towards them. There was nobody close so he decided to hook the shunter on himself.

The little locomotive puffed in, Jack stepped out on the rail to reach for the connecting hook when he slipped. In those few seconds it happened! Jack slipped and landed on the track, just as the shunter arrived!

*

Amanda was devastated.

Friends and family arrived. Even her father and his wife of three years came and stayed with her for two weeks. Everything was done for her but, in some ways, it made things worse for her as she had more time to think. Jack her husband, friend, lover and father of her child, was dead, taken from her in a blink of an eye just like her mother and brothers in the avalanche.

It wasn't fair! Dearest Jack had hurt nobody but even if it was only for Dot's sake, life must go on.

'I will be fine, Father,' she said as Sean stood by the steps leading up to a carriage of the *Great Northern Express* and gave his daughter a final hug before leaving for Washington.

'Visit us,' Amelia O'Donnell added softly and her expression was genuine. Sean's wife gave Dot a kiss and the little girl grabbed her mother's hand.

'I'll look after Mommy,' she said. Her eyes were dry and the look serious. 'There's just us now. Daddy's in heaven.'

Sean O'Donnell glanced at his granddaughter and bent to kiss her. 'I know you will, Dot but remember Grandpa is always near.'

'I will Grandpa,' Dot said and squeezed Amanda's hand. The little girl had grown up quickly in just two weeks.

With tears rolling down her cheeks, Amanda and Dot walked off the station together to where an unexpected carriage was waiting.

Molly opened the carriage door. 'I couldn't let you go home alone, she said while Peter waved at Dot from the back seat. 'You're both coming to my place tonight.'

It was times like this when real friends showed their worth.

*

CHAPTER SEVEN

Tuesday 25 June 1907
Dear Diary

My entries are becoming few and far between, I am afraid, but there is little of value to write about. Since my Dear Jack's tragic departure all those months ago I have immersed myself into the business. Dot is coming on well in her studies at school. Every night I have to hear her read and she is already writing whole stories with beautiful penmanship. I am, indeed proud of her.

Whether I am proud of my actions this very afternoon, though, remains to be seen but I am a woman, still young and missed what Jack could provide. Who was responsible, I do not know but Samuel made me a woman again today.

Sincerely,
Amanda Williams

*

'Come on, Amanda, it's a beautiful summer's day and I want to get some photographs of the countryside. Why don't you make up a picnic lunch and accompany me?' Samuel said.

Amanda sighed. It was true, the day was grand and a break was needed. She turned to her staff photographer and nodded. 'There's no time, Samuel. I have to be back in town by three to pick Dot up from school.'

'It's only nine thirty,' Samuel added. 'We can take the ferry across the harbour. I have hired an automobile on the other side. Half an hour's drive, an hour's photography then home. We should be back by two thirty. Anyhow, Molly can meet Dot if were late.'

Amanda looked at the sun blazing down in what was going to be one of the hottest days in the summer. The thoughts of the harbour crossing and walk in the wilderness did sound inviting.

'Yes, Samuel, I'll come,' she said.

*

The Capilano Suspension Bridge that looped down across the canyon like an inverted coat hanger was reputed to be one of the highest in the world. Narrow wooden boards and wires for the walkers to grasp looked highly dangerous and even on this still day, appeared to be vibrating in the breeze.

'I can't walk across that!' Amanda gasped as she stared down the dizzy depths. Massive trees below looked like models and the distant rumble of water, way below seemed to make the bridge even more fragile.

'You can,' Samuel said, 'I want to photograph you on the bridge.' He grinned. 'Right in the middle.'

Amanda had watched enthusiastically as the photographer set up his tripod and camera so it was aimed at the structure. She looked through the lens and was enraptured by the latest of equipment.

'Is this how the photograph will come out?' she asked after she took the black cover off her head and gazed up from the viewer.

'More or less,' Samuel replied. 'I usually trim the edges in the final picture. It should make a wonderful postcard.'

Samuel had taken four different photos of the bridge and canyon when he made this suggestion to go onto the bridge and be in the final shot.

Amanda gulped but she was no coward. The bridge had been there over twenty years so would not collapse now. Logically it was quite safe, but emotionally... She stared at the man beside her and bit on her lip.

In stature and looks, Samuel was quite different from her Jack. He was no taller than herself, slim and had a bushy black beard compared with Jack's clean-shaven and muscular features. But his smile was the same, that slightly twisted smile of compassion.

'Go on,' he urged. 'You'll look grand in that beautiful frock.'

Amanda flushed. She was dressed in a new white gown that, in the latest trend hung to just above her ankles so it did not need to be held up as she walked through the track leading to the bridge. Underneath, she'd only put on one petticoat and a new lightweight bosom amplifier. On such a hot day she had decided to wear only light sandals and no gloves or coat. A wide straw boater hat to shade her nose and parasol completed her attire. With her auburn hair combed up under her straw boater she felt quite a genteel lady. She laughed. 'Well, here goes, Samuel. Wave at me when you want to take the photo.'

She bent over to place her parasol against a tree trunk when she felt two hands on her waist.

'Samuel, she cried 'What are you doing?'

The man was obviously nervous but one hand reached up the back of her gown and undid a button.

'Samuel!' Amanda gasped.

She stood up but still faced the tree with her back to the man. The gown loosened slightly as a second button was undone while she put both arms out so her hands were resting on the rough bark of the fir. She knew she should be furious and swing around to slap his face. Strangely, though, she wasn't annoyed. After all she was a widow. In the months since Jack's death she had gone from being very sexually active to being celebrant in one move. Often she'd dreamed of Jack in the dark hours of the night and had stimulated her own body before crying herself asleep.

And now on this hot summer's day, this young man, he'd be younger than her, was undoing her gown. She knew it was naughty but hoped he wouldn't lose his nerve.

This was when she spoke in a hoarse whisper. 'Not here, Samuel. Someone may come. We need to move into the trees.'

She grabbed his hand and led him through the trees until they found a secluded spot where she kissed Samuel passionately, turned and let him finish unlacing her garments. Nothing more was said but she knew what was about to happen. She smiled and helped when he appeared so nervous his fingers failed to work. Moments later, she removed her top underwear and pantaloons and stood before him naked and confident while he fumbled with his own clothes. He was only the second man she had seen and she suppressed a gasp for his male organ was larger than Jack's. But he wasn't Jack. He was Samuel! What was she committing herself to?

"I'm sorry," he said. With his face red with embarrassment and a hand over his organ, he turned away and reached for his trousers.

"Don't you dare," Amanda whispered.

She grabbed his arm, spun him around and held him so close her breasts flattened against his chest. She knew he could not stop now. She kissed his lips, lay down and spread herself wide to receive him.

His lovemaking was unrestrained with a passion that left her gasping in a frenzied orgasm that, after two ejaculations deep within her body left her moaning for more. Not even Jack had satisfied her the way Samuel did.

*

A close up photo of Amanda dressed in her white summer gown, straw boater, holding a parasol above her head and smiling into the depths of Capilano Canyon was an instant success. Hundreds of copies of the postcard were printed and sold in the *"O'Donnell and Williams"* stores, other outlets in Canada as well as Washington State. Amanda was offered several modelling positions, one from as far away as San Francisco, but she gracefully turned them all down.

Nobody except Samuel and herself knew why she looked so ravishing that fateful day and they had a silent pact to keep it a secret. Three months later Samuel proposed marriage to Amanda but she turned him down. 'I like you as a friend, Samuel,' she replied in a quiet voice. 'I love you bedding me but I do not wish to remarry. Do you understand?'

Samuel nodded but looked hurt. Their intimacy had been repeated dozens of times in the intervening period at his place and hers. Though never quite as exciting as that first experience under the firs way out in the country, they were passionate and caring and she was sure there was love involved and not just lust.

'Cheer up,' said Amanda with a grin. 'I happen to have an apartment in the cellar of my place. It is very compact and has internal access to the house. Would you like to rent it? It can be dangerous for Dot and myself living in a large house in these wild times.'

'You don't mean?' spluttered Samuel.

'Only if you're discrete, young man,' she said. 'I may not want to get married but I need you Samuel' She felt her cheeks grow hot. 'Often!' she added.

Samuel grinned. 'It's a deal,' he said.

A week later he shifted into Amanda's apartment to become Uncle Samuel to Dot. Their life together was fruitful and exciting but remained discrete. Amanda doubted if even Molly not realised that she was having a passionate love affair with the firm's photographer. Also, for the first time since Dots birth, Amanda was glad she could be a woman without any fear of pregnancy. Perhaps that was why she found no need to marry Samuel. She had all the benefits without loosing her freedom.

Slowly, the visions of Jack faded as Samuel filled her life. He was a man, a real man who made even Jack's loving seem that of an amateur. Yet Samuel was so gentle and kind Amanda wondered if she should marry him, after all.

*

'Mom,' none year old Dot moaned one October evening two years later. 'I've got a terrible headache and sore throat.'

Amanda glanced up from some bookwork she was doing and frowned. Dot was a happy child who rarely complained about being ill. The youngster did, though, look quite flushed and Amanda could tell by the tight look across Dot's eyes that something was wrong.

'Come on, Dear,' she said as she stood up and put an arm around her daughter. Dot was growing and her head already came to her mother's chin. 'Have a hot bath and then to bed. You can stay home from school tomorrow.'

'But Mom,' Dot complained. 'We've got an arithmetic test tomorrow.'

'I'm sure Miss Nolan can give it to you when you return, Dear.' She grinned to herself. Dot was very bright and it wouldn't be that long before she would graduate to high school. Only a few of the girls moved beyond elementary school but Amanda was determined her daughter would be one. That was why the test marks, even at Dot's young age, were so important.

After a steamy bath and a spoonful of medicine, Dot seemed a little better and cuddled into her bed in the bedroom opposite Amanda's.

'Night Mom. I love you,' Dot said sleepily.

'Night Dear. No reading tonight. You go straight to sleep.' Amanda kissed her daughter as she did every other night and quietly left the room.

*

Frightened screams awoke Amanda. She leaped out of bed, switched the lights on and rushed into Dot's room. The girl was thrashing around the bed so violently that all the blankets and sheets had slid onto the floor. Amanda could see at once that something was seriously wrong. Perspiration covered her daughter's face and hair but though her eyes were open, she was not awake. They were just sort of staring vacantly into the air.

Amanda rushed over and bent down to Dot. Her daughter's face and body were hot like fire and cheeks covered in a red rash. Amanda looked further and saw Dot's chest and arms were also covered. The girl moaned and thrashed around and did not reply when she tried to pacify her.

Dot was in a fever!

Amanda stood back and, most unusually for her, slipped into a state of almost panic. She remembered another girl the same as this. Her only sister, Elizabeth, had become ill with a fever. She remembered watching from the bedroom door as her mother tried to help. The doctor came in a black suit and tall hat. He had a large clip up bag and stethoscope around his neck, stayed a while and left. The next morning their house had been quarantined. For days they were not allowed to leave but on the second day Elizabeth slipped into a coma from which she never recovered. It had taken Amanda months to recover from the shock of her sister's death and now her daughter was in the same situation.

But there was someone to help. Samuel! Amanda rushed along the corridor and down the cellar stairs. At the bottom beyond the furnace was Samuel's apartment. She ran in and switched on the light in his bedroom.

'Samuel,' she screamed. 'Come quickly. Dot's got the fever.'

Samuel woke from deep sleep and squinted. As soon as he orientated himself, though, he leaped out of bed and grabbed her shaking body in his arms.

'Come on Sweetheart,' he whispered as he held her close. 'We'll go and check on Dot.'

The girl, if anything looked worse when they arrived back in the bedroom. Moans and violent shudders filled the air as the youngster tossed her fragile body around.

'Call the doctor and I'll get a cold towel to try to cool her down,' he directed. It looked bad.

Amanda nodded and cranked up the telephone, talked for a few moments and came back. Her expression was grave. 'The doctor can't come for at least three hours,' she stuttered with tears building in her eyes. 'Apparently there is an outbreak and he has dozens of other patients. They advised us to give her fluids and keep her cool until he arrives.' She stared at Samuel. 'Elizabeth, my sister was like this, Samuel.' Her lips dropped. 'She died.' Tears ran down her cheeks. 'I don't want Dot to die. She's all I have.'

'There may be someone,' Samuel whispered.

'Who!' Amanda gasped. Her eyes stared up at him.

'A Chinese man. He's not really a doctor but is an acupuncturist. That's an ancient Chinese practice. It is used a lot in Chinatown but few Europeans have knowledge of how it works. I've seen fevers such as this completely controlled.'

'How?' gasped Amanda.

'Needles,' Samuel explained. 'Something to do with controlling the nerves. I don't understand it myself but the Chinese swear by it.'

'... And you know someone.'

'Yes, remember those photos of Chinatown I took? I got to know the Chinese quite well and made a few friends there.'

Amanda nodded. Vancouver had the largest Chinese population in Canada with thousands of workers brought in to build the railway. However, the two cultures tended to stay apart and she had never been to Chinatown.

But Dot was more important than ethnic differences. 'Get him!' she snapped.

'There's little time,' Samuel said. 'We'll need to take Dot there. Wrap her up in coat and blanket and I'll get the automobile.'

Amanda had recently entered the modern age and had purchased a single cylinder Cadillac Model M automobile. While Samuel ran outside and cranked the motor, Amanda found a coat, gathered her daughter up and staggered along the corridor.

Samuel met her at the kitchen and reached out. 'I'll take her,' he said quietly. 'You go and get dressed.'

Amanda nodded and realised she was still in her nightgown. Samuel lifted Dot up and carried her out to the Cadillac. By the time she had dressed Samuel had Dot her in the tonneau, the separate passenger's compartment attached behind the front seat, lit the three gaslights and adjusted the spark control so the motor made an even rumble.

Amanda climbed in the tonneau and cuddled Dot onto her lap while Samuel slammed the doors and the vehicle moved forward.

*

They were soon away from the suburb and inner city buildings but Amanda had no idea where. All she noticed was the cold wind blowing on her and the sick child in her arms. The gas lit lights of the vehicle showed the road ahead like a tunnel in the dark world between the few gas lamps attached to lampposts every half a block. The streets were narrow now and quite deserted, fog clung around the lights and the rumble of the motor and wind howl blotted out the other city noises. A distant freight train hooted and Amanda's thoughts jerked to memories of Jack.

Samuel turned into an even narrower road with buildings squashed together and built right up to the narrow pavement. The street lamps now disappeared altogether and only their Cadillac's blue flickering lamps showed the way ahead through the dark buildings. Amanda stared around and held Dot closer. It was not a part of the city she liked.

'Almost there,' Samuel shouted over his shoulder. 'We have to stop and walk soon. These roads aren't designed for vehicles.'

He clunked down a gear and swung into the curb. 'Come on, Sweetheart,' he said to Amanda. 'I'll take Dot now.'

'She seems to be asleep,' Amanda replied as Samuel reached under Dot's body and lifted the youngster out of the automobile.

He disconnected one of the gas lamps and handed it to Amanda. 'It's quite heavy but well need it for light,' he said. 'Can you manage?'

'Of course,' she retorted.

With Amanda holding the lamp behind, he turned into an alleyway with Dot in his arms. For more than ten minutes they threaded their way through alleyways, wider lanes and more alleyways. Amanda could see little but the smell of human habitation enveloped her. There was the occasional call or jabber of voices in Cantonese or Mandarin, what language Amanda didn't know or care.

'Daddy,' Dot suddenly said. 'Is that you Daddy?'

Tears flushed Amanda's eyes at the words but they turned to a tiny smile as Samuel replied. 'I've got you, my little angel. A man is going to help you. Just hold on to me tightly.'

'Is Mommy here, Daddy?'

'I'm right behind you, My Love,' Amanda cried and reached up to brush her daughter's cheek.

'My throat hurts, Mommy. I feel so hot! Mommy, I'm scared. Why are we out here in the dark? Everything smells funny.'

'We'll be there soon, Angel,' Samuel repeated and hoisted Dot up a little in his arms.

'Thank you, Daddy,' Dot replied and lapsed back into a semi-coma.

*

Finally, Samuel stopped beside a small green door decorated with Chinese symbols. Amanda glanced at him, placed the gas lamp on the cobblestones and took Dot back into her arms. Samuel stretched up and pulled on a piece of red twine hanging down from the roof. Amanda heard a distant tingle of a bell.

They waited.

The door opened a fraction and light from a weak electric bulb cut across the alleyway. Two eyes appeared and the blunt face of a Chinese lady. She stared at Samuel for a moment and seemed taken back that he was a European.

'Yes!' she croaked in English.

Amanda began to shake. A sort of terror began to creep up her spine. The situation was totally alien. It was as if they were suddenly transported across the world, not just a few miles from home. She'd been foolish in allowing Samuel to bring them here. How could they help Dot?

'I have a sick child I wish Mr. Sing Woon to see,' Samuel said. 'You may remember me. I'm Samuel Hutchkins.'

'Mr. Hutchkins?' the woman said but made no attempt to open the door. 'Go to your own doctor, Mr. Hutchkins. We cannot help.'

'Wait,' Samuel snapped as the door began to close. 'Remember. I'm the man who took the photos of your beautiful grandchildren...'

The door opened again and the face reappeared. Eyes glanced at Amanda and the child.

'Your wife?'

'Yes,' he replied and Amanda saw his eyes stare at her.

'Fever?'

'Yes.'

Amanda waited impatiently but decided it would be futile to say anything.

'Come in. I shall get my husband.'

The door opened and Amanda found herself in a small room with bamboo curtains and mats. The only furniture was a low kidney shaped table and a tiny wall cupboard.

Samuel touched her on the shoulder, and indicated she should remove her shoes and sit down. He gathered Dot from her arms and placed the youngster on a mat. Everything was quiet compared with the alleyway outside and a smell of spices filled the air.

The old lady shuffled back in and gave a mere hint of a smile. 'Come,' she said and disappeared behind some bamboo curtains.

Amanda carried Dot into another room that made her give a silent gasp. It was a surgery, every bit as clean and well equipped as the one her own doctor had. Samuel placed Dot on a wooden platform covered in a crisp white sheet and shook hands with a slim, serious faced Chinese gentleman.

'Pleased to meet you Mrs. Williams,' the man said in crisp English after Samuel introduced her. 'Now, with your permission, I shall examine the child.'

'Certainly,' Amanda answered and watched as the Chinese doctor peered into Dot's eyes, felt her pulse, gently undid her nightgown and gazed at her heaving, rash covered chest.

'She is a very sick child,' he said. You were correct in bring her to me.' His soft eyes turned to Amanda. 'Europeans are sceptical of our methods, Mrs. Williams but I assure you we can help the child. Please understand that.'

Amanda nodded. 'Please,' she replied and felt her throat tighten. She swallowed back the tears. 'Please help my Dot.'

'Take a seat,' Sing Woon invited and spread his hand out to a western style cane chair.

Amanda smiled nervously and sat down.

Meanwhile Dot spluttered and coughed. She appeared to have trouble breathing. Sing Woon gave a slight frown, lifted her head slightly and brought a small porcelain mug of liquid to her lips.

'A herbal relaxant,' he noted as Dot coughed and swallowed a small portion of the concoction. But it seemed to work. The coughing stopped and the squirming body settled down into a troubled sleep. Amanda reached out and grabbed her sweaty hand that hung down from the bed.

The next moves, though, were almost too much for Amanda to bear. She trusted the Chinese man but when he brought out a jar of long thin needles and began to push them into Dot's body, she had to look away and divert her thoughts.

A hand appeared on her shoulder and Samuel looked into her eyes. 'She is in good hands, Sweetheart,' he whispered. 'Mr. Sing Woon is one of the leading acupuncturists in British Columbia.'

Amanda wiped tears from her eyes, nodded again but still could not bring herself to look at those long needles piercing her Dot. She sat and listened to her daughter's gasping breath and afterwards her voice, as Dot again appeared to be hallucinating.

'Mommy, Daddy, are you here? ' Dot suddenly shouted out.

'I'm here, Darling,' Amanda cried and squeezed the little hand that was still in hers.

'Daddy? '

'I' m here, Little Angel,' Samuel replied.

Satisfied, Dot nodded off into sleep but this time it appeared peaceful.

*

Amanda had no recollection of the time but when she stole another look, Dot's face looked calm and quite beautiful. The perspiration had gone and the blue lips looked cherry red. Even the rash on her chest seemed to be less raw.

'She will sleep for many hours,' Sing Woon said quietly. 'The fever has broken. Apart from nausea and the itchy rash, when she awakes she will be fine. You have a beautiful child, Mrs. Williams. I am glad I could be of assistance.'

Amanda smiled, glanced at Dot and realised there were no needles poking up from her tiny body. More important, though, the fever had gone. Dot eyes suddenly flickered and she looked at her mother then Samuel.

'You brought me here, didn't you Samuel?' she asked.

'I did, little angel,' he said.

'And Daddy wasn't here?'

'No, I'm afraid your Daddy couldn't be here,' Samuel whispered.

'I know,' replied Dot. 'Daddy is dead but Mom...' Her eyes turned to Amanda.

'Yes, my Darling,'

'Don't you think it's about time you and Samuel got married?' She gave a little smile. 'Then he can be my new daddy and you wouldn't have to slip down the stairs late at night.'

Amanda's felt her face turn hot and knew it had flushed bright red. 'That's up to him,' she spluttered. Her daughter was growing up.

'No it isn't, Mom,' Dot retorted. 'He's waiting for you to make up your mind. I know.'

It was now Samuel's turn to look embarrassed. 'It's morning,' he muttered. 'I'll go and see if I can get the Cadillac closer.' He shook hands with Sing Woon and disappeared.

The little Chinese man gazed at the two visitors and sighed. 'Our customs may seem strange to you, Mrs. Williams,' he said. 'However, yours are strange to us at times, too. I think your daughter is right. That man loves you with all his heart. It would be a pity to lose him because you're clutching at past memories, now wouldn't it?'

Amanda nodded and hugged her daughter. 'I believe you're right, Mr. Sing. One's happiness is more important than living on memories, isn't it?'

'It is time to move on in your life, Amanda,' Sing Woon replied using her forename for the first time. 'For Dot's sake as well as your own.'

*

The wedding in the Vancouver Methodist Church, their selected faith, was one of most reported events of the winter. For it was here where the attractive auburn haired beauty, envy of the business community, became Mrs. Amanda Hutchkins. At the reception, the two bridesmaids, Dot and Molly smiled across at a slight Chinese man and his equally small wife who toasted to the couple's future happiness. He caught Dot's eye bowed his head slightly to acknowledge her attention and walked through the guests to speak to her.

'Dorothy,' he began. 'Your blue gown looks exquisite. Your mother must be proud to have such a beautiful daughter.'

'Why thank you, Mr. Sing,' Dot replied in a shy voice, 'but it is my mother who is the beauty here today.'

'The generations of spring and summer, Dorothy.' He smiled. 'A blossoming flower compared to a full bloom. Both are of equal beauty.' He smiled at Molly, gave a slight head bow and disappeared back into the crowd.

'Strange man,' Molly whispered.

'Yes,' Amanda replied, 'but a true friend.' She glanced around the crowded room. 'More so than many of the social climbers here today.'

Molly grinned and dug Amanda in the ribs as a businessman nearby avoided her eyes. 'I know what you mean,' she whispered. 'That's a former client of mine.'

*

'Happy?' Samuel asked his wife as they drove away from the reception in the Cadillac a few moments later.

'Yes, My Darling,' Amanda sighed. 'And if it wasn't for Dot's fever it may not have happened.'

'True,' Samuel said and bent across to kiss her.

'Careful,' Amanda said and slapped his arm. 'You're driving an automobile, you know.'

*

Dear Diary

I notice there is but one page left in this volume and what can be more fitting than to sign off with my new name. My only regret is that I cannot produce a child for Samuel but, as he said, we both have Dot. Tomorrow is Christmas day and Dot is so excited. She spent over an hour picking a present for Samuel and another wrapping it. She's in her bedroom right now; wrapping mine, I guess, for I am not allowed to enter. I close with a photo of our wedding to complete the last page. Doesn't Dot look so grown up? Merry Christmas, Dear Diary.

Sincerely
Amanda Hutchkins

*

PART 2   DOROTHY 1918

CHAPTER EIGHT

18 April 1918
Dear Diary,

I guess I am following in Mom's footsteps by starting this diary. I remember as a child, watching her sit on her bedside with the cloth bound blue diary in her hand, either reading it through, deep in thought or writing another section. At times she'd write with flourish while at other times, I guess when nothing much happened, her diary would just lie in her drawer waiting for new adventures.

Mom and Daddy (I've called Samuel that since their marriage) are well and the family business prosperous. At times I miss them so much I almost cry. (Well, to tell the truth, I do on lonely nights like this.) Right now it is a little before two in the morning and I have a lull in my duties as staff nurse at North Dover Military Hospital, England; a facility for wounded soldiers transferred back from that terrible front line in France. I am part of the Canadian nursing contingent in England to help our boys the best we can.

The hospital here was once a private school (which in England is a public school) taken over by the army for the duration. It is a strange country here and I'll never get used to their enforced class system. However, this Great War must be drawing to a close with thousand upon thousand of American troops joining the battle. Though it makes me quite proud of my ancestry I feel they could have come sooner.

I shall endeavour to keep this document going but in this busy hospital with long hours it may be difficult.

Dorothy Williams

*

Dorothy, who hadn't been called Dot since school days, reread her first entry in the cloth bound diary, grinned and shut the covers. She had bought one almost the same as her mothers but with a red instead of blue cover. She glanced up at the wall clock and moaned. It was time to do the ward rounds again. At least in the middle of the night Sister or Matron weren't cruising around looking over one's shoulders.

She straightened her starched cape and walked into the long dim corridor. Blackout curtains and the half a dozen light bulbs dangled from the high ceiling. These enhanced rather than stopped the shadows of the hospital. Grunts, snores and an occasional groan came from the wards as she made her way to the main stairwell. On this graveyard shift, it was usual practice to start at the far ward and work back. Half way along the corridor Dorothy stopped and swung around. She could hear sobs come from one of the single rooms.

Well, the night round was to check on problems and this was obviously one. Tears were not unusual in the hospital even though they were frowned upon by the military hierarchy. She was about to open the room door when a hand touched her shoulder. Dorothy leaped in fright and swung around.

A military police sergeant with MP stitched on his lapel stood eyeing her. 'You cannot go in there, Nurse... err,' and read her name tag, 'Williams. The occupant is a military prisoner.'

Dorothy pouted but her mother's determination came through. 'So why is he in hospital?' she asked.

'I don't know, Ma'am. My orders are to let nobody in or out of that room.'

'Including the medical profession?'

The man nodded.

Dorothy snapped. 'In that case, it is a waste of time having him in hospital.' She looked the M.P. in the eyes. 'I have orders too, Sergeant, and that is to care for my patients. That man in there is a patient. He is obviously in distress and needs help. If I do not tend to his needs I am failing in my duty.'

The sergeant's eyes were hard but he stepped sideways and barked as if he was addressing a parade ground. 'You can have five minutes, Nurse.'

'Thank you,' Dorothy replied, pushed the door open and flicked on the light.

The man in the bed wasn't more than a slim boy. He had a grimy blood stained bandage wrapped around his chest. Huge brown eyes darted at her before he looked away and stopped sobbing. He tried to wipe away tears with a dirty hand.

'Hello,' said Dorothy. 'Can I help?'

'No,' he said. 'It is too late for any help.' Those eyes, though, told a different story. They were almost pleading for attention.

'You do,' Dorothy said. 'Sit up and I'll change your bandage. It is filthy. When was it put on? '

'About a week ago,' the boy muttered but he sat up and let Dorothy unwind the material.

Dorothy retorted. 'A week!' she gasped. 'You've had this blood soaked bandage on for a week?'

The smell of stale blood and perspiration made her nose turn up but she continued until the wound was exposed, a deep bullet wound. Worse, though was the condition it was in. Deep welts of purple swollen flesh and puss covered the entire length of the wound. Dorothy took one look and frowned.

'I'll be right back,' she whispered and walked out.

'That man has not been looked after, Sergeant,' she snapped. 'I'm getting some gear to clean him up and will be back. If you hinder me in any way I shall file a report with the matron.'

The sergeant stared at her. 'Won't do him much good, Nurse,' he said in a quiet voice.

'Why not?' Dorothy snapped.

The soldier shrugged. 'He's being court marshalled for desertion and cowardice next week.'

'I see,' Dorothy replied in an equally quiet voice. 'What will happen to him?'

'It's cut and dry, Ma'am. He'll be found guilty and shot.'

'What?' Dorothy gasped. 'That boy in there is hardly out of high school.'

'Private Robertson is nineteen, Ma'am and subject to military law. Desertion of one's post is a capital offence. It cannot be allowed to happen.'

'That's barbaric,' Dorothy retorted. 'My God, you English are no better than the Germans,'

The sergeant stared at her cold eyes. 'It's not up to me, Nurse Williams,' he replied. 'It's the law.'

'Damn the law,' Dorothy retorted and stalked away to find some clean bandages and disinfectant for Private Robertson's wounds. Her whole body shook in anger. She'd seen terrible things in this hospital but for a young boy to shot by his own side was criminal. No matter what had happened he did not deserve this.

*

'What is your first name?' Dorothy asked as she bathed and cleaned Private Robertson's wounds with warm water and disinfectant.

'Tim,' he replied as he gritted his teeth in an attempt not to cry out. It was obvious he was hurting.

'Well, Tim,' Dorothy commented. 'You don't look like a coward to me. Would you like to talk about it?'

Tim fixed his eyes on the nurse and sat up a little. 'My cobber, Ron Franklin and myself were shot at the same time. By the trenches, we were,' he started in an accented voice Dorothy couldn't trace.

'Are you Australian?' she asked.

'I wish I was. That's the trouble. Ron's Australian and he's going home but because I'm a bloody New Zealander I'm up on court marshal.'

Dorothy frowned and completed cleaned Tim's wounds before reaching for a new bandage. 'What's the difference?' She corrected herself. 'Between your countries, I mean.'

Tim gave a slight smile. 'You Americans don't know much about us, I guess.'

'Canadian,' Dorothy corrected.

'Well we're a bit like that. Australia and New Zealand are two different countries in the South Pacific. The Australian government has allowed some of it troops to return home. There was a row about how the British commanders treated them or something but our government hasn't so Ron goes home and I get shot.' His face tried, unsuccessfully, to look brave.

Dorothy looked exasperated. 'It couldn't be that simple. What did you do?'

'Walked away,' Tim replied. 'Ron just couldn't stand the trenches any more. The killing, the disease, being treated like shit and bullied so one morning Ron walked away and I followed.' His chin quivered, body shook and without warning, he erupted into massive tears. For several seconds it heaved and shook as the young man broke done and cried. 'I was only trying to bring Ron back,' he sobbed. 'He just sort of snapped...'

Dorothy sat on the edge of Tim's bed and reached across to wipe his brow with a damp cloth.

'Go on,' she whispered.

*

Morning dawned over the ANZAC section of the western front; another day of grime and boredom. The rumour was that the Germans were preparing a major attack over the top but, like all rumours, there were no facts to back it up. Tim and Ron sat with their backs against the trench wall and completed their breakfast, cold bully beef and stale bread. Ron had just poured himself a mug of hot tea when Stanley came stalking up.

The two youngsters stared at the dark expression and knew there was trouble. Stanley was their sector bully, a monstrous man in his mid twenties who achieved his objectives by intimidation and sheer brute force.

He went straight to Ron and grabbed the boy's chin so his head was thrust back. Ron's tin mug dropped and landed on his leg. Only the rough khaki material stopped a major scold.

'Where's my cigarette, Worm,' he snarled. 'I had three left last night and one's gone!'

'Leave him alone, Stanley,' Tim cut in. 'You know Ron doesn't smoke.'

Stanley flung Ron aside with a violent push and turned his blood shot eyes to Tim. 'Oh yeah, I forgot the wimp hasn't got the guts to do anything. I reckon he needs to ask his mother if he wants to fart.'

'Leave him alone. He's done nothing to you.'

Stanley grabbed Tim's shoulder and squeezed so hard he dropped sideways and grimaced in pain. 'So I guess you took my cigarette, Timmy Boy.' He moved his stubby face and glared into Tim's eyes. 'I'll be kind to you and Worm. Have two cigarettes back in my pack by twelve hundred hours and well forget it happened.'

'We haven't got any cigarettes,' Tim argued. 'Even if we did I wouldn't give them to you.'

Stanley snarled and grabbed Tim at the back of the neck. In one pitiless thrust, Tim found himself lying in the stagnant sticking water with his head pushed under. He tried to struggle but it was hopeless. Water was up his nose and he found himself spluttering and choking for breath. Ron gave a cry of frustration, leaped on the bully and started to cuff him around the ears.

'Leave Tim alone, you gutless bastard. You're twice his size.'

His bravado worked. Stanley shoved Tim aside and swung around to grab Ron. The youngster, though, had anticipated the move and ducked back out of reach. The bully stepped forward but heard a footstep squelch in the mud and stopped.

Lieutenant Whiting, clean and immaculately dressed, stared at the three.

'Trouble?' he asked in almost a sarcastic tone.

'No Sir,' replied Tim. Experience taught him it was useless complaining to an officer. They weren't interested in these minor disputes. Stanley would simply wait until later and continue the bullying, but with interest.

'You look a mess, Robertson. Go and change into dry clothes and make sure the ones you are wearing are washed,' Whiting snapped.

'Yes Sir,' Tim muttered and stood up.

As he passed Stanley, the bully whispered. 'It's three cigarettes now, Timmy Boy and you're bloody lucky it's not three each.'

Three, six or sixty, Tim and Ron both knew there was no hope of getting any. New rations weren't due for distribution for three days, Stanley had smoked all his cigarettes and this was his way of getting some before ration day. That night they were due for a beating and nobody would prevent it.

Half a dozen other young soldiers along the trench grimaced. With Tim and Ron being picked on, they were left alone for another day. The lieutenant nodded to them and strutted on as if the dirty stinking trench was a parade ground.

'I've had this,' Ron announced with a strange expression in his eyes. 'I'm leaving.'

He stood and walked straight towards the exit trench that headed back at right angles to the main concourse. Further back, steps lead to ground level and a track continued to buildings a quarter of a mile further away. Ordinary soldiers were banned from leaving the trench without permission.

'Are you crazy!' hissed Tim and ran after his friend. 'You'll be up on charge.'

'Oh, let Worm go,' Stanley sniggered. 'He might find some cigarettes.'

'Shut up!' Tim retorted and ran after his friend who, by now had disappeared.

*

'I'm not going back,' Ron stormed and Tim noticed tears in the boy's eyes.

The steps to the surface loomed up but the determined boy continued on. Tim hesitated and followed. The two were on the surface and walked along the muddy track. Tim still pleaded with Ron but was ignored. He never noticed the guard by a distant building with his rifle loaded and ready until the soldier called out.

'You men halt!' he called and brought his rifle up into a firing position.

However, Tim was still trying to persuade his friend to return to the trenches and did not hear or notice grim faced man with pips on his shoulders and a large moustache who appeared beside the rifleman.

'Deserters, sergeant. Bring them down.'

'Yes Sir,' replied the sergeant and fired.

*

Dorothy gasped, 'You were shot by the British?'

'Yes,' Tim replied in a whisper. 'If they'd waited I might have persuaded Ron to go back.' He shrugged. 'They never gave us a chance.'

'Didn't you report this?'

'What's the use? I was arrested and brought here to be patched up so I can go on trial,' He shuddered and was almost reduced to tears again. 'The British are going to make a show trial of it as there are men leaving all over the front and they want to stop it.'

'... And your friend?'

'The Australian government stepped in and overruled the British. As I said, he's going home. They even filed a complaint with the War Ministry complaining about Ron being shot but for me; nothing!' He gulped. 'The court marshal is next week.'

Dorothy stared in utter horror and revulsion. Here she was, volunteering to help in this ghastly war and the British were shooting their own men and because his own country didn't support him, the British were going to get away with it. The bastards!

'Thanks for the clean bandage,' Tim interrupted her thoughts. 'I'm feeling much better now.'

Dorothy suddenly made a decision. 'Look Tim,' she said. 'I'll see what I can do to help. I'll be back tomorrow night and drop in to see you. Okay?'

Tim's eyes met hers. 'In eighteen months you are the first kind person I've talked to,' he whispered. 'Apart from Ron and my other mates, that is, but we're all in the same position. Can you tell me your first name, Nurse?'

'Dorothy,' she replied and reached over to squeeze his shoulder. 'Now rest, Tim. I'll be back.'

'Thank you Dorothy,' Tim smiled and leaned back on his pillow. 'You can't do anything but still thanks.'

*

Dorothy knew that if she was to help the boy it had to be done soon. Though by now used to horrendous patient injuries from massive burns to rasping mustard gas victims, the sight of Tim and the sad story twisted something inside her. Perhaps it was because politics played so much in his fate and nobody was interested in him as a person. He was a number to be put to trial for nothing but propaganda reasons and his friend was going home. In her mind this was the opposite of everything they'd been told the war was being fought for. Dorothy hardly slept that day and returned at twenty-two hundred hours, tired but with an embryo of a plan.

When she walked in the nurses' office, Nicky the nurse she was taking over from handed her, amongst other items, a notebook with *"Deaths"* written on the cover.

'Six so far tonight,' she muttered before continuing with her report on acute patients to watch, problems and so forth. Dorothy wasn't listening. Six deaths in one evening were probably average. Surely out of those, there could be one that would fit her plan.

'I'll tend to them first,' Dorothy replied and took the notebook. After the initial disgust at this job, it had now become a routine. The bodies were not men any more and if she thought of it that way it wasn't too hard.

She wheeled the trolley into Ward 3 where three beds had the ominous white sheets over the deceased soldiers. She moved up beside the first body so the trolley was adjacent to the bed, then placed a wooden platter under it, lifted and pushed it up so the body slid across to the trolley. Like most corpses, this soldier had been extremely undernourished so the manoeuvre wasn't too difficult. She ignored the jibe from the patient in the next bed, pulled a sheet over the head and wheeled the trolley down a zigzag ramp to the morgue.

There, she removed the dog tags from the body and recorded the details in her notebook as well as a cardboard tag tied to the body's big toe. The dog tags were placed in a locked drawer she had the key for. Her job was complete.

In the morning a doctor would walk through issuing death certificates. The dog tags and personal items would be sent back to the regiment the soldier came from. If they were not claimed by relatives within three days the corpses were buried in a nearby military cemetery. A vicar or priest, depending on the decease's religion recorded on the dog tag, would officiate. The funerals were held with military precision. Dorothy knew there would be ten Anglicans, three Catholics, a Presbyterian and a Methodist waiting to be buried the next morning. It was all recorded in the morgue's records. Death in the Great War was a common occurrence.

Dorothy's plan hinged on the fact that there appeared to be no follow up check made between the dog tags and actual corpses. Once the information was written on the toe tag, the doctor used this to write the death certificate. Her idea might just work but she needed a body similar to Tim in size.

The fifth one she wheeled in would do. According to the dog tag the soldier was Australian. That was even better. There would be no local parents wanting a body. With her heart beating furiously in her chest she placed this body near the door, slid the dog tags in her pocket and completed her collection of corpses. Next she headed for Tim's room, nodded to the M.P., a different man from the previous night, and found Tim asleep inside.

'Tim,' she hissed. 'Wake up.'

The boy opened his eyes and stared at her. 'Hello, Dorothy.' He gave a sad sort of smile. 'It's good to see you.'

'I have a plan,' she whispered. 'Now listen...'

'You can't do that,' Tim complained when she had finished explaining everything. 'If anyone finds out they'll shoot you.'

'They don't shoot nurses,' retorted Dorothy. She knew discovery would mean immediate discharge and probably a jail sentence but the consequences of her action meant little to her at the moment.

'When you hear me come back and talk to the guard, pull the sheet over your head and don't move a muscle. I'll do the rest.'

She smiled at Tim and stalked out of the room as if she was in a hurry. Dorothy depended on the guard not knowing the routines as she pushed the corpse she'd selected, still covered in a sheet, back along the corridor up to Tim's room. Also placed on the trolley was a large first aid box painted with a red cross against a white background.

'You won't have much to guard, tonight, Corporal.' She smiled at the M.P. and tried to sound frivolous. 'I don't think this poor boy will last the night.'

The young soldier smiled and ignored the trolley she was wheeling.

'Is that so, Nurse?' he said as his eyes strayed down to her figure.

Dorothy pushed the trolley into the door and shut it behind her. Tim immediately staggered up and, together, they rolled the body onto his bed. Tim took his dog tags and placed them around the corpse's neck while Dorothy undid the tag tied to the toe and shoved it in her skirt pocket. She shuddered. If the morning nurse or doctor remembered Tim and recognised the body as someone different the consequences could be disastrous. This could happen but with so many patients and a changing duty roster, the changes were in her favour.

She hoped!

'Up you get,' she whispered and pulled the blankets up so the head was poking out. She nodded and Tim climbed onto the trolley and covered himself with the sheet. Dorothy swallowed and pushed the trolley out.

If they were challenged now everything would be ruined. She left the room with an enforced slow casual walk past the guard who watched her but didn't say a word. It was one in the morning and he watched as Dorothy swayed her buttocks as she pushed the trolley away. If he was looking at her he wouldn't worry about the man on the trolley.

Back in the morgue Dorothy sank onto a seat and gasped. 'It's okay. Nobody will come in here until the morning.' She looked at Tim with concern. The boy looked quite ill but was grinning. 'Stay here. I have to do my rounds but will be back as soon as I can.'

'Thank you, Dorothy,' Tim said. He sat on the bench with a grimace on his face.

'Does it hurt a lot?' Dorothy asked but her companion smiled and shook his head.

'Hardly feel it.' reached up to squeeze Dorothy's hand. 'I'll be okay, really I will.'

'See you soon,' Dorothy whispered and disappeared out the door. So far the plan had worked but anything could still go wrong.

She returned an hour later to find Tim sitting almost exactly where she had left him. He looked quite ill.

'How are you feeling?' she asked.

'Not too good,' he admitted. 'I think my wound is beginning to bleed.'

He went to stand up, gave a tiny moan and staggered back onto the seat. Dorothy watched in anguish, bent down and felt a racing pulse. Her original plan was to walk out of the hospital with him, go down to the railway station and buy him a ticket for London. She had not thought beyond that, but now he couldn't even stand, let alone walk out of the hospital.

In almost a panic, she glanced around with her mind racing. Of course, the dead man had dog tags so why couldn't Tim take the other man's identity? It might work. She still had them in her pocket.

'Look, put these on,' she said and glanced at the dull metal plates. 'You're Corporal Adrian Campbell. Remember that!'

Tim shrugged doubtfully.

'Listen,' Dorothy persisted. 'You're too ill to leave the hospital. I'll find you a bed in a different ward...'

'But what if I'm recognised?'

'Well what do you suggest?' Dorothy retorted. Her plan seemed to be falling apart already.

Tim looked at her. 'I'm sorry, Dorothy. You've really put yourself out for me. I don't want you to be caught, that's all.'

'Thanks,' she replied and her anger disappeared. 'I'll get a wheelchair and take you to Ward 7. We often make changes in the early morning to get ready for new patients who arrive from the boat after breakfast. Nobody will think anything about it.'

Even though the corridor was empty, Dorothy's heart raced as she wheeled Tim along to the ward, found an empty bed near the door and helped him in.

'There,' she whispered. 'Now everything is as it should be. I'll dress your wounds.'

After she had completed helping as best she could, there was no more she could do so she completed her rounds. She handed over to the morning staff and walked across the quadrangle to the nurses' home. She felt exhausted but strangely calm.

Tim seemed such a nice boy but was really just a bag of bones. She liked his accent, too. Dorothy gave a giggle at what she'd done. He was actually older than her but didn't seem to be. Boys were like that.

*

The next evening when Dorothy walked into the hospital she immediately sensed something was wrong. Doctor Cowan's ancient Austin car was still parked in the drive and Matron's office lights were on. She was intercepted by Nicky as soon as she walked through the front door.

'Matron wants to talk to you,' the other eighteen year old whispered in a worried voice. 'And Doctor Cowan is there, too.'

Dorothy's face drained and her heart thumped. 'Thanks Nicky,' she gasped.

She put a brave face on but felt almost dizzy as she knocked on Matron's door and was invited in.

'Sit down, Nurse Williams,' the stern autocratic woman directed.

'Yes, Matron.'

Dorothy sat down and stared at the floor with her hands shaking and teeth biting on her lower lip. She turned her eyes up and noticed the doctor watching her. His expression was calm and compassionate, quite different from the distant remote composure usually reserved for nursing staff. Dorothy glanced away and sneaked a view of Matron who looked almost bemused.

'How old are you, Nurse Williams?' the matron asked.

'Eighteen, Matron.'

'And you're a member of the famous O'Donnell and Williams publishing family, I believe?' Doctor Cowan added.

'It's my mother's firm, yes.'

'So why did you come to England?' Matron added.

Dorothy looked up and saw both Matron and the doctor looking intently at her. 'I wanted to help,' she muttered. Suddenly her eyes flickered and huge tears appeared. 'I know I did wrong,' she burst out, 'but it is not fair. Nobody should be killed for trying to help a friend. Why should a bunch of dithery old men play with boys' lives? If the British are like this, they are as bad as the Germans.' She jerked her head back then realised her emotional outburst wouldn't help and burst into tears. 'I'm sorry,' she blurted out, jumped up and ran out the door.

*

'A young woman ahead of her time, Matron,' Doctor Cowan remarked dryly.

'Yes,' the woman replied. 'We spend a month trying to devise a method to save these young boys from the "dithery old men" as Nurse Williams put it and she sorts it out in one night.'

Doctor Cowan nodded. 'I heard her mother speak in Toronto a couple of years back. I'd say if she knew about this she'd be proud of her daughter.'

'And imagine what "*The London Dispatch*" would say,' Matron added.

"*The London Dispatch*" was a syndicated weekly column, appearing in over sixty American and Canadian newspapers that were often highly critical of the way people were treated in the war. A censored version was even printed in "*The Times*" of London. It was owned by *O'Donnell and Williams* and often written by Amanda Hutchkins, herself.

'They'd make the British Army into mincemeat,' retorted Cowan, 'and it bloody deserves it.'

There was a knock on the door and Dorothy's head appeared. Her eyes were red but she'd stopped crying. 'I apologise Matron, Doctor,' she said. 'Can I come back in?'

'Please do,' the doctor replied and waved his hand back to the seat the nurse had only recently vacated.

*

Dorothy sat and stared at the wall. Visions of disgrace and even criminal proceedings shot through her mind but she was determined to defend herself and the young New Zealand soldier treated so unjustly. She could not bring herself to look at her superiors.

. 'You cannot take matters into your own hands, Nurse Williams.'

'No Matron,' Dorothy whispered

'There are many terrible things happening in this war,' Matron continued.

'Yes, by the enemy,' snapped Dorothy with anger replacing nervousness. 'Not by our own side. So much for the British justice we were taught about at school.'

Matron glanced sideways at Doctor Cowan before going into a long lecture about hospital rules and regulations. 'And what about the relatives of the poor Australian soldier you took the dog tags from? They would never have known what happened to him.'

Dorothy's eyes filled with tears again. 'I didn't think about that but only tried to save Tim. I had nothing personal to gain.'

'Your motives are commendable,' Doctor Cowan interjected. 'We'll see what we can do for Private Robertson.'

'You will?' gasped Dorothy. She realised, perhaps for the first time, the doctor and possibly even Matron were on her side.

'An indiscretion like this cannot go unpunished, I'm afraid.' Matron was her old self again.

'I realise that, Matron.' Dorothy wiped away her tears and waited for the worse.

'Your three day leave at the end of the month is cancelled and you'll do two hours extra duties every day for six weeks...'

'Yes Matron.' The days off didn't really matter; there was nowhere to go anyway, but the extra hours would mean at least twelve hours duty every day.

'Your extra time will be spent providing acute care to a very ill soldier in Room Sixteen. That begins immediately. Normal duties commence afterwards. You may go nurse.'

Dorothy stared in amazement. 'Is that all?' she spluttered.

'No,' Doctor Cowan replied. 'Everything discussed here is confidential. Understand?' He raised an eyebrow.

'Oh yes, Doctor,' Dorothy replied, gave a smile of gratitude and left.

Room Sixteen was one of the single rooms on the ground floor. Deep in thought, Dorothy made her way there and walked in. The soldier inside wasn't asleep.

'Hello Dorothy,' he said from the pillow. 'I was told a nurse would be along soon to change my bandages. I'm glad its you.'

'Tim!' she gasped. She had no idea it would be him. 'I've been assigned to look after you.'

*

CHAPTER NINE

26 April 1918

Dear Diary

Nothing more has been said but Tim has been given a completely new identity as an Australian soldier called Kevin Smithers. After having to swear on the bible to secrecy (he told me, though), he has been issued with new dog tags, identity papers and a partly used ration book. He even has an honourable discharge due to war wounds from the Australian Army. I have a strange feeling that my Mom's importance has helped. The British are very impressed by such things.

I returned the dog tags of the late Corporal Adrian Campbell to the locked drawer and no doubt, his regiment and relatives will be informed of his death.

Yesterday, Tim heard that Ron, his friend, is now on a hospital ship heading home to Australia. As an "Australian" Tim could have gone too, but chose to take his discharge here in England. As he said, Australia is unknown to him and he cannot return to New Zealand to visit his family, not that he really seems very interested. He told me he is one of seven children and never really got on with his parents, anyway. With my own Mom and Daddy so caring and loving, I find this quite sad. I would hate to be all alone in this world.

Anyhow, hospital life goes on and I spend much of my time with Tim. We seem to have so much in common, even down to the books we read. My feelings for him now are strange. I have never felt this way before. It is like my love for Mom and Daddy but is also different. I wish Mom was in England so I could talk to her about it. Meanwhile, I'll care for Tim until he gets better. He is still quite ill and, though I dress his wounds regularly they still look terrible.

In other news, a letter arrived from Mom yesterday and it wasn't even censored. Daddy and her are well and want me to go home when my tour of duty is over in a few months. Funny, though, with Tim here, England now seems like home, too. The papers say the war will be over soon but, of course, that was rumoured last year. Time will tell.

Dorothy Williams.

*

Work at the hospital was busy and often frustrating as young men, and some not so young, received treatment for their wounds. Bullets were removed from bodies and diseases diagnosed, with patients often sent on to other hospitals or clinics for tuberculosis or venereal diseases. Psychological problems, though, were rarely understood or treated and often only partially cured soldiers were sent back to the front. Manpower in 1918 was becoming difficult to maintain so mere boys and older men were called up to serve their country in the trenches of France.

After a brief response to Dorothy's tender care, however, Tim reverted into a state of just lying on his bed, soaked in perspiration and lapsing into troubled sleep. His wounds did not respond to treatment and still appeared ugly and purple when Dorothy bathed them.

'Oh, Tim,' she said one morning after he had vomited into a basin after she had tried to give him some solid food for his breakfast. She washed his face and found his pulse racing and temperature was just under a hundred degrees. The boy was burning up.

Tim attempted to smile but instead gave a low groan and his eyes turned up into the sockets while his body shuddered and writhed around.

'Don't die on me, Tim,' Dorothy whispered. She put aside the basin and rushed out of the room.

Doctor Eddie Douglas, one of the overworked house surgeons, was in the adjacent ward when Dorothy rushed up and stood beside him. Even in an emergency there were procedures to follow.

'Trouble, Nurse Williams?' he asked in his slow Scottish accent.

'If you could spare a moment, Doctor.'

Eddie frowned but nodded. 'I'll just finish with this patient and be with you,' he said.

A few moments later he was examining Tim.

'I see,' he muttered and picked up the clipboard of Tim's medical notes. He was unaware; of course, the original notes had been methodically rewritten under his patient's new identity. 'This is not correct.'

'What, Doctor?' Dorothy's voice was apprehensive.

He has a "M" on his notes. That is for seriously wounded patients who have no hope of survival. You know that.'

Dorothy bit on her lip. 'I know,' she whispered and quoted the regulations. 'Maintain and keep comfortable but treatment is kept for patients who'll benefit more.' She was almost in tears as she looked up. 'But please help him, Doctor.'

'Skinny young laddie. Got through to you has he, Nurse?' Douglas grunted but he did bend down to examine the patient. 'He wouldn't be Scottish by any chance?'

'No, New Zealand...' Dorothy corrected herself. 'Australian.'

'Aye. These colonials are quite tough.' The doctor grunted, unwrapped the bandage around Tim's chest and examined the wound. He frowned and turned to the nurse. 'Can you get my surgical kit, please? It is at the end of Ward 4.'

When Dorothy arrived back with the bag, the doctor took out a surgical knife and anaesthetic.

'He just vomited up his breakfast so should have an empty stomach,' she said as she checked Tim's pulse. Though still high, it appeared more stable.

'Good,' said the doctor and began to administer the anaesthetic. When the patient was in a deep sleep he made a long slice along the wound. Blood and putrid puss squirted out and Dorothy used a sterile cloth to soak as much as possible up.

She watched, white faced and shaking as the doctor cut deeper before giving a satisfied grunt and asking for tweezers. Dorothy could see nothing except blood and wounded flesh. The doctor peered into the wound, cut a piece of dried flesh away and manipulated the instrument. Finally, he found the object of his search, pulled a long blood covered object out and dropped it into a metal tray Dorothy held out.

'A large splinter of wood,' he retorted. 'That was why the wound wouldn't heal.'

Dorothy frowned. 'How, Doctor?' she gasped.

'I'd say a bullet didn't hit this man at all. More likely a bullet hit a wooden object near him and his chest was pierced by this large wooden splinter.' He looked annoyed. 'If it was found and taken out immediately, he would not be suffering these recovery problems.' He glanced at Tim's fake serial and regiment numbers. 'This is not good enough. I'll file a report to his regiment's medical officer.'

'I'll do it,' Dorothy gasped almost too quickly. If authorities discovered Tim's new identity, everything would be ruined.

'Why thank you, Nurse Williams,' Douglas grunted and began to clean and stitch up the wound. 'Aye, he's still a sick lad but with care and a temperature drop, he should survive.' He shook his head again. 'If it wasn't for his "M" ranking the trouble would have been picked up earlier. Thank you for your conscientiousness, Nurse.' He shook his head. 'To classify him as serious was ridiculous.' He gave her another smile of acknowledgement and left.

Dorothy stared at the sleeping patient deep in thought. Two things had been revealed; the soldier aiming at Tim had either been a bad shot or had purposely tried to miss him. She believed it was the later. The bullet had missed but shrapnel had caused the damage. Secondly, someone higher up had classified him as "M"; probably in the hope he'd die and save the trouble of a court marshal.

Dorothy shuddered at the callousness of this unknown officer. 'Bastard!' she swore and began to rebandage the wound. 'If that military policeman purposely tried to miss you, the least I can do is to help get you better. We'll show them, Tim.'

*

After early signs of recovering, though, the soldier's condition slipped back to be bad as, if not worse than before the splinter was removed. He became feverish and seemed to have trouble swallowing. His rasping breath made Dorothy frown with worry.

'What's wrong, doctor?' she asked Doctor Douglas who was in the room when she arrived.

The doctor glanced up. 'Not good, I'm afraid. Our young patient here has tetanus probably introduced into his wound by the wood splinter.'

'Is it fatal?' Dorothy asked.

'In his condition I'd only give him about forty per cent chance of survival. If he can get through the next week those odds will improve to ninety per cent. We'll need to perform minor surgery to remove any infected tissue and I'll inject a muscle relaxant to control the spasms.' He looked at her. 'I'm sorry, Nurse Williams. This type of thing is happening far too frequently lately. The initial wounds are followed by diseases. I'm afraid the medical profession still has a lot to learn. Keep the room shaded, his temperature down and fluid intake up. If there is a sever heart murmur or he slips into a coma, contact a staff doctor or myself immediately.'

Dorothy nodded and looked at her patient with determination. For the next three days, she spent well beyond her two hours extra duty with Tim. She would bathe his sweaty brow with cool water, try to get him to swallow weak limejuice and remain with him so long, sheer exhaustion would take a hold. Often, she would fall asleep in the bedside chair.

Tim remained in a dazed condition where he didn't really know what was happening or slip into restless sleep. Occasionally, though, he became alert and talked to Dorothy.

On the fourth day after the diagnoses, Dorothy awoke to find Nicky shaking her shoulder. 'Wake up Dorothy. Go back to the nurses' home and sleep,' she said. 'I'm off duty so can keep an eye on Kevin.'

'Kevin?' muttered the half asleep Dorothy before she realised Nicky was using Tim's fake name. 'No, I'll be okay. I'm not on duty until this afternoon. You need your rest, too, you know.'

'Look go,' said Nicky and pulled Dorothy up from the chair. 'I'm not doing twelve-hour shifts. You've hardly left this room for three days. You won't help Kevin if you collapse from exhaustion, now will you?'

'Guess not,' Dorothy replied and smiled in appreciation. She looked at Tim and was about to take his temperature when Nicky interrupted.

'Go!' she ordered. 'I'll do that.'

Dorothy grinned, squeezed Nicky's arm and left.

Six hours sleep resorted much of her energy and she returned to Room Sixteen to find Tim sitting up alone in the room with a couple of pillows propped being him.

As she bent over to pull the blankets up, the young man suddenly grabbed her shoulders. Before she could say a word he reached up and kissed her on the cheek. Dorothy flushed and jerked back but noticed the tenderness in his eyes.

'I'm not going to apologise, Dorothy,' Tim said in a resolute voice. 'I know you've been here for hours and hours. I wanted to kiss you as a thank you and decided I would.' Suddenly his nerve gave out. 'I like you a lot,' he muttered and looked away.

Dorothy smiled, bent down and kissed him back. 'Next time, ask first,' she whispered and finished tucking the blankets in. She'd wanted him to do that for a week.

*

After the crisis of that first week drew to a close, Doctor Douglas said Tim's progress was looking good.

'Mind you, Lassie,' he said to Dorothy. 'He'll be still on the seriously ill list for at least two more weeks and needs to remain in hospital for a while beyond that time. Your care has certainly helped. I hope the young fellow appreciates it.

'I do but tell her to look after herself, Doctor,' interrupted Tim. 'She pays no attention to me.'

Doctor Douglas looked at the dark rings under Dorothy's eyes and nodded. 'I see what you mean, Lad,' he said and winked at the nurse. 'Count yourself lucky. I doubt if many soldiers in this hospital received the help you've got.'

Tim reached out and found Dorothy's hand. 'I know,' he whispered and gave a smile before his eyelids grew heavy and he drifted asleep.

'By the way,' Eddie Douglas said to Dorothy. 'Matron asked me to write a report on how you've been performing.' He coughed. 'I recommended you should be taken off the extra duties and have your leave reinstated.'

'I appreciate that, Doctor,' she replied. 'Thank you.'

*

When or how the friendship and empathy turned to love, Dorothy never knew. Perhaps it was after Tim became fully alert and began to talk about himself, his disillusionment with the war, his reasons for enlisting in the first place, life in New Zealand as a child and everything about himself. He just talked while Dorothy listened and watched the young man gradually recover.

The ugly wound lost its purple puffy look and the weeping sores dried up. Healthy skin began to show, his swollen neck went down and Tim finally managed to retain solid food in his stomach. His temperature returned to normal and fluttering heart became steady.

Late one evening, Doctor Douglas called Dorothy into his office and told her the tetanus bacteria had been conquered. She had to tell Tim but had other urgent duties so it wasn't until well after midnight that she entered Room Sixteen to find him in a restful sleep. She knew the doctor had left and except for the guards patrolling outside, everyone in the hospital was asleep.

When she looked at her patient lying there in the reflected light from the corridor, emotions she had only dreamed about rushed through her body. There was Tim sleeping peacefully in front of her; not another person was around. Her mind went back to her mother's diary. That was the section about the love making with Samuel in the Capilano Canyon. When she had read the description it had disgusted her at the time but now, she could understand. If her mother did it without being married so could she. Tim could still have a relapse and die and he she would never know what it was like to be loved by him.

She gulped but instead of suppressing her responsive body she made the decision to proceed. With shaking hands, she shut the door and, with it, the light from the corridor. Adrenaline rushed through her veins as she removed her cape, garters, white stockings and shoes, pulled back the blankets and slipped in beside the sleeping man. Dorothy tucked her arms around the slender body and kissed his lips. What would happen next, if anything, was completely unknown. She felt excited but, at the same time very calm. Tim awoke with a twitch and his vibrant male body could be felt through the thin pyjamas.

'What are you doing?' he whispered through the charcoal darkness. Dorothy's body was shaking and she could feel strange things happening. But she could tell Tim, too, had become aroused. His male organ was suddenly tight and rubbing against her.

'It's okay,' she replied and kissed him. 'Don't talk.'

'Oh Dorothy,' Tim gasped but folded his arms around her. 'We shouldn't.'

'I know,' Dorothy whispered, grabbed his hand and brought it up to her uniform top where he fumbled with the buttons and undid them.

Suddenly they were kissing frantically and Tim had his hand down the valley of her bosom while his other hand moved around her back and undid the clips of the brassieres she wore. With the garment loosened the nervous man pulled it aside and stretched trembling fingers out to touch the soft flesh of her breasts.

'It's okay,' Dorothy whispered, kissed him open mouthed and run her tongue around his lips while clutching him so close he could hardly breathe.

He fumbled in embarrassment for several minutes and Dorothy hoped they could continue without making fools of themselves. Their kisses and petting continued into a passionate until Tim moaned and rolled onto her. His gentle thrusts became desperate as he entered her body and warm sperm burst into her.

'I love you, Dorothy,' he whispered afterwards and caressed her hair.

Dorothy sniffed back tears and stared at him in the darkness. She could see little but all her other senses were on full alert. 'Oh Tim,' she replied and kissed him on the lips.

Suddenly she thought of the time, flicked on the light and glanced at her little pocket watch attached to her breast pocket. She'd been in the room over half of an hour.

She grinned. 'You're a real man, Tim. Be proud.' She bent forward and squeezed his hand. 'You can help me with my brassieres if you like.'

Tim smiled and, with firm but sweaty hands, did the clips up and afterwards, the buttons on her uniform. Finally, Dorothy stood up, brushed her skirt down and reattached her cape.

'I must be going,' she said, leaned over, kissed him and left.

'Mom, I understand now,' she whispered to herself as she made her way towards the toilet to clean herself up before starting the rounds. She knew she loved Tim, they had made love and she had no regrets what so ever.

*

'You what!' exclaimed Nicky a few hours later in the nurses' home after she heard of Dorothy's activities. 'Let's hope the Good Lord doesn't strike you down for your sins. Do you want to have a baby?'

'Oh come now,' Dorothy retorted. 'You're a nurse. I worked my time out exactly. There was no risk.'

'Yeah,' replied Nicky. Then how come there are unwanted babies being born all over the country. What makes you so special?'

Dorothy pouted and put on a great show of confidence but it was only skin deep. Underneath, with the light of the new day she felt totally nervous. She still did not regret losing her virginity with Tim but Nicky's comments shook her confidence. What if the worse had happened and she was pregnant? The trouble was she was certain she wanted to make love again, the mere thought of the action sent tiny quivers of anticipation through her body.

Nicky noted Dorothy's expression and gave a slight grin. 'Look Dorothy, I'm sure you had everything worked out well. Tell me about it.'

Dorothy flushed. 'I started it,' she confessed. Then once we began we couldn't stop. I can't explain. You need to do it.'

Nicky frowned. 'I don't think so, but Dorothy, be careful. There are things you can use to stop getting pregnant.'

'Yeah but they're only available to married people.'

'Oh for God's sake, you're naive,' Nicky retorted. 'Soldiers on leave are issued with them. Talk to Kevin about it. I am sure there are supplies somewhere in the hospital. I'll have a look if you like.'

Dorothy nodded. 'I guess,' she said. 'It doesn't seem right, though.'

Nicky grinned. 'Of course it isn't but neither is leaping into a hot blooded soldier's bed, is it?'

'It wasn't like that,' Dorothy retorted. 'Tim... I mean Kevin and I have feelings for each other. You make it sound just crude.'

Nicky smiled. 'I'm sorry, Dorothy. I didn't mean it that way. I've seen all you've done for Kevin and the way he looks at you. Don't spoil it now and ruin your life. I'm only thinking of you.'

Dorothy nodded but her confidence was undermined. It was only when her period arrived right on time a few days later that she sighed in relief. Meanwhile Nicky produced some little rubber packs of something called condoms that an embarrassed Dorothy handed on to Tim.

He, though, thoroughly agreed with her worries and their lovemaking was repeated several times, especially when Dorothy was on the graveyard shift and they could use his bed. Their love physically and emotionally grew through the next few weeks and the physiological affect on Tim was noticeable, too.

*

Gradually Tim's body began to heal, the poison in his wounds disappeared and one day the Doctor Cowan pronounced him fit enough to be discharged the next morning.

'When you leave you'll be a civilian, Son.' He reached out and shook his hand. 'Is everything set?'

'Yes, thanks to your help,' Tim replied. He glanced around the room to see that nobody could eavesdrop on their conversation. 'Will I ever be able to use my real name again, Doctor?'

Doctor Cowan frowned. 'I would be careful, Kevin,' he added and stressed the name he used. 'Stay away from anyone in your old regiment. Marry that young nurse of yours and move into the country, Wales or Scotland, at least until the war is over. Once peace comes...' He shrugged. 'Anyhow, has your war disability pension come through?'

Tim grinned. 'It starts officially on my discharge. I get my final army pay next week and my pension money a month later. The Australians sent me a very nice letter.' He gulped. 'I feel like a criminal. They're so good to me and I'm not even from their country. They even got me accommodation in a Dover hostel for discharged soldiers like myself.'

'Don't feel guilty,' the doctor said. 'Whether you're from Australia, New Zealand, England or Canada, you did your duty for the British Empire. Think of it that way.'

'Thank you, Doctor Cowan,'

Tim looked up when he heard a tiny cough at the door.

Dorothy was standing there dressed, as usual in her nurse's uniform, crisp and white and with her blonde hair and slim figure so beautiful Tim could hardly believe she was his love.

'I bought you some civilian clothes,' she said and placed a shopping bag on his bed before turning to the other man in the room. 'Hello Doctor Cowan. Our patient looks well, doesn't he?'

'Indeed he does,' the doctor replied. 'Thanks to you, Nurse.' He brushed her arm and walked out.

Dorothy turned and gave Tim a kiss. 'Well, Kevin,' she said. 'Are you ready for the big wide world?'

'Only if you're with me,' the young soldier replied and gazed tenderly into her eyes.

A whole new world was indeed waiting, one that involved Kevin, as he had to remember to call himself, and the young nurse who had helped to get him better.

*

That night Dorothy wrote her mother a coded letter. This consisted of a simple use of words to escape the censor. When she referred to the word "birthday" in the first sentence her mother would know that particular code was in operation from the next sentence on. It was a crude code but one she'd used before to help her mother write a scathing article about hospital conditions a couple of months earlier.

For two hours she thought and wrote until her five page, seemly innocent letter of hospital and personal life contained an explanation of what had happened to Tim. She knew her mother would be able to write an article that couldn't be traced back. Amanda's flare for imagination and knowledge of regimental positions on the western front made many commanders think she was writing directly from France. She'd even learned that one infuriated British Brigadier had assigned military police under his command to find this journalist undermining the war effort.

*

Ten days later the New York Tribune carried a *"London Dispatch"* headlined *"Young British Soldier Shot by his Own Side for leaving his Trench on a Toilet Call,"* and continued...

"The terrible case of a young Australian soldier who was shot by a British officer for merely leaving the trenches because he had diarrhoea and then left to die without medical attention has been reported to London Dispatch."

The article was censored out of the British press but blazed across German newspapers in a major propaganda scoop.

The full story exposed the "M" classification and desertion trials in a fictitious account of Tim's suffering. It also reported that the military secret service was called into 10 Downing Street to explain to Mr. Lloyd George, the prime minister, why this happened.

A later article reported that the "M" classification had been dropped from medical files and four other young soldiers due to go on trial for cowardliness and desertion, had their charges reduced to Absent Without Leave and sent back to their regiments.

Dorothy smiled when the news filtered back from her mother who had other, quite extensive, British sources. In her own modest way, Dorothy felt she had contributed something towards helping several other anonymous young soldiers and, of course with her love for Tim, her own life would never be the same again.

*

CHAPTER TEN

2 July 1918

Dear Diary

The war is on everyone's lips with massive battles seemly everywhere but I have done my part. My nursing duties are over at the end of the month but with high U-boat activity in the Atlantic, we have been advised to stay in England until the war's end. I can continue my nursing on a casual basis if I wish or move on. I am fortunate in that Mom insisted on complementing my meagre salary with an allowance when I decided, against her wishes, to come over here. I am not, therefore, about to become destitute if I give up nursing.

Kevin (Yes, I always call him that now) has never looked better. He quite enjoys his lodgings and, I think with Matron's help, has an orderly's position here at North Devon Military Hospital so we are together all the time.

Dorothy Williams.

*

Dorothy gave a sudden scream when the diary was snatched away and a hand grabbed her wrist.

'You spend all your time writing in that book,' Kevin chuckled and held it up out of reach as she jumped to grab it back. After a brief scurry he deposited a sloppy kiss on her lips and pretended to read the book.

"Kevin,' Dorothy screamed.'Don't you read my diary. Its personal.'

'Okay,' he said and handed it back.

'What are you doing in my room, anyway?' she snapped as she put the diary away. 'Men aren't allowed in the nurses' home.'

'I was missing you and had a job over here and thought I'd see how you are.' He gave a grin and shut the door. 'I must say, you look particularly sexy in your uniform and with your hair down.'

'Kevin!' Dorothy eyed him suspiciously. 'You wouldn't!'

'Why not?' he replied. 'It's early afternoon and the building is deserted.'

He grabbed her and though she struggled and beat on his back, he was too strong and held her down while one hand undid the uniform buttons. Within seconds her objections stopped and she let him continue to remove unwanted garments and lay her across the bed. As usual, their petting, once started continued with two steamy passionate bodies climaxing in full intercourse after Dorothy's orgasm almost, but not quite, wore Kevin out.

It was only after they had redressed and Dorothy had warned Kevin about trying to do it again in the middle of the day when they realised they had taken no precautions at all.

'I'm sorry, dearest,' Kevin gulped. 'I even had one in my pocket but you looked so beautiful sitting there with your diary, I forgot.'

Dorothy grinned. 'Don't worry, Sweetheart. It will be okay.'

*

But it wasn't. Even though their sex over the next three weeks was thoroughly protected, Dorothy's period did not arrive and a visit to a Dover doctor not connected with the hospital confirmed she was pregnant.

'For a small fee, I can have your... err ...problem taken care off,' he said.

'What do you mean?' Dorothy eyed the elderly man with wariness.

He glanced up. 'You're a single woman who made an error. We can remove the foetus quite easily as long as it is done soon. Our service is entirely safe and only takes a few moments. It'll cost twenty pounds,' he added bluntly.

'An abortion,' Dorothy gasped. 'That's illegal and the cost is outrageous.'

'It is wartime, young lady. The cost is necessary to cover our expenses and maintain our secrecy.' He coughed. 'If this conversation is repeated, I'll deny it took place, of course.

'Can I think about it?' Dorothy whispered. Her face was gaunt.

'Certainly, but you'll need to make your mind up within a week. I'll give you a number to phone. Payment is in advance and in cash.' He handed her a card with nothing except a phone number on it.

'Of course,' Dorothy retorted but took the card. The man wasn't interested in her welfare one little bit, only the money.

The doctor smiled. 'Remember, within a week. It becomes complicated after that.'

Dorothy stared at him and nodded. The doctor wasn't a very pleasant person but the offer was tempting. She had the money and didn't even need to tell Kevin.

That night she felt terrible, physically and emotionally. Thinking back over the last few days she had felt different. Her breasts felt swollen and her nipples so tender she had to dissuade Kevin from touching them. In fact, it was the nausea that morning that had motivated her into seeing the doctor to confirm her suspicions.

'Oh hell,' she retorted to herself as she tossed and turned in bed. Kevin was working late and she hadn't seen him since her doctor's visit. Finally sleep arrived but she woke up in the morning feeling violently ill and still with the problem to solve. The one decision she had made as she returned from the bathroom and had a drink of water to clear away the awful taste in her mouth; was that she would tell Kevin. After all, it was as much his fault as hers.

*

Somewhat unexpectedly, Kevin gave a broad grin when Dorothy plucked up the courage and told him of her condition three days later. Without saying a word he smothered her in kisses and held her so close she could barely breathe.

'I thought you'd be annoyed,' she stuttered.

'I love you Dorothy. Why should I be annoyed?'

'I'm not nineteen until February and you're less than a year older, we have our whole lives in front of us and the burden...'

'I've fought in a war and was almost shot as a coward. You've been a nurse for over two years; the war will be over in a few weeks. Oh My Darling...' He kissed her neck and just held her while tears built in his eyes.

'What's wrong?' Dorothy asked with concern in her voice.

'Nothing,' Kevin replied. 'I'm just can't realise how lucky I was you were a nurse at the hospital. Without you I'd probably be dead by now and this news...'

'I can get rid of it if you wish,' Dorothy gulped and told him of the doctor's visit.

Kevin's face turned serious. 'Would you like to hear what I want?'

'Yes.'

'I want to marry you, Dorothy and have our wee baby together. Will you?'

Dorothy bit on her lip. 'Is it only because of my condition?

Kevin stared at her. 'No,' he whispered. 'I've been planning to ask you. I have a wee secret, too.'

Dorothy frowned. 'What?'

'You know how we were advised to go away so I wouldn't be recognised?'

Dorothy nodded.

'Well, I've been looking around and have been offered a job as a printer's assistant with the *Evening Herald*, a little newspaper in the town of

Kettingham, northeast of London. There is a cottage with the job.' He flushed. 'I told them I was married.'

'Why did you do that?' Dorothy asked.

'Oh Dorothy. I love you so much surely you want to…

Suddenly the young woman grinned. 'Yes, Kevin, I think I'd like that.'

All words were smothered as Kevin's lips covered hers and they just clung together.

'So we keep the child,' she finally said.

Kevin smiled. 'Yes, Sweetheart. It's our little love child and I want to give it my name.'

'Which one?' Dorothy asked with a cheeky sparkle in her eyes.

'I'm Kevin Smithers now and don't mind staying that way. Doesn't Dorothy Smithers sound right?'

'Not bad, not bad at all. Thank you, Sweetheart. I've been so nervous about telling you.' She glared at him. It was that day you practically raped me that afternoon at the nurses' home that did it.'

Kevin chuckled. 'If I remember correctly, you were very cooperative indeed.'

They linked eyes and both laughed. With so much love between them, Dorothy was certain everything would turn out just fine.

*

The Weekly Dispatch, the flagship of *"O'Donnell and Williams Publishing Company"* was fast becoming one of the most sort after Canadian newspapers. Printed in two editions in Vancouver and Toronto every Tuesday, it could reach most of English speaking Canada by the weekend. Its cream coloured front page and five sections included a pictorial section of photographs printed on higher quality paper, latest war news, sports news, and an editorial and columnist section called "Afternoon Coffee" as well as a large classified adds section that gave it financial security. Even the trick of dating the Dispatch "For the Week Ending Saturday …" made the Canadians away from the metropolitan centres think their three or four day old edition was right up to date.

The paper caught the hearts of the people and circulation had doubled since the beginning of the war with photographs of the western front and other battle scenes. Exclusive articles and hard-hitting editorials mainly delivered with woman readers in mind added to the paper's popularity.

"O'Donnell and Williams," owned the *Weekly Dispatch* and Amanda Hutchkins often worked twelve-hour days at the newspaper.

Now forty, Amanda's auburn hair, cut short in the latest fashion, carried a few streaks of grey and a few lines radiated from around her eyes. Her anatomy though was as petite as it had been for twenty years and marriage rock solid.

Since Captain Samuel Hutchkins had returned on leave from Europe where he was an official photographer for the Canadian Army, their life together had become quite romantic with desires and needs for each other as exciting as ever.

It was Tuesday morning, 20th August 1918 and Amanda was inspecting the front page of the *Weekly Dispatch*. The massive headline *War will be over by Xmas* was followed by the smaller, *But not until after Germany throws a secret weapon into the Western Front in one final push to obtain satisfactory surrender terms.*

'It looks good, Harry,' she said to the editor. 'With Samuel's latest war photographs he brought back and the exclusive on the U.S. Army Martin MB-1 heavy bomber, we should sell well.'

Harry Sannazio nodded and was about to make some suggestions when one of the young women from the telegraph section came in.

'A telegraph cable has just arrived from London, Mrs. Hutchkins. It's personal and I thought you'd like to see it straight away. She looked quite red as she handed the copy she'd just made to her managing director.

'Thank you, Mary,' Amanda replied as slit the envelope open and extracted the one page document. Her face clouded over as she read the brief message.

'Trouble?' asked Harry.

Amanda looked angry as she stared at her editor. 'It's from Dorothy,' she hissed. 'The stupid girl has got herself pregnant and wants my permission to marry the boy.' She reread the cable and shook her head in disgust. 'Not if I can help it,' she muttered and turned to Harry. 'Is my husband in yet?' she snapped.

'I think he's in the photographer's room,' he replied.

'Thanks,' Amanda almost shouted.

*

'Now calm down, Amanda,' Samuel urged. 'At least Dorothy contacted you.'

Amanda glared at him. 'But she's only eighteen, Samuel. How could this happen? She's such a sensible girl. When she signed up to go to England she wasn't the slightest bit interested in males now she's pregnant and wants to marry the boy.' She swore in frustration. 'I knew we should never have let her go away. Her life's ruined.'

'We don't know that,' Samuel comforted. 'Dorothy is a very mature young lady. I doubt if she would do anything without really considering it.'

'Sleeping around with men is not what I call mature,' Amanda snapped. 'Where has all the morality gone?'

'Think back, My Dear,' Samuel said. 'I don't believe we had taken the vows before our trip out to Capilano Canyon that day.'

Amanda stopped and pouted. 'That was different,' she replied but her voice became calmer.

'Was it?' Samuel answered and took both Amanda's hands in his. 'Dorothy is perhaps too much like her mother, don't you think?' He reached forward and kissed her lips.

Amanda responded to his kiss and sighed. 'I guess I'm getting old, Samuel. It's just that Dorothy is my only child and I do want her to have a happy life. This doesn't seem to be a good beginning.'

'Then go and talk to her.'

'How?' Amanda retorted again. 'Its not like she's across the city or even in Canada.'

'As you know, my leave is almost over and I'm due to head back to England next week. The troop ships always carry a few civilians, reporters, politicians and so forth. Why don't you come along? It will be good for your column to see wartime England. I'm sure it will add a cutting edge to your writing.'

Amanda eyes focused on her husband for almost a minute before they blinked and she replied. 'I just might do that, My Dear. Daughters need their mothers at a time like this.'

Samuel watched as she swung around. Even after all these years he still admired her colouring and graceful figure. She was, though, a very determined and stubborn woman. The meeting with Dorothy could be interesting.

*

'My Dad's given me permission to marry.' Kevin said and flapped a letter in front of Dorothy's face.

She frowned. 'Your Dad? How is that possible?'

'Come here and look, My Darling,' He yanked her down so she ended up in his lap on the sofa. Dorothy put an arm around his neck and read the letter Kevin was holding out.

'Frank Smithers,' she said. 'Who's he?'

Kevin grinned. 'Fictitious father,' he explained. 'There is a telephone number I can contact at the Australian High Commission if I need any help with my identity. I rang last week and explained about wanting to marry you. I was told to write a letter exactly as I would to my real father and post it to them. I did and this arrived back,' he said. 'It's all go, My Love.

Dorothy smiled. 'There's only Mom's reply. I wonder what's keeping her. I sent an overseas cable over two weeks ago.'

'Mail takes a while,' Kevin said and squeezed Dorothy around the waist. 'I'm sure it'll be here soon. Shall I book the venue?'

Dorothy shook her head. 'No wait a bit,' she said. 'I'm still a bit worried about my mother. I expected her to send a cable straight back.'

She stood up off Kevin's lap and gazed around the tiny Kettingham cottage. Even though it was tiny and almost two hundred years old, the atmosphere was perfect. They'd bought a small amount of furniture and she had, only that morning, put up the last curtains and rolled out several new mats on the polished floor. Kevin's had been at his job for a week now, and everyone in the workplace and village had been introduced to Dorothy as Mrs. Smithers. This was lucky, for her slim figure was already showing signs of the growing baby within.

Dorothy kissed Kevin and chuckled. 'I'll get the vegetables on,' she said. 'I'm afraid there's only cold meat from yesterday.'

'My Darling,' Kevin replied. 'Anything you cook is superior to the hostel food. Can I give a hand?'

'Take the ration book and wander down to the village store. I've made a list up and put it in the basket.'

'As good as done,' Kevin said, smacked his partner's bottom and ducked away out the low door as a wet sponge came hurtling through the air in his direction.

*

Another ten days slipped by with no word whatsoever from Amanda. Dorothy said little but Kevin could tell by her actions that she was worried. There was, though, little he could do except give her moral support.

It was a Wednesday when Bill Kirkpatrick, Kevin's foreman tapped him on the shoulder. 'There's a lady to see you, Kevin,' he shouted above the clang of the press in full operation. 'I don't know why but the Boss is as nervous as hell. I'd clean up first if I was you.'

Kevin grinned and grabbed an oily rag to wipe printing ink off his hands. He thanked Bill and went into the men's room to wash his hands further then ambled through to the administration section.

'Hurry up, Smithers,' an elderly man with a worried frown whispered. 'And watch your "ps" and "qs". She's a very important person but wants to speak directly to you. Go into my office.'

'Okay, Mr. Burnett,' Kevin replied and wondered why he was suddenly so important.

He opened the editor's office and fixed his eyes on the woman facing away from him gazing out the window. Hells bells, she looked familiar but Kevin couldn't really think why.

He gave a slight cough and the woman turned around. Her hair was auburn but the face…

'Mr. Smithers?' she said with a soft Canadian accent and held out a gloved hand.

Of course! Kevin realised why he recognised the woman. Except for auburn instead of blonde hair she was almost an older version of Dorothy; the facial features and even build were much the same.

'Hello Mrs. Hutchkins,' he said and shook the hand firmly. 'Have you seen Dorothy yet?'

It was Amanda who now appeared surprised. 'No, I haven't but how do you know me? Nobody knew I was visiting.'

Kevin gave a nervous smile. 'You look alike,' he confessed, 'and when you talked with that Canadian accent it couldn't be anyone else. Dorothy's been worried about you. Take a seat, Mrs. Hutchkins.'

'Call me Amanda,' the visitor replied and sat in one of the comfortable leather chairs 'Why would Dorothy be worried?'

Kevin was beginning to lose his nerve in front of this powerful woman. 'You never replied to the cable we, I mean, she sent you.'

'I see.' Amanda glowered at him.. 'You are the Tim Dorothy sent me information about?'

'Yes,' Kevin replied, 'but please don't tell anyone here Mrs.…. I mean Amanda.'

'Of course not,' Amanda replied. 'You got Dorothy pregnant?' she added in a cutting voice.

Kevin nodded, 'I love her,' he muttered. 'It's not as bad as it seems.' He glanced up and saw Amanda's eyes boring into him. 'With the war on we couldn't wait. We even took precautions but…' he looked away. 'Well, it just sort of happened.

'I see, so the love came first then the sex, not visa versa?'

Kevin gulped. Hell's bells, she was blunt!

'You don't know Dorothy if you think she'd just sleep around,' he retorted in a surge of anger.

Unexpectedly, Amanda smiled with her lips curling up in the same manner as Dorothy's. She laid her hand on Kevin's shoulder and he could smell a whiff of perfume. 'Thank you, Kevin.' The slow Canadian accent sounded friendly. 'I believe you but had to be sure. Now, tell me, how can I find Dorothy? I walked here straight from the railway station.'

Kevin smiled back. 'It's called Rosevale Cottage,' he said and gave Amanda the directions. 'She'll be pleased to see you.'

'I hope so,' Amanda grunted. 'I'll see you after work.'

'Right Mrs. Ha... I mean Amanda,' Kevin answered and watched as the graceful woman departed. He shook his head in wonder and didn't know what his reactions were. Dorothy's mother here in England... Bloody hell!

George Burnett intercepted him on the way back to the printing room. 'Do you know that was Mrs. Amanda Hutchkins who owns the *"London Dispatch"* column and half a dozen Canadian newspapers. What did she want you for, Smithers?'

'Oh, didn't I tell you, Mr. Burnett.' Kevin smirked. 'That's my mother-in-law.'

'What?' the man, who was both editor and manager of the newspaper, spluttered and his abrupt manner softened. His face filled with a new respect. 'I know your good wife is Canadian but never realised...' he muttered.

Kevin grinned. Mr. Burnett was a pompous little man who hadn't made him welcome at all. Perhaps things might change now.

*

Dorothy was stretched up hanging the washing on a line behind the cottage when she happened to glance up. She often admired the view of the village dominated by massive oak tree that towered over the cottages and even the church steeple but today something else caught her attention. A woman walked out from the shadow of the tree and down the lane towards her. Dorothy frowned, looked closer and her heart began to thump wildly.

'Mom!' she screamed, dropped the sheet that was only half pegged up and tore out the tiny gate between the stone fences with her skirt flying. In seconds she was hugging her mother, laughing and talking.

'Mom. What are you doing here?' Dorothy brushed tears of excitement from her eyes and held her mother's hand. 'Come inside. I'll show you the cottage.'

'You're looking chubby, Dorothy,' Amanda commented. 'Is the pregnancy going well?'

'Oh Mom,' Dorothy exclaimed, 'I'm just fine. The first five weeks were a bit rough but it's okay now. Want some tea?' She turned her nose up. We can't buy coffee here. How did you get here? Why are you here? Oh my God, Mom, I was worried about you.'

'Slow down, Dorothy.' Amanda laughed. 'There's plenty of time.'

'Oh Mom,' Dorothy said. 'You'll have to meet Kevin. You'll like him. I know you will.'

'I have met him and he impressed me very much.'

'What? How?' Dorothy stopped. Her voice turned serious. 'Why did you go to see Kevin first, Mom?'

'I wanted to see what he was like and find out why he put my daughter in the family way.'

Dorothy's face flushed. 'You had no right to do that.'

Amanda met her daughter's gaze. 'Well, you're only eighteen and aren't married, Dorothy. When I got the cable I was extremely disappointed.'

Dorothy's lip dropped. 'Why?' she whispered.

'It's morally wrong for one,' Amanda retorted.

Dorothy sat down and turned her head towards her mother. 'I just followed your actions,' she whispered.

Amanda stopped and fixed stern eyes on her daughter. Her business voice filled the room. 'Would you like to explain that statement further, Dorothy?'

'Yes,' Dorothy answered. 'Just before I left school I was cleaning up in the attic at home and found a clothbound diary.' She swallowed. 'I read how I came into the world in the train accident, your elopement with Jack, my real father, and how you had sex before you married Daddy... Everything Mom.'

Amanda flushed but said nothing.

'It disgusted me at the time, Mom. I was only fifteen but after I met Kevin this year, Tim he was called then, I understood.' She couldn't stop the tears that built in her eyes and rolled down her cheeks. 'So don't quote morals to me, please Mom. I'm just like you. I didn't elope but you never had the war...'

Amanda's reserve broke and her own eyes became moistened. 'Oh Dorothy, Sweetheart, I didn't know. I'm an old hypocrite aren't I?'

'No Mom,' Dorothy smiled and blew her nose. 'Just a concerned mother and I love you for it.' She stood up. 'That cup of tea, now?'

'Yes please,' Amanda replied.

*

Amanda watched her daughter and felt guilty about her real reasons for visiting. Fancy reading her diary! The naughty girl. But Dorothy wasn't a girl any more but an expectant mother who would soon produce her a grandchild.

'It had better be a girl,' she added and her face softened. 'Did you read the bit about your grandmother's legacy?'

'I did,' Dorothy replied and grinned. 'It took weeks but I read everything. I used to sneak up there and read a few pages at a time. It was like a serial in a magazine.'

Amanda smiled. 'I wrote it for myself but never dreamed my own daughter would read it. However, I guess there's no harm done. I can't keep any secrets from you now, though, can I?'

'It was only the first volume, Mom and stopped about ten years ago, if I remember correctly.'

'I guess it did,' Amanda said. 'The second volume fizzled out when I became too busy. I'm glad you told me about it, though. I came here, hell bent on stopping your marriage and had visions of persuading you to terminate the pregnancy. Now I realise how wrong I was.' She gazed at her daughter. 'Samuel was the one who never lost faith in you, Sweetheart. He told me you had your head screwed on and could look after yourself.'

'How is Daddy?' Dorothy added.

'Fine. You'll see him soon. He's in England, too.' She studied Dorothy and changed the topic back. 'You love Kevin, don't you?'

'Yes Mom,' Dorothy replied. 'The baby wasn't planned but Kevin and I would have had one later, anyway. I was offered an abortion but Kevin and I decided against it. That's when I sent you the cable. Without your approval, we can't get married.'

'Well,' Amanda replied. 'We'd better get on with it then, otherwise you won't fit in a wedding gown, will you? '

'Oh Mom,' Dorothy said. 'I knew you'd understand.'

*

'I'm nervous Daddy,' Dorothy whispered to her stepfather as they approached the small Anglican Church in a massive Austin taxi.

The pair both looked very smart with Captain Samuel Hutchkins in full dress uniform of the Canadian Army and Dorothy wearing a white wedding gown that Amanda had insisted on providing. The bride grinned as she thought back to her mother's comments.

'I was married twice and never had one,' she retorted when Dorothy had protested about the cost and that she wasn't a virgin bride. 'As for the second reason, I reckon half the brides in white aren't virgins anyway.'

'Yes, but not many are as far on as I am.'

'Why worry,' retorted Amanda. 'I gave up worrying what society thought years ago.'

'You look a stunning bride, Dorothy,' Samuel's voice interrupted her thoughts. 'One of the most beautiful woman in the world.'

Dorothy smiled and raised an eyebrow.

'After your mother, of course,' he added with a grin.

'Of course,' Dorothy said. Her hands shook a little as the Austin pulled to the curb; a Canadian soldier opened the car door for her, and stood back at full attention then saluted as her foot touched the pavement. The timing was perfect.

'Not bad,' Samuel commented after saluting the soldier back. 'Our timing isn't too bad, either. We're only five minutes late.'

Dorothy tucked her arm in his and walked forward into the church as the traditional wedding march played on the organ. Kevin was waiting while friends filled the pews. She caught her mother's eyes and could see the pride there.

Kevin turned and looked so handsome in his dark suit; their hands slipped together and clasped. The service was about to begin.

*

CHAPTER ELEVEN

20 October 1918
Dear Diary

It is Sunday and we're home in our Rosevale Cottage. While the world has entered one of its darkest days in history with hundreds of newly manufactured tanks pounding through the battlefields and the first bomber aeroplanes inflicting mayhem on innocent victims, Kevin and I had our honeymoon in a delightful tiny guesthouse in Wales. The peace and tranquillity makes the war seem a million miles away and even the rainy weather seems to enhance, rather than deter our love.

For the first time since I've known him, Kevin has begun to put on weight and, much to my amusement, his facial hair is growing at such a rate he needs to shave daily. Apart from weariness in the afternoon I am in perfect health. Baby is starting to show his presence, though. Kevin even says he can feel the little thumps when he places his hands on my tum.

Dorothy Smithers (New name- same author)

*

Like all honeymoons, the real world jolted the newly weds at Kettingham back to reality somewhat quickly. It was eight on the Monday morning and Kevin had only just walked in the Evening Herald buildings when Elaine, the office woman approached and said Mr. Burnett wanted to speak to him immediately.

The editor-cum-manager glowered at Kevin and pointed to a wooden chair. 'You'd better sit down. We have to discuss your future with our company.' He sat behind his massive desk and produced a document that Kevin recognised as the application form he had originally filled in.

'You stated here, Smithers, that you were wounded on the Western Front and returned to England. Afterwards, you had an honourable discharge from the eighth regiment of the Australian army.' He glanced up. 'Is that correct?'

Kevin turned pale. He was certain his false identity been discovered. Visions of arrest and being dragged off to jail raced through his mind. He stared at the manager and almost blurted out his full story but stopped when he noticed the other man's actions. George Burnett did not seem to be taking an interest in that section but had continued on without waiting for a reply.

'You further stated that accommodation was required for your wife and yourself.' The manager stopped and drummed his fingers on the table. 'You were married only two weeks ago so were living in sin with your present wife when you arrived here, weren't you?'

So that was it! Kevin didn't know whether to feel relieved or concerned. His identity hadn't been discovered. Mr. Burnett was querying his relationship with Dorothy.

'It's true, we weren't married but we are now,' he replied. 'Dorothy and I were engaged...

'That's all very well,' retorted the manager. 'However, you won this position under false pretences by stating you were already married and brought this company into ill repute by blatantly fraternising, indeed living, with a young lady who was not your wife.'

'I guess you're right,' Kevin mumbled and stared at the floor.

'Your neighbour, Mr. Gregory has contacted me about your ...um... wife's and your own unseemly behaviour in a public place...'

Kevin swallowed. This was too much. 'What was that?' he snapped.

'You were kissing and stroking each other in an unseemly manner in your back yard.'

'So what! It is none of his business,' Kevin retorted.

'Don't get that tone of voice with me, young man,' Burnett growled. 'In a village such as ours there is a high moral standard we adhere to. Even taking into account you are Australian, your wife Canadian and there is a war on, does not excuse your behaviour.' He fixed Kevin with his beady little eyes. 'For that reason, I have no option but to terminate your employment with this company as from the end of the month. You will, of course be required to move out of the cottage that will be needed for your successor.'

'That's not fair? Kevin gasped and sat back in his chair as the full impact of the words filtered through his mind. 'Where do I go?'

'That is your affair,' Burnett snapped.

'But my work?'

'I have no complaints about your work, Smithers. You have a conscientious approach and are learning your trade admirably. It is your personal life and the fact that you lied on your application form that brings about this dismissal. That is all.' The manager stood up and turned away.

'You narrow minded little bastard,' Kevin retorted and stood up. He was a head and shoulders taller than the manager. 'I came across the world to fight for this country, Mr. Burnett and you treat me like shit.'

The manager turned with his face purple in anger. Kevin guessed nobody had ever dared speak to him in this manner before. Burnett lifted his hand and almost struck out at his employee.

'Go on, do it!' hissed Kevin. 'Lay one hand on me and I'll file a complaint of assault with the local constable.'

'Get out!' screamed Burnett. His face was still contorted in rage while his sweaty hands clenched into tight fists. 'You'll be paid for three weeks but will not enter these premises again.'

'Oh I won't!' Kevin replied and stalked out.

When he went to gather his coat and cap from the men's room, Bill Kirkpatrick, the foreman came up.

'So the old bugger sacked you, did he, Lad?' he said.

Kevin nodded in an almost trance like condition.

'I know it's of little help to know, but he's done it before.' Bill put a hand on the younger man's shoulder. 'I've been impressed in your work.'

'Thanks Bill,' Kevin replied. His anger had turned to despair and he was almost in tears. 'If there was only me, I wouldn't worry but with Dorothy...'

'I know, Lad. Keep your chin up. Drop in tomorrow and I'll have a reference written out for you. With most men in uniform and your honourable discharge, it shouldn't be too hard to pick up another job.'

Kevin nodded. If Bill realised that was even a sham! He nodded, shook hands and walked away.

*

An hour later after just wandering through the village and country lanes trying to console himself, Kevin finally walked into Rosevale Cottage to find Dorothy in the kitchen. She glanced up and saw his face.

'Kevin, what's wrong?' she exclaimed and rushed over to him.

'They fired me,' he whispered and attempted, unsuccessfully to stop tears forming in his eyes. 'I've always tried to do the right thing,' he cried. 'Even at the front, I tried ... Oh what's the bloody use?' He flung himself down on a kitchen chair. 'You know, the old bugger next door complained about us cuddling in the back yard.' He stopped. 'I hate this country!'

Dorothy crouched down on the floor and grabbed Kevin's hands. 'Tell me what happened, Sweetheart,' she said with her eyes filled with compassion. 'Everything!'

*

Even though Kevin wanted her to do nothing, Dorothy was determined to help. She persuaded her husband to accompany her and headed down to the post office, one of only a handful of places in the village with a telephone. Armed with a pile of pennies and threepences to deposit in the coin box, she asked the operator for the *Evening Standard* in London, where she knew the British headquarters of the *London Dispatch* was located.

It took almost an hour but finally the toll operator rung back and Dorothy heard a crackly voice at the other end. There was another five-minute wait and two more pennies deposited in the coin box before Dorothy got through.

'Amanda Hutchkins, speaking. Can I be of assistance?'

'Mom,' Dorothy yelled into the mouthpiece. 'It's Dorothy. We need some help.'

'Yes Dear,' Amanda's voice showed concern as if she realised there must be an emergency or her daughter wouldn't be ringing.

Dorothy explained Kevin's plight and glanced wide-eyed at him standing by her as she listened. 'Mom wants to talk to you,' she said and handed Kevin the mouthpiece.

'Tell me, Kevin,' Amanda said. 'Is the *Evening Herald*, the paper you worked for?'

'That's it,' Kevin replied and screwed his nose up at Dorothy.

'... And is that part of the *United Provincial Newspapers* group?'

Kevin shrugged then realised he was talking over a phone line. 'I'm not sure but the name seems to ring a bell in my mind.'

'Good,' Amanda replied. 'Now don't you worry. Put Dorothy back on please.'

'Mom!'

'It will be fine, Dear. I may drop in and see you later in the week. I'm glad you confided in me. Bye.' The line went dead.

Dorothy knew her mother and grinned at Kevin as she hung up. 'I have a strange feeling Mr. Burnett is going to regret sacking you, Sweetheart.' She grabbed his arm. 'Come on. With your spare time, you can take me shopping. I need a new maternity frock.'

*

At the newspaper plant a week later, George Burnett was nervous but confident for he'd done everything to impress the new owners of the *Evening Herald*. After months of negotiation the *United Provincial Newspapers*, a small chain of half a dozen newspapers sprinkled throughout smaller southern England cities, had fought a take-over by a large London paper. This hostile bid would only result in the smaller papers being closed and subscribers being offered the metropolitan paper to replace the local one.

However, at the last moment an unknown company had made a better offer for the group, together with a promised not to close any papers.

'I want everything spotless,' Burnett snapped and Bill Kirkpatrick grinned at the other senior staff members gathered in the manager's office. As if a bit of spit and polish would make that much difference in the long run!

The arrival was at ten o'clock and, on the stroke of the village clock, two large Worsley automobiles pulled into the curb. Five gentlemen and a lady climbed out and walked in the front door where Burnett was waiting in his best suit, with Bill and the senior staff assembled behind.

He shook hands along the line with the gentlemen but stared at the woman at the end of the queue.

'This is Mrs. Amanda Hutchkins, the managing director of *"O'Donnell and Williams Publishing Company"*, who, as you know, are purchasing the *Evening Herald*," one of the visitors introduced.

'We have met before.' Amanda smiled but the smile never reached her ice cold blue eyes. she held out a gloved hand. 'Mr. Burnett, before we depart, there is one small personal item I need to discuss with you. Remind me, won't you?'

George Burnett turned a slight shade of grey but managed to maintain his dignity. 'Certainly, Mrs. Hutchkins,' he whispered.

After a tour of the premises, inspection of the books and a lavish dinner, the visitors were about to depart when Amanda approached George Burnett.

'Mr. Burnett, if you please,' she said quietly and walked towards the manager's office where she sat down behind his desk so he had to take the visitor's chair.

'I shall be blunt' she said with her Canadian accent sounding very business like. 'I have not told my fellow directors but have decided to make a completely separate arrangement for this newspaper.'

Burnett stared at the ice blue eyes but could only find the courage to nod.

'The *Evening Herald* is to become a subsidiary company independent of the other newspapers...

Burnett gave a slim smile and relaxed a little. 'That sounds interesting, Mrs. Hutchkins,' he began to gush. 'Can you elaborate?'

'I shall,' Amanda continued. 'The ownership is to be given to my daughter, Dorothy Smithers as a wedding present. Now, whether she wishes to keep you employed as managing editor after the way you treated her husband is entirely up to her.' She glowered and leaned forward. 'We take over on January the 1st, 1919, Mr. Burnett. My advice is that you reconsider my son-in-law's apprenticeship with this firm. Alternatively you could look in the classified ads for new employment, yourself.' She waited while the full impact of her words penetrated the man's brain then stood up. 'Good afternoon to you, Sir.'

She lifted her frock and walked out with head held high and not one look backwards while the manager just stood in horror staring at the empty doorway. In those few minutes, his little empire crashed around him. Now he had to desperately claw his way back into favour.

*

'Mom, you didn't?' Dorothy chuckled that evening after her mother told of Burnett's discomfort.

'Yes, the pompous little man' Amanda said. 'I must admit, though, he's running quite a profitable paper. I'd keep him on, if I was you.'

'What's it got to do with me?' Dorothy frowned.

'Your grandmother, the one you're named after, helped me all those years ago, Dorothy. Now I want to do the same for you, Kevin and my grandchild. I am giving you a majority share holding in *Evening Herald Newspapers Ltd.*, sixty per cent, actually.' She turned. 'You're being given thirty percent, Kevin and ten percent will be held by the parent company we are buying out.'

Dorothy just stared at her mother then slipped her hand into Kevin's.

'Mom!' she exclaimed. 'You can't!'

'Why not?'

'I'm a nurse and know nothing about newspapers.'

'That's why you have a manager. George Burnett may be an arrogant little twit but he knows his job.' She grinned at her son-in-law. 'How much would you like to bet you'll be offered your job back before the end of the week, Kevin?'

'How about two shillings, Mom?' he replied. He grinned to himself for in New Zealand, as in England, the term Mum, not Mom was always used but Dorothy's mother was Canadian, after all.

'You're on.' Amanda shook hands and then coughed. 'The ownership includes plant and buildings. As well as the newspaper building, this cottage and the three adjoining properties are part of the deal.'

'So we'll be in nosy parker next door's landlord?' Dorothy said.

'Yes,' Amanda replied with a laugh. 'Bloody foreigners owning half the village. How will he be able to swallow his pride?'

Kevin suddenly walked over to Amanda, threw his arms around her and deposited a kiss on her cheek. 'Thank you. I don't know how but I'm going to make this generosity up to you, Mom.'

'There is no need.'

'He will,' Dorothy responded with her eyes dancing like a child's. 'I'm certain of that.'

*

It was the very next morning when George Burnett knocked on the cottage door. He flushed when Dorothy answered but Amanda was sitting in the kitchen behind.

'Do come in, Mr. Burnett,' Dorothy said. 'You met my mother yesterday, of course.'

'I did,' the man stumbled. 'Good morning, Mrs. Hutchkins. I really came to see Kevin.'

Amanda nodded and briefly spoke before continuing her late breakfast. Kevin walked in and, in his best manners, invited the manager through to the parlour. Twenty minutes later he returned, placed two silver shillings on the table beside Amanda and grinned at Dorothy.

'I'd better get dressed in my work clothes,' he finally stated. 'The press is giving problems and they need my help. It seems my dismissal was just a small misunderstanding and, owing to the new owner's more liberal attitudes, I have been invited to continue my apprenticeship.'

Amanda nodded. 'I think Mr. Burnett was very gracious to offer you the position back so quickly.'

'More like damned scared,' Dorothy retorted.

Amanda looked at her daughter. 'True, but this is a different country, Dorothy, a very old country steeped in traditional class and moral values. Many people are afraid of change. Don't be too quick to condemn the man for trying to uphold society's values. In the newspaper world in particular, you cannot afford to go against popular opinion.' She took a sip of tea and screwed her nose up a little. 'Take this tea, for example. I would much prefer coffee but if the corner shop here sold coffee instead of tea it wouldn't make many sales.'

Dorothy nodded and sat down. 'Go on, Mom,' she said.

Amanda smiled, 'It's the same with newspapers, Dear. If I produced an edition of *"The Weekly Dispatch"* here in England, it would probably go broke in six months. It's the same with this little paper. To us, it might seem conservative and old fashioned but if that's what the locals want, it shouldn't be changed.'

'But if people don't find out about new technology and change?' Kevin put in.

'That's business,' Amanda added and glanced up at him. 'Without change we stagnate. It's a thin line so, with your paper, just go slowly when you introduce new ideas. For example, I noticed there are no photographs in the *Evening Herald*. I'm sure adding these would benefit the paper, especially local photos of village happenings. Don't try to compete with the London papers with war news but find out about local boys to write about. I noticed that is what George Burnett does very well.'

'I see why you're so successful, Mom.' Dorothy studied at her mother. 'I'll remember your advice.'

'Mind you,' Amanda couldn't suppress a laugh... 'Brute force also works at times.'

*

November 1918 hit Kettingham and the rest of the world with two sufficient events; the Great War was finally won with an exhausted Germany signing an armistice on the eleventh day of the eleventh month. Even more devastating, though, was the influenza epidemic that circled the world. It was believed the strain started in United States and was brought to Europe in the lungs of soldiers.

The worst aspect was the sheer speed and severity of the scourge, as the local papers called it. Some victims died extremely quickly. Within three days their lungs had filled with fluid that practically drowned the hapless victim. Other people survived longer only to develop secondary infections with bacterial pneumonia, a disease for which there was no known cure so it was random luck whether the sufferer survived or not.

Medical knowledge knew the disease spread through the air when people sneezed and by skin contact such as shaking hands so steps were taken to avoid contact between people. Social events were cancelled and families affected encouraged to stay at home and, if possible in bed. For unknown reasons it also appeared to be family based. In Kettingham, the *Evening Herald* printed statistics that became horrific reading with one family of ten having nine people affected and two deaths while, only a few doors away another equally large family had nobody affected at all.

Throughout that tragic month, Dorothy put her nursing skills into practice and volunteered to help the hard pressed local doctors and nurses. Though, now quite obviously pregnant she would visit families in the streets allocated to her and provide as much help as she could. Distressed mothers with sick children were advised on how to cope while many elderly people in the village eagerly looked forward to Dorothy's visit.

It was due to her conscientious approach, the young Canadian nurse became accepted in the community. She was not a foreigner or colonial any more but a local who was willing to help her neighbours in distress. However, in late November it was probably inevitable that Dorothy caught the disease herself. She woke one morning with a terrible sore throat and aching limbs; her whole body shook in a rasping cough and perspiration saturated her nightgown.

'It's got to me,' she spluttered to Kevin who woke and heard his wife's rasping breath.

'Oh My Darling,' Kevin responded. 'You stay there. I'll help.

He immediately rushed and filled a basin with warm water to methodically bathe Dorothy's face and arms. 'You tried to do too much,' he complained. 'How many houses have you visited this week? Dozens I'd say....'

Dorothy gave another dry cough and attempted a weak smile. 'If I was going to catch it, I would have even if I sat here with the curtains drawn,' she spluttered. 'Isolating infected families hasn't stopped the spread at all.'

'I know,' Kevin replied and kissed his wife. 'And that's why I love you, My Darling. Now, though, you can rest and I'll look after you.'

'But you have work to do.'

'I am staying home today, Dorothy,' Kevin replied. 'Half the staff is off anyway. Nobody will expect me to turn up with you ill. Anyway, there's two of you, aren't there?'

For two days Kevin stayed with Dorothy and did everything he could to help, from making hot honey drinks to rubbing her down in a hot bath and just holding her close as they lay together during the long nights. They both knew the three first days were crucial and if the fever was broken by the third day she would be well on her way to recovery.

On the second afternoon just after lunch, Dorothy had slipped into a restless sleep. Kevin heard a knock and opened the door. Three middle-aged ladies stood there.

'Hello, Mr. Smithers,' one woman said. 'We're from the Women's Guild and I, for one, was visited by your good wife when I caught the scourge. Now we hear she's ill. How is she?'

'I'm not sure,' he replied but then shook his head. 'I'm afraid she's pretty low,' he confessed. 'I've tried but....'

The ladies nodded.

'We would have come earlier but...' Helen Flanshore, the leader of the trio said.

'I know,' Kevin answered. 'I think every family is affected but come in. I appreciate you coming.'

He stood back; the ladies came in and immediately set about helping. Unnoticed by Kevin, one had been carrying a pot of steaming hot food that she set out on the table.

'This is for you,' she said. 'If you don't feed yourself you won't be able to look after Mrs. Smithers, will you?'

Another went and tended to Dorothy who seemed to be only semiconscious while a third filled the washhouse basin with warm water and began to wash the pile of clothes and sheets Kevin had tossed in a corner.

'We're only paying back what Dorothy did for us,' Mrs. Flanshore replied.

'You know, Dorothy looked after my three children for two days while I lay in bed,' She looked sad for a moment. 'My Henry hasn't returned from France, yet.'

So kindness replaced remoteness as neighbours pulled together to cope as best they could. Often hundreds of silent mourners would attend funerals of neighbours who had hardly spoken before the epidemic hit and volunteers would cook meals, tidy houses and baby sit.

On the fourth night Dorothy awoke feeling much better, only to find Kevin sleeping fitfully beside her. 'Oh, you poor dear,' she gasped, forgot her own aching head and immediately set about helping him.

Luckily, Kevin's flu was a comparatively mild version so, within two days the Smithers were back in health and Dorothy continued her nursing rounds. By early December 1918, the *Evening Herald* reported that sixty-three per cent of the district's population had had influenza. Of these seven thousand, eight hundred people, one hundred and seventy-one died. A little over three hundred were still ill and less than four and a half thousand people had remained healthy. It appeared that the worse was over and the village could return to normal life.

*

On New Year's Day 1919, Dorothy and Kevin officially took over ownership of the *Evening Herald* and the biggest compliment heard was in the local grocery shop where Dorothy overheard Mrs. Gregory, wife of their grumpy neighbour who had initially complained about them, talking to the shopkeeper.

'Matthew, my husband, reckons were lucky that nice Smithers family bought out the Herald,' she said while the grocer weighed out some flour for her. ' "Better than those bloody foreigners from London", he told me.' She spied Dorothy behind her and flushed. 'Oh hello, Mrs. Smithers, I was just saying how pleased we are you bought the Herald out. Matthew doesn't like outsiders.'

'And we aren't?' Dorothy couldn't help saying.

'Oh Lordy no, not after all your help during the scourge, Mrs. Smithers. You're one of us.' She gave a grin, 'Even with your Canadian accent.'

'Why, thank you, Mrs. Gregory. That is kind of you.'

The other lady smiled. 'Call me Maude. We're friendly folk in Kettingham, not like London or even Cambridge.'

'And call me Dorothy,' the young pregnant woman replied but wondered what the locals would have been like if the epidemic hadn't hit the country.

'Oh yes... Dorothy,' Maude replied. 'I'll bring the rent money around tonight. You're my landlady now, you know'

'No hurry,' said Dorothy. 'We're still getting all that sorted out.'

She walked out with her bag of groceries and went to meet Kevin at the newspaper office. 'Hi Sweetheart,' she said when he appeared from out the back alley. 'How are you going?'

'Fine,' he replied, grabbed her in a bear hug and kissed her on the lips while the locals pretended they never saw. After all, the war was over and the colonials were more demonstrative than English folk. The Smithers were locals, of course.

'Oh, just gossiping at the shop,' she replied with a laugh. 'When you've finish here, I'll walk home with you.'

*

On Friday, 28 March 1919 after several hours in labour, Dorothy's baby arrived.

'Congratulation, Mr. Smithers,' the nurse said to a nervous Kevin in the waiting room. 'Your wife has just given birth to a dear wee boy. Would you like to go and see the happy pair?'

Kevin grinned in excitement and walked in to the room and saw Dorothy sitting up with several pillows behind her. In her arms was a tiny bundle of humanity, all wrinkly red skin and wide blue eyes.

'You have a son, Sweetheart,' she said, 'and we both thought it would be a girl.'

'No,' said Kevin. 'Your mother said it had to be a girl but she didn't have the final say this time.'

Dorothy smiled. 'Would you like to hold him? I'm sure the nurse won't mind.'

'Can I?' Kevin asked and nervously picked his son up. 'Oh Dorothy,' he gasped. 'He's perfect. Look at his fingernails.'

'They're mine,' Dorothy said. 'You still bite yours.'

At that moment the nurse returned and politely but firmly took the infant off Kevin and placed him in the bed. 'You'll have to leave, Mr. Smithers,' she said. 'Your wife is very tired and needs to rest and we don't want Bubbs here to catch germs from you, now do we?'

'No Nurse,' said Kevin and kissed Dorothy before retreating out of the room. He walked down the stairs grinning to himself. They'd been so convinced the baby would be a girl, a boy's name hadn't even been thought of.

The next day he returned to the maternity home with the *Evening Herald* in his hand. 'I have a surprise for you, My Dear,' he said and handed her the folded up paper.

Dorothy unfolded the paper and gasped. On the front page was the very first photograph the Evening Herald had ever printed, a photo of Dorothy holding their son.

A headline beneath said, *"The Managing Director of the Evening Herald gives birth to son while we launch our new paper... Welcome readers to the new Evening Herald. With our new press we now have the ability to include photographs in our paper and for the first time, also have news on the front page..."*

Dorothy stared at the paper and gasped in surprise, 'Who took the photo?' she gasped.

'Thomas, our staff photographer sneaked in and took it through the glass observation windows. Like it?'

'Like it! It's wonderful! Come here.' She reached up and kissed her husband with a huge sloppy kiss. 'Oh Sweetheart, it's so clear. How did you get everything done so quickly? I was told the new press wouldn't be in operation for two months and to have the news on the front page...' This was an innovative step as most English papers used the front page for classified advertisements. She bit on her lower lip. 'I hope we haven't gone too far. Remember what Mom said about not rushing changes?'

'My Dear, the first edition sold out by four and we're, at this very moment, printing off another two thousand copies.'

'But how did you get it done so quickly?'

'We tricked you,' Kevin said. 'Bill had the equipment installed by the end of November but we pretended there was a delay. George agreed to wait.'

'You devious man,'

'Where's baby?' Kevin asked as if he'd just remembered the addition to their family.

'Down in the nursery. Hungry little fellow. All he wants to do is drink his milk.'

'And you?'

'Me?' Dorothy said and pulled off her blankets. 'Look I'm all slim again." She grinned. "Well almost. The doctor said I had an amazingly straightforward first birth and I can come home in a week.' She gave a giggle. 'Did you get that telegram off to Mom and Daddy?'

'Oh yes, I forgot,' Kevin replied. He pulled a crumpled envelope out of his pocket and handed it to Dorothy.

"Congratulations," the cable read. *"We really wanted a grandson, you know. Love Mom and Daddy."*

'That's a lie,' Dorothy said, 'but I love her still. Perhaps we'll have a daughter next time.'

Kevin gazed into her eyes then reached down and hugged her close. 'I love you with all my heart, Dorothy,' he said. 'Thank you for just being you.' He stood and wiped a tear from his eye. 'I'm not very good at the English stiff upper lip stuff,' he added.

'Don't worry,' Dorothy said. 'Our son is part Canadian, American, New Zealander and adopted Australian. There's not much English in him.'

*

1 November 1922

Dear Diary

Well, they say third time lucky. After two gorgeous sons, Albert now three and a half and Timothy just over two, today at ten in the morning I presented Kevin with a daughter. We are going to call her Cindy Amanda. (Sounds lovely, doesn't it?)

Kevin and the boys are thrilled to have a baby sister and Mom just walks around with a satisfied grin on her face as if she did all the hard work. (Yes, Daddy and she are on another of their frequent visits to Kettingham.) I'm sure with all her papers in England sold, except for ours of course, she doesn't need to come over here all the time but except for spoiling the boys, she is no trouble.

It was sad about George Burnett. Heart attacks can take one from us so quickly but in a strange way his departure helped. I remain on the board of the Evening Herald, even though with three youngsters now, Kevin does most of the work. His appointment as manager is quite appropriate. It was Bill who recommended Kevin and Mom, being a board member, backed him up. We still have to appoint an editor to replace George but Mom knows of several suitable candidates.

Good news, too. The paper now sells thirty thousand copies compared with sixteen thousand when we took over in 1919. Of course the collapse of the paper in the next village last year helped but our modern layout and features from Mom's Canadian papers are a big bonus. (And she said our readers would be conservative.) Oops, Cindy is crying and here comes Kevin with the boys (Also Mom and Daddy) so I'll sign off for now.

Dorothy Smithers

CHAPTER TWELVE

26 September 1932

Dear Diary

The good news is that, after the stock market crash of 1929 and two years of anguish, we have cleared our debts with everyone except Mom. (She refuses to take any money back). The Evening Herald is our only remaining publishing venture now but I guess we were a little ambitious in trying to compete with the big national companies by having those three country life magazines plus another provincial paper. Mom warned us about expanding too quickly back in 1928 but we thought we knew better.

The Evening Heralds circulation is building and is almost back to the heights of 1928 when it reached 35,000 copies. Compared with many other small newspaper owners, Kevin and I came out quite unscathed but I fear there will still be tough times ahead.

I find being editor of our paper hard but enjoyable work and it certainly saves us money by not having to pay a high editor's salary to an outsider. I guess we are a real family business now. To relax, I enjoy having early afternoon break at 'The Creamed Scone' a small tearoom just around the corner from the Evening Herald before going home in time for Cindy's arrival home from school.

By afternoon, the paper is rolling off the press and my work is really over for the day. Kevin, as manager, is in charge of distribution and the physical side of getting the paper out to the public. I must admit, it does get hectic at times.

On the home front, the new school year has started. Timmy, can you believe it, started grammar school, much to Bertie's annoyance but they really do get on together. Our baby, Cindy is in Standard 3 and growing like a mushroom. Having three children and two at secondary school makes one feel old. I thought passing thirty would be the end of my youth but I feel no different. They're only numbers Kevin told me on my last birthday and I believe that's true.

Dorothy Smithers

*

Dorothy was alone in The Creamed Scone sipping her coffee and deep in thought when she heard a polite cough. She jumped in fright and glanced around.

'Mrs. Smithers?' said a quiet voice.

A slim, almost skinny woman dressed in modern up-market clothes stood beside the table. It was her face, though, that caught Dorothy's attention; hollow hazel eyes stared out at her above pinched lips devoid of any makeup. Her hair was greying and cut in a short straight style under a modest bonnet. In those few seconds, Dorothy also noticed that the woman's skinny hands and bony fingers were shaking. It was as if the stranger was apprehensive about something.

'Yes,' Dorothy replied. 'Can I help you?'

'Can we talk in confidence please?' The woman's frightened eyes gazed around the tearooms.

Dorothy frowned. 'Nobody will overhear us here,' she replied. 'Please take a seat. Can I order you a drink?'

The woman nodded and sat in an opposite chair. 'Just a cup of tea will be fine, thank you' Her eyes again flickered around the room.

Dorothy called the waitress over and ordered the tea and two more jam scones. If the woman didn't want one she could easily eat two herself.

'Now,' she said. 'You have my full attention. What would you like to say? '

'Please don't deny anything until I have finished explaining,' the woman began.

Dorothy nodded but said nothing.

'My name was Ruth Whiting.' Her voice became more confident. 'I'm here because of my husband but you probably haven't heard of him.'

'Pleased to meet you Ruth. No, I'm afraid I have never heard of your husband.'

The woman licked her lips and continued. 'To be brief, Conrad my husband came from an aristocratic family but the family's fortune was wiped out in the stock market crash of two years ago,' she said, 'Not that they had a lot before then and were really living on borrowed time. The crash really just hastened the inevitable.'

Dorothy nodded. 'That happened to thousands of families, Ruth but how does it affect me?'

'You know Tim Robertson, don't you?' The eyes zoomed in on Dorothy.

Dorothy gasped and subconsciously brought a hand up to her mouth. She had not heard Kevin's real name mentioned in years. It was something they had successfully tucked away into the past but now, out of nowhere, this mousy little woman knew Kevin's identity.

'Go on,' she hissed.

Ruth began to scratch her arm nervously. 'I can see from your reaction that the name has meaning to you. You don't need to confirm it but I know it is your husband's real name.'

'What do you want?' Dorothy retorted.

'I'm here to help, Mrs. Smithers; not to destroy your family.' Ruth Whiting's voice became more confident. 'My husband was a lieutenant in the Great War and Tim's commanding officer. He recognised Tim in London about three months ago. At least he thought it was him.'

Dorothy sighed. After all these years of never being recognised she guessed they'd become complacent. Her heart began to beat faster and thoughts twirled through her mind as she stared at the woman.

'Conrad is a very bitter man,' Ruth Whiting continued. 'Instead of accepting he is now bankrupt he wants to blame others. In his warped mind, your husband and yourself are enemies to be brought down.'

'But why?'

'Because of your success. You're a very attractive and successful woman, Dorothy.' Ruth coughed, sipped her tea for a moment and accepted the jam scone offered her. 'Conrad immediately set about trying to trace your husband after he recognised him, but failed.'

'Then how come you're here?' Dorothy retorted.

'He traced a Mr. and Mrs. Kevin Smithers but can't prove your real identities. Therefore, he is going to attempt to trick your husband or yourself into making a mistake that he'll home in on.' Ruth gave her first smile. 'For example, I knew straight away I was onto the real Tim Robertson by your reaction when I mentioned his name just now. That is all Conrad would need. Do you understand?'

'I think so,' Dorothy whispered.

'He is using a man called Stanley McKee, a brute of a man and hardened criminal, to help him. Have you heard the name?'

Dorothy blinked. In the dark folds of her mind the name Stanley meant something. 'He knew my husband in the war, didn't he?'

'Correct. Conrad and McKee came here to Kettingham recently and watched your newspaper office. Stanley said he recognised Tim but he could have lied because he could see a financial award coming his way. Anyhow, they will be trying to get your husband to panic. If any mail arrives for Tim Robertson, don't open it. If anyone rings asking for Tim, don't even gasp as you did with me. They may even attempt a surprise frontal approach like I did. Once it is established who you are, they'll probably attempt some sort of blackmail. McKee is completely ruthless and I'm afraid my husband is little better.'

Dorothy felt her body grow sweaty but she swallowed and maintained a dignified control.

'Why have you told me this Ruth? What's in it for you?' She looked hard. 'Are you part of the plot?'

'I've left my husband,' Ruth smiled in a sad but determined way. 'For years I put up with his physical and emotional abuse. I even have a court order out against him, not that it will do much good.' She screwed her face up. 'I found out about you, too, Dorothy and envy you.' Her mouth dropped and she glanced away. 'I don't want Conrad to ruin anyone else's life. He can't bear to see people like yourselves, so called commoners, succeeding while he is a failure. All his life he had his aristocratic background making him believe he was superior to the ordinary people. The Great War brought his life of luxury to an end then the 1929 crash finished it off completely. We have nothing now, except an ancient castle deep in debt and a useless title.'

'Title?'

Ruth smiled again. 'My maiden name and the one I have reverted to, is Viscountess Ruth Hartford-Beaumont. I'm a cousin about twelfth removed to King George V. That's the only reason Conrad married me.'

'Oh you poor dear,' Dorothy exclaimed. 'I think I understand now. Thank you so much for your help, Ruth. I'm afraid I don't know this Tim Robertson but if, through our newspaper we come across him we'll warn him of the danger.'

Their eyes met and Dorothy was certain Ruth knew that she was lying.

'I'll leave you my lawyer's telephone number,' Ruth said and produced a tiny cream card from her handbag. 'I can be reached through him. I hope everything turns out for Kevin and yourself. God bless you both.'

'You too, Viscountess Hartford-Beaumont,' Dorothy whispered and reached across to shake the thin hand again. 'Thank you.'

'My pleasure,' the slim woman replied and walked away out of the tearooms.

Dorothy watched the empty doorway and frowned as she reached for the last scone. She knew the visit would be a help but somehow wished the woman had never come. This one conversation had set her life back thirteen years, thirteen happy years with a man she deeply loved and had produced three children for.

For several moments she sat thinking then stood and headed for the door determined that nobody would take their lives away from them. Nobody!

*

Viscountess' Hartford-Beaumont's warning almost arrived too late for it was only a few days later when a letter arrived at the *'Evening Herald'* addressed to Mr. Tim Robertson. Kevin studied the envelope and, like Dorothy, memories of the past raced through his mind. His first impulse was to throw it into the fire, his second was to rip it open but finally he decided to take a pragmatic approach and discretely slipped it in his inside jacket pocket to take it home to discuss with his wife.

It was late and the children had all gone to bed when he took it out and showed Dorothy.

'The fun begins,' he said and placed it on the little table in front of where Dorothy was listening to a radio serial.

Her face paled as she stared at the name. 'Oh Sweetheart,' she whispered. 'I'm so sorry.'

'If that Viscountess whatever her name was hadn't warned us, I'd be certain this was a genuine letter. Look at the envelope.'

Dorothy nodded. The envelope had New Zealand stamps cancelled in Auckland, the city near to where Kevin had lived before the war. The handwriting was curly and slightly shaky almost as if an elderly person had written it. Even the message on the bottom left hand corner could have been written by an older person. *'Please check before returning. My son may be using a different name.'*

'My Mum,' Kevin said. 'It's meant to be from her.'

'Would she still be alive?' Dorothy replied.

'Could be,' Kevin shrugged. 'She'd be about your mother's age. What shall we do?' Dorothy frowned and turned the envelope over. It was not very bulky so probably only contained a page or two inside. Out of interest she sniffed it and shut one eye in thought.

'How long would it take for a letter to get here from New Zealand, Sweetheart?'

'At least two months, probably three depending on the shipping.'

Dorothy handed the envelope back. 'Sniff it,' she said.

Kevin did and grimaced. The paper had that crisp tingly smell of something new. Even though it looked several months old with slightly tatty corners it smelt new. 'It's not three months old, is it?' he whispered.

'No,' replied Dorothy. 'They slipped up on that. I'd say the stamps came off a genuine New Zealand letter and the cancellation stamp faked. If it was dropped in a post box, the Post Office would assumed it was redirected mail and send it on without adding a local cancellation stamp.'

'Crafty but what shall we do with it?'

'Wipe it clean with a damp sponge so your fingerprints aren't on it then we'll steam it open and read the contents. I'll put my gloves on. I doubt if they have your fingerprints on record but it pays to be very careful.'

While Kevin watched, she slipped some gloves on and held the envelope over a steaming kettle. Little by little the glue dissolved and the back flap opened. Dorothy pulled a two-page letter out and placed in on the table for them both to read.

Kevin recognised the address at once. 'That's Mum's place,' he whispered. The date was four months old and the letter written in blue ink just like millions of other private letters being delivered around the world. Even the paper was typical of that one would buy in a stationery shop.

'*Dear Timmy,*' it stated. '*The New Zealand Army approached me and said you may still be alive. It seems there was a mix up in hospital records in 1918...*'

Kevin read on orally while Dorothy listened and read along, too. 'So please, Timmy, if you receive this letter contact your old Mum. Even if you have a new name or perhaps a wife and family, I'd like to know. The New Zealand Army has a special London number you can phone or you can write to me there.' The number and address was included and the letter concluded with another personal plead. It was quite an emotionally charged letter.

Dorothy felt sad as she folded it up but Kevin merely grunted and looked angry.

'What's wrong Sweetheart?' Dorothy said and placed an arm around Kevin.

'It's a fake,' Kevin said. 'I admit it's well researched and probably done by a professional but it's still phoney, just like the envelope.'

'How are you so certain?' Dorothy asked.

Kevin sat down on the couch and pulled Dorothy in beside him, kissed her tenderly on the lips and left an arm tucked around her. 'My mother never went beyond primary school,' he explained. 'In all my two years in the army she only wrote to me once.'

With his fingers covered by a handkerchief, he opened the letter again and illustrated his point. 'She would never write *approached me* but more likely *sent me a letter*'. Also, her spelling was terrible and the one letter I received was full of them and other mistakes. This is far too neat and accurate. Mum was almost illiterate and, even if she copied something written by someone else she would have made errors.' He coughed. 'We didn't really get on, so she would not have written that emotional crap at the bottom. She was a hard old lady.'

Dorothy bit on her bottom lip and nodded. 'What now Sweetheart? I'm out of ideas.'

Kevin grimaced. 'We'll reseal it. I'll write, "Unknown. Return to sender" on the envelope and post it back. Our friend who wrote it must have thought of some way of intercepting any reply back. He couldn't be certain we'd use the telephone number or London address given here.'

'No,' Dorothy said and placed her hand on Kevin's. 'I'll write on the envelope. We don't want them to have a copy of your handwriting, do we?'

Kevin smiled. 'You aren't just a dumb blonde, are you?'

'No Sweetheart, but remember, this is only the first approach. I have a horrible feeling there is more to come.'

'I know,' grunted Kevin. 'The only good point is that Lieutenant Whiting has not broken my cover and only suspects who I am. The Australians did a thorough job and it is thirteen years.'

'And you've put on weight and lost some hair,' Dorothy pointed out. 'Even I would hardly recognise you from that skinny bag of bones I looked after in the hospital.'

'Guess not,' Kevin smiled and grabbed Dorothy in a huge embrace, 'and through all these years, you've remained as beautiful and sexy as ever.'

'Oh Kevin,' Dorothy sighed. 'No wonder I still love you.' She cuddled in close and felt eighteen again. 'Let's go to bed.'

Kevin grinned. 'Why not? It will take more than one letter to spoil our life, My Dear.'

The lights went off and for a few moments the two came together as they had so many times but Dorothy hung on just that little bit longer after their lovemaking and tears appeared in her eyes. 'Oh Kevin,' she cried. 'I hope nothing happens to you.'

'It won't,' Kevin cupped her face in his hands and kissed her lips tenderly. 'That's a promise.'

*

Even though the next encounter was anticipated, when it arrived Kevin was able to survive the onslaught only with the help of his friends. He was sitting at the bar of *The Fox and Hound*, the pub most of the workers at the *Evening Herald* frequented after a hard day's work, when Tom, the newspaper's foreman gave Kevin a dig and grunted. 'Don't look now, Kevin but there's a mean character over in the far corner taking an intense interest in you. I noticed he was here last night, too.'

'Thanks Tom,' muttered Kevin and continued to sip his pint of ale. Tom was one of the friends he'd told to keep an eye out for strangers around inquiring into his family's affairs. 'Will you get the others?

'Sure, Kevin,' Tom muttered. He stood and moved away while Kevin continued to drink from his mug.

'He's coming up,' Brian, the publican, whispered and Kevin gave the slightest of nods.

'Well if it ain't from old friend Timmy from the Great War,' a voice boomed and Kevin felt a slap on the shoulders. He stiffened, turned his eyes to meet the stranger but even being forewarned didn't stop the surprise.

Stanley McKee, the bully from the trenches, was leering at him. The face was lined and puffy from too much drink, the hair grey, but the smirk was still there and the massive body towered over Kevin.

Kevin, though, only tightened his fists and stared at his old adversary as one would with a complete stranger. 'I'm sorry,' he replied. 'You must have me muddled with someone else.'

'Oh come off it, Timmy,' boomed the other man. 'You put on a bit of weight but I'll never forget you. Left us in the lurch, your mate and you did. The lieutenant was as mad as shit when you and that Aussie bloke walked out. What was his name, now?'

Kevin stared coldly at the man. 'Look,' he said. 'I have never met you before in my life. It is obviously a mistaken identity.'

McKee stared and squinted closely through shaggy eyebrows but did not give up. 'I hear you leaped in bed with that young blonde nurse at the hospital they repatriated you to and put a bun in her oven. That took a bit of guts, I reckon. Of course, we all knew she was an easy lay. I reckon half the blokes at hospital had her pants down behind the boiler room. Wasn't she the one with enormous tits?' He laughed just as he did all those years before and never took his eyes off Kevin's face.

Kevin felt his fists contract and blood rush into his face and only with the utmost of self-control did he stop lashing out at the man. Instead he clutched his mug, gulped some ale down and stared ahead. He could not even bring himself to speak.

Tom arrived, placed a hand on the visitor's shoulder and squeezed so hard; Stanley gave an audible gasp of pain.

'You are wearing out your welcome very quickly, my friend,' the foreman grunted.

Stanley swung himself away and turned from staring at Kevin. He was about to lash out when his eyes moved up to see the two other men glaring at him. He shrugged. 'Okay,' he said. 'Just catching up old days with an old mate.'

'Mr. Smithers said he never knew you, Sunshine,' Tom continued. 'That's good enough for me. Drink up your ale and be on your way. Get it!' He stood to his massive height of over six feet and positioned his massive frame beside Stanley. 'We don't like intimidation in our friendly little pub.'

Stanley glowered and turned to Kevin. 'Bye Timmy,' he snickered. 'Say hello to Dorothy, too and that darling little daughter of yours. Ain't she a sweetie?'

Kevin stood with his face red and swallowed. 'I can forgive a mistaken identity but nobody has the right to insult my wife and family.' He stood up with his fists clenched and was shaking in rage but Brian grabbed his arm.

'Steady, Kevin,' he said softly. 'Don't you see he's trying to provoke you?'

Kevin hesitated and sat down with his face staring straight ahead. 'Let the man have his beer,' he said.

'If you say so, Kevin,' Tom replied and switched his attention back to McKee. His look was black. 'We'll regard it as a mistaken identity mister just like Mr. Smithers said,' He cracked his knuckles. '... This time.'

McKee glanced around, saw he was outnumbered and walked out of the bar without saying another word. 'Blimey, he's a mean customer,' Brian commented. 'Do you really know him, Kevin?'

Kevin shook his head. 'I would have remembered a face like that. I think he was just spoiling for a fight.'

'Could be,' Tom muttered. 'The boys will keep an eye out for him around the village, just the same.'

*

The meeting the next afternoon was in another neighbourhood public house but this one was in northern London. Stanley McKee sipped his ale and stared across the small black table at Conrad Whiting puffing away on a pipe.

'It could be him,' he retorted, 'but if it is, he's certainly changed a lot. He's bigger than I remember and doesn't lack confidence. If I didn't know better, I'd say he was expecting me.'

'How come?' Whiting snapped.

'Just his mannerisms and the three or four heavies waiting around ready to protect him. Even when I made comments about his family he resisted thumping me. Oh yeah, he was as mad as hell but he left it to this massive great bugger to warn me.' Stanley rolled his eyes. 'I must admit, I was sure I'd be thrashed. They were quite mean until Smithers settled them down.'

'What about his wife?'

Stanley smirked. 'She's one great tart. Even now, I wouldn't mind having her in my bed for a couple of hours. All my information confirms what you found out; she is the majority owner of the newspaper, not her husband, and was financed into it just after the Great War by her mother who owns a publishing company in Canada. She was a nurse at North Dover Military Hospital at the end of the war and met Smithers there. That doesn't prove he is Robertson, though. The documents I checked said Robertson died of war wounds. However, there was one strange thing.'

Conrad Whiting jerked up and listened. 'Go on,' he grunted.

'Kevin Smithers' record goes right back to the high school he attended in a town called Gosford near Sydney, Australia. I talked to some old Australian soldiers from his regiment but nobody remembers him. I reckon I spoke to a twenty or more men and not one remembered him or the name; not even remotely.'

'I see,' Whiting said and blew a cloud of blue smoke into the air. 'That's interesting. Okay, McKee, you've earned your fifty quid. Stay around. I may need your help again later. Meanwhile, stay away from Smithers. We don't want to frighten him off.'

'Right Mr. Whiting,' Stanley replied and put the money in his pocket. 'Any time. You've got my address. If you'd like me to rough up his wife, I'll only charge you half my usual fee.'

'Stay away,' hissed Whiting. 'If you start anything like that you'll only get the police onto our tail.'

'Okay,' Stanley muttered with a thin grin. 'Just joking. She's getting a bit old, anyhow. I like them in the twenties.'

*

After his henchman left, Conrad Whiting ordered another whiskey and sat gazing out the window. He was certain now that this Smithers was Robertson but was equally sure there was no way to prove it.

The last comment McKee made though had possibilities. Whiting retorted. He would get to the leech through his wife. From all accounts, Smithers was devoted to his wife and family; the silly bastard didn't even have a mistress. Now with a little pressure in that direction he could get the bugger to confess. What's the bet he'd do anything to stop his wife being hurt!

Conrad Whiting banged the ashes out of his pipe, refilled and lit it. My God, that's the way he'd go but it would take careful planning.

*

CHAPTER THIRTEEN

1 November 1932

Dear Diary

It was Cindy's day today. She is ten years old and I don't really know where the last decade has gone. There was the usual party after school with over a dozen little girls screaming around the house, eating ice cream, jelly and everything else put in front of them. (As long as it was sweet). Games were played and the boys, including Kevin, were noticeably absent. With a bedroom full of presents, I'm afraid our daughter is becoming quite spoiled.

Write about being spoiled; Kevin has gone absolutely crazy and spent a small fortune on a new completely impractical car but I guess it is one of our few luxuries. He said it was for me but I know better. A two-tone green MG sports car is now parked in the car shed and what a thrill it is to drive.

We have heard no more from that horrible man but I don't think he has vanished forever and the peace is more like a lull before the next storm. I don't even wish to think about it, so I won't.

Dorothy

P.S. It does seem so silly signing my name every time I make an entry but I guess I'm just carrying on Mom's tradition. She's well, still living in Vancouver where she shifted after the crash and writes regularly.

Dorothy

*

The MG 'J Type' sports car was dark green, low and wide with a long narrow bonnet and shiny vertical radiator at the front. Huge headlights on the front fenders peered out above bicycle spoke wheels. Wednesday, November the second, 1932 was a cold morning so the canvas roof was pulled over and triangular shaped Perspex side windows were in place above the cut away doors. The tiny vehicle was overflowing with people. Cindy and Timmy were squeezed in the rear seat while Bertie sat at the front and admired the polished wooden dashboard.

'Are you children ready?' Dorothy called and reached across to turn the ignition on.

'Yes, Mum!' they chorused and held on as their mother reversed out, changed the tiny gear lever to first and roared off up the road. She loved driving and was quite an expert, too. The sports car had a reputation of being capable of eighty miles an hour and Dorothy had driven it well over sixty. At that speed the ride was exhilarating with the throaty roar of the motor and howl of wind in her ears.

After the boys bundled out at the grammar school and grinned at the envious stares of fellow pupils, Dorothy was off around to Kettingham North Primary School where Cindy squealed in delight. Miss Martin, her teacher, was just walking into the school and saw her waving out the tiny side flap.

'Bye Mummy,' Cindy said, gave her mother a peck on the cheek and ran off to point out their new car to her teacher.

Dorothy also waved to Miss Martin and headed out of town. She was off to Cambridge, the closest city, to a meeting of the district press club. There was plenty of time as the journey only took a little over an hour and the meeting didn't start until eleven. The outside air was frigid and the heater, the first car they owned with one, could barely cope. However, Dorothy wore long leather gloves, a scarf, coat and leather helmet to keep herself warm so the chilly frost outside didn't worry her.

Twelve miles along the highway she changed down and turned into a narrow side road. This was a short cut she used regularly. It avoided three villages and, even though no shorter in distance, saved at least a quarter of an hour's driving time. Though the shopping in Cambridge wasn't that much superior to that in Kettingham, Dorothy enjoyed the atmosphere of the university city and had given herself time to wander around before the meeting.

The narrow road was hardly wider than the MG and almost like a tunnel with hedgerows towering above her low-slung car. Every so often a driveway appeared between the hedges but otherwise the road curled around to the left so she could only see fifty yards or so ahead. For this reason, Dorothy slowed to thirty miles per hour and changed down a gear. It was lucky she did, for around one almost right angled bend, a gigantic traction engine, bellowing smoke and steam, was chugging along in front of her.

'Damn!' Dorothy grunted and braked. There was no room to pass so she'd have to wait until the driver in front pulled into the next driveway.

But he didn't. The traction engine slowed and stopped. Dorothy cursed and also pulled to a halt. She wondered if she should reverse back to the last driveway and go back to the crossroads she remembered passing half a mile back.

It was only when a large black car appeared from behind and came right up to her bumper that she realised nothing could be done. She glanced in her rear vision mirror as two men stepped out of the car. One man walked on each side of the road towards her. Dorothy frowned, opened her door and stepped out.

It was at that moment that she sensed this was more than just a minor traffic hold-up and a gasp of alarm escaped her lips. The men were wearing Balaclavas and motor goggles so were totally unrecognisable. Dorothy turned to run but one man intercepted and grabbed her.

'Oh no you don't, Misses,' he hissed and Dorothy found her arm grabbed in a vice like grip.

'Let me go!' she screamed and aimed a kick at the man's shins. This must be a hijacking of her new car. She'd heard of this happening. The cars were stolen, stripped down, repainted and sold, often in Ireland or Scotland.

'Oh no, Mrs. Smithers. I'm afraid we need to detain you for a while,' said a muffled voice. Even though the Balaclava covered his mouth Dorothy could see cold leering eyes beneath the goggles. She screamed and struggled but her arms were pinned back and there was no way to escape.

'What do you want?' she screamed.

'You!' said the man. He reached forward and started to undo her coat buttons.

Cold fear crept through Dorothy's body like a nightmare when one wakes up with beating heart and perspiration soaked nightgown but this was no bad dream. It was real and was happening to her! In spite of her screams and struggles she found her coat undone, yanked back and pulled off her arms. Cold air enveloped her but she was hot with fury, not cold. The second man grabbed her right arm and pulled up the sleeve of her cardigan.

'You're a nurse, Mrs. Smithers,' he stated in a clipped upper class accent. 'So hold still and it won't be so bad for you.'

Dorothy stared in horror. The man had a hypodermic needle in his hand. 'You bastard. Let me go!' she screamed and managed to bite the hand held over her mouth.

'Bitch, you'll regret that later,' the man snarled but his grip did not slacken. Instead he purposely reached around and squeezed one of her breasts so hard, it hurt. 'On second thoughts this could be fun!'

She was terrorised but struggles became futile. The man holding her was just too powerful. Grinning eyes peered into her, his breath stunk and the prickly knitted Balaclava rubbed against her cheek and a hand was inside her blouse. She tried to scream again but could hardly breath with the hand over her mouth and pushed up against her nose. God it stunk of tobacco! She felt her blouse sleeve pulled up so a bare arm was exposed, there was a sharp prick and the world around began to go fuzzy.

She heard the first man snap in an angry voice. 'Cut it out! Don't fondle the woman, Stanley... ' The words drifted away.

Thoughts rushed into her foggy mind. Stanley? Of course, that man at the pub Kevin had trouble with. Her thoughts clouded over as she slumped down and heard no more.

*

'You didn't have to say my name,' McKee grumbled as he let Dorothy go so she crumbled down on the road and lay on the wet surface. 'She could have heard.'

'I doubt it,' Conrad Whiting muttered as he waved up to the traction engine and the vehicle started rumbling away. 'This is a fast acting drug. Get her into my car and you take the MG. No reckless driving, though. We don't want to attract attention to ourselves.'

'Okay,' muttered McKee. 'We've been through all that.'

Whiting glowered. 'I also said no fondling, didn't I? You leave this woman alone.'

'You're the one paying.' The other man shrugged. 'The bitch needs to be brought down a peg or two, I'd say.'

'Possibly but not yet,' Conrad Whiting grunted. 'Come on before another vehicle arrives.'

He helped McKee drag the unconscious woman to his car and, none to carefully, threw her into the back seat; Stanley climbed into the MG and the traction engine turned into an opened gateway. Within two minutes the lonely road was empty as if nothing had happened and Whiting knew it would be at least two hours before anybody realised Dorothy was missing. Everything had been thoroughly researched.

*

Oh her head pounded and stung. Her whole face stung and the eyelids were like lead.

'Go on wake up.' The voice sounded as if was spoken in a foghorn.

Suddenly she was slapped across the cheek. It was cold, dim and quiet; too quiet. She jerked away and saw the man, the smaller one with the upper class voice.

'So you're awake, Mrs. Smithers,' he said and stared at her through the gap in the Balaclava.

Dorothy's throat felt dry and she erupted into an uncontrollable coughing fit before lubricating her throat with constant swallowing and finally becoming aware of her surrounds.

She was in a stone room with a naked light bulb dangling down. The one tiny window, much too small to crawl though, was about eight feet up. Sunshine filtered through dirty glass in a dusty ray of light that cut diagonally across the room. The angle of the light meant it must be mid afternoon, hours after her abduction. She sat up but felt terrible. The room spun and a lump of vomit lodged in her throat.

'Where am I?' she gasped.

'Listen,' the man replied. He grabbed her shoulders and shook her violently. 'You're okay, now. Just a bit of an overdose, what! '

Dorothy nodded and shook her head. It cleared a little, the spinning stopped and she managed focus her eyes. She was on a bed.

The man who had been bending over her now stood back and waited with his arms on his hips.

'This will be your home for a while,' he said. 'Don't try to get away. The cellar is solid and nobody will hear your screams.'

'What do you want?' Dorothy tried to remain defiant but the last word turned into a sob. Her whole body was shaking and she expected to be attacked at any moment.

'Don't worry I am not about to rape you and my companion is not here. I apologise for his wandering hands. That was not part of the bargain.'

'You bastard,' Dorothy hissed. 'I advise you...'

The man laughed. 'You are in no position to advise anything, Dorothy. Lovely name, much better than Mrs. Smithers or even Mrs. Robertson, don't you think?'

Dorothy stared and shrunk back into the pillow behind her head. 'You're the men who were annoying my husband,' she gasped.

'No, Dorothy, we were just trying to establish the truth but that is not your concern at the moment.' His eyes looked mean and the voice sounded hard. 'I'll say this once, so listen.'

The woman nodded.

'This will be your home. Not as comfortable as yours, I guess but quite self-contained. There's a bathroom and toilet, a heater and blankets. I even brought a change of clothes and toiletries for you. There is also food for three days by which time I'll be back.' He hesitated. 'Of course, if your husband is uncooperative I may send my friend in. He's not as self-disciplined as me.'

'You wouldn't't!' gasped Dorothy.

The man's eyes grinned. 'You'd better hope your husband sees reason. My friend has taken quite a fancy to your, shall we say ample proportions, what!'

'You vile little man,' snapped Dorothy but her fear returned like a sheet of ice running in her veins.

The man merely laughed. 'Oh yes, I left a few magazines and books for you to read, even a pencil and some writing paper. I heard you are excellent at writing feature articles. Bye.'

Dorothy swung her legs off the bed and considered making a rush for the door but it was too late. The man had departed and the solid oaken door slammed shut. Dorothy heard a steel latch being thrust across before everything became quiet.

After waiting in trepidation for what seemed to be an eternity she shivered in the musty air stood and examined the cellar. Beyond the window, a wall protruded half the way out across the floor. Dorothy walked around and saw a second door. It opened to show an ancient shower, tin hand basin and flush toilet. She screwed her nose up and tested them. The shower, tap and toilet all worked.

Thank God! At least she could maintain some dignity.

'Oh hell!' She sighed, wiped away a tear and walked into the main room again.

Three boxes sat on a small wooden kitchen sink. They contained groceries, toiletries and a selection of books and magazines. A tiny electric stove, a table with two kitchen chairs and the wire bed with several blankets on a lumpy mattress completed the furnishings. The main door would not budge. Everything felt musty and dirty and she shivered with cold. She looked around for her coat and saw it folded neatly over a brand new suitcase.

It was unlocked and inside she found a complete set of clothes from warm jerseys to two sets of underwear. She stared at it and again fear shot through her body as her trembling hands took the clothes out. The new clothes were her exact size, variety and brand that she usually wore. How did this man know so much about her personal habits?

It was at that moment that her bottom lip dropped and she erupted into tears. Long sobs filled the air as the seriousness of the situation rebounded into her mind. Then she found one other thing. Her wristwatch was missing from her wrist. She frantically hunted around but it was nowhere in the room. She had no way to tell the time.

'The bastards!' she shrieked and flung herself down on the bed. Her body erupted into a flood of tears while her hands kneaded in acute distress.

*

Dorothy blinked awake and realised she had been asleep. It was freezing cold and the lone light bulb shone down. Her blankets were on the floor and she was remembered where she was. A rat ran across the corner of the room and disappeared down a hole she didn't know was there.

She sat up and felt tears welling in her eyes. 'Oh Kevin,' she sobbed and stood up. The rat was gone but bleak shadows flickered around from the swinging light she must have bumped. She sat on the edge of the bed and tried to take a grip on herself.

She reached for a blanket to tuck around herself and stared at the tiny window. Moonlight was glowing faintly through to give her strength and a method to overcome the panic. She walked into the kitchen, found another light with a dangling string that she pulled. It came on and somehow the two lights seemed friendlier than one. She went to the toilet and felt so grubby she ran the shower. It was well into the night and the chance of the men coming seemed remote now she was wide awake so she removed her top clothes and showered in bras and panties. No way was she going to remove everything. The water was only warm but made her feel better as it ran through her hair and over her body. It seemed to wash away the touch of the horrible men who had imprisoned her.

Finally she found a towel, dried herself and changed into clean underwear and clothes. Once again, she was too afraid to put on the nightgown tucked in the suitcase. She found a hairbrush, mirror and lipstick; yes it was the sort she used. For several moments she brushed her hair, dressed in clean clothes and applied the lipstick. She felt so much better until she walked out and the truth hit her like a pickaxe.

She was still a prisoner and that nightmare could become true. She had no doubts what so ever that Stanley was quite capable of rape.

'Oh Kevin,' she cried again and climbed back in the bed. Sleep was difficult but finally arrived, dreamless and even comforting until she awoke to see light in the window. It was morning and by the look of the square of blue sky, a beautiful day.

The day dragged and with the next night came a nightmare. Stanley was chasing her with a knife between his teeth. She was running but was knee deep in mud. He grabbed her and in one swoop, her clothes were ripped away and she woke up, trembling and covered in perspiration. Dorothy lay there shivering and decided enough was enough. She was going to find a way to escape!

*

At eleven thirty on Wednesday, Kevin was handed the telephone in his office. 'Good morning, Kevin Smithers speaking,' he said.

'Mr. Smithers this is Ruth Hartford-Beaumont speaking. I am trying to contact your wife but your home phone is not being answered. It's quite urgent I contact her.'

Kevin frowned. 'She's in Cambridge, Viscountess Hartford-Beaumont,' he said. 'Can I help?'

Ruth gave a tiny gasp. 'Did she take the train, Kevin?'

'No, our car. Why?'

Then I'm afraid I might be too late,' the woman continued. 'I rang to warn her not to travel out of the village. I've learned my husband is planning to kidnap her.'

Kevin's face paled. 'Have you any details, Ruth?' he said, forgetting to use her title.

After listening for several moments he hung up and immediately rang long distance. His fingers drummed on the desk as he waited impatiently while the call went through to Cambridge. Moments later he hung up with his face twisted in horror. It was confirmed that Dorothy hadn't arrived there.

'What's wrong, Kevin?' Tom, who had witnessed the two conversations, asked.

'I think they've got Dorothy,' Kevin replied and repeated everything he had learned. He then stared at Tom and decided to tell his friend more. 'He's about to blackmail me,' he continued and in a hushed voice told Tom everything; his assumed identity; the lot. 'I had to tell someone,' he concluded and blew his nose to hide his true feelings. 'I can't just do it myself.'

Tom nodded. 'You shouldn't have to, Kevin. We now have to decide what to do. Firstly, I'll ring Kath and get her to pick Cindy up after school. She can also meet the boys then I think someone should follow Dorothy's route but not you. If it is a blackmail bid, you'll need to be here for any contact.'

'I don't want the police in yet,' Kevin whispered. 'I've heard they can often make things worse.'

'Okay, but what about this lady you were talking to. We have one advantage. We know who the man is. Wouldn't it be a good idea to go to the police and tell them your fears.'

Kevin frowned. 'But...'

'Listen, Kevin, from what you said, it seems this character can't prove who you really are. Don't tell the police that part but include everything else. After all, you're quite a rich man. That could easily be the motivation for a blackmailer. I say do it now even before the Whiting rings you.'

Kevin bit on his lip and nodded. Feelings of utter frustration flowed through him. He remembered when he was nineteen in hospital with Dorothy there to help him.

'We can't fight it ourselves, Kevin,' Tom said. 'If your identity has never been discovered since the war it must be pretty secure. Military Intelligence doesn't work with the police, you know.'

Kevin frowned then appeared deep in thought. 'There is another way. I was given an emergency number at the Australian High Commission to phone. There was a code to say if I ever had my cover blown. I've never used it but have always kept the number and remember the code.' He took out his wallet and a small notebook that he thumbed through for a moment. 'Here it is under *'Aunt Alice,'* he said.

'Okay Kevin,' Tom replied. 'Do it now and I'll tell Bev on the switchboard that we want no incoming interruptions on your line. ' He frowned. 'Just in case the blackmailers call I'll have any calls for you diverted to my phone.' He looked his friend right in the eyes. 'But if there is no response from this number, you're to ring the police, right!'

Kevin nodded and seemed to be in a trance. Tom clapped his shoulders. 'We'll come through this okay, Kev. Dorothy's an intelligent woman and I'm sure Viscountess Ruth will help.'

Kevin sucked on his lip and nodded. He was himself again as he picked up the phone and asked for an emergency long distance number.

'Australian High Commission,' said a woman's voice with the distinct Australian accent. 'May I be of assistance?

'I would like Extension 17, please,' Kevin said.

The line went quiet before the woman spoke again. 'Are you sure... Sir,' she asked in a severe tone.

'Sorry,' replied Kevin. 'Extension 71, I meant.' This was all part of the prearranged code.

'Wait one moment Sir,' the woman seemed to have a tremor in her voice.

'Is the weather hot there?' a harsh male voice asked.

'Not as hot as Alice Springs,' Kevin replied. After thirteen years the code was working perfectly.

'Are you on a secure line?'

'Yes,' Kevin replied.

'Your code number please.'

'Kevin repeated it and several other identifications, including his real date of birth, his mother's maiden name and his real and assumed military numbers.'

The voice sounded less formal. 'I'll put Major Denton on, Kevin. He has been in on our whole conversation. It may take a couple of minutes to find your file.'

Kevin waited and smiled briefly at Tom.

'Denton here,' said a new voice. 'Tell me everything, Kevin no matter how unimportant it may seem.'

'Yes Sir,' Kevin replied and proceeded to explain everything. He spoke for almost fifteen minutes with only minor grunts of acknowledgement from Major Denton.

'You were right to contact us. We'll follow it up. Don't tell your local police anything yet. If you are contacted, make no commitment no matter how sever the threats are and ring the number I give you straight away, day or night. Understand.'

'Yes Sir,' Kevin replied answered a few more questions and listened to instructions before hanging up.

'They're going to help,' he whispered.

*

The call from the kidnappers came at ten at night at Kevin's place. An Australian army captain had arrived at seven and the living room was filled with equipment including four telephones and gigantic recording devices Kevin had never seen before.

Kevin's boys were present but Cindy had been taken home by Kath, Tom's wife, so she would not become too upset.

'Pick it up when I say,' snapped Captain Doug Fraser. 'On three...'

'Kevin Smithers speaking.'

'Hello Timmy, My Lad,' cackled the voice. 'I'm glad you never told the police after my original call. By now you may realise Dorothy won't be home for a while and is under our care.'

'My name is Kevin but go on.'

'We want two things Kevin, if you must be called that. Firstly ten thousand pounds would ensure your wife's safety from my boys. We'll ring later with details.'

'And the second.'

The voice laughed. 'You're going to ring the army and confess who you are, my lad.'

The captain poked Kevin and made a *'Keep him talking''* movement with his fingers.

'I am Kevin Smithers so I see no advantage in telling the army that. Can you elaborate.'

'Oh you're a calm one. Perhaps a few screams from your wife might change your mind. I'll be back to you some time tomorrow. Tell the police

and dear Dorothy will be floating down the Thames. Good night, Timmy.'
The line went dead.

'We have a trace, Sir,' a sergeant in the room said.

'Good,' replied Captain Fraser and turned to Kevin. 'You did well,'
he said. 'That last little conversation gave us the time.'

Kevin looked afraid. 'But what about Dorothy?'

The captain grimaced. 'Kevin, to put it bluntly, if they were going to
kill her it would have been done by now. If they haven't, twenty-four hours
will make little difference. We have men following both suspects right
now. If they go to where your wife is imprisoned or contact a third party
they will be immediately intercepted. My guess is she is locked somewhere
secure and will be just left until they make a deal.'

'Poor Dorothy,' Kevin choked. 'It's not bloody fair.'

'It never is, Kevin,' the captain said kindly, 'but I'd say at this very
moment she'll be worried about you and the family.'

*

CHAPTER FOURTEEN

5 November 1932

Dear Diary.
This is written on a scrap of notepaper in my bleak prison. Hopefully, I can paste it in my diary later.

Thoughts of My Loved ones, Kevin so gentle and kind, Bertie and Timmy, two fine sons and my Cindy are all with me in my mind. I even think of Mom and Daddy and wish they were close. Without my family to think about, this horrible place would have broken me but I know Kevin is out there looking for me and with his help, I shall survive this terrible ordeal.

I realise it is Guy Fawkes Day and we had planned bonfire and fireworks for Cindy and the boys. I hope Kevin still has it for my thoughts will be with them all. I cannot waste time writing so will sign off.

I have never been a religious person, but if things go wrong I trust God will look after my family.

Dorothy.

*

With grim determination, Dorothy set about inspecting her prison. The door was solid with no exposed hinges. It had a new type of lock fitted and the locking mechanism looked foolproof. As well, Dorothy knew it had been latched from the outside. She dragged the bed across under the window and by standing on it with tiptoes, could see down a slight slope to a grove of trees. There was nothing else in view. The glass in it could be easily broken but that seemed to be of no value as the window was only a foot high by one and a half long. Two vertical iron bars were fastened to the outside.

Next she examined the toilet. The outlet pipe fitted perfectly and was held in place by concrete. The rest of the cellar was made of thousands of stones ranging in size from the width of her hand to large ones over two feet in diameter. The gaps between them were concrete while the bottom section of the whole cellar up to a height of her knees was plastered over with smooth grey cement. This, unlike the rest of the walls seemed to be a recent addition. Perhaps it was done when the toilet was installed.

She prepared herself a cold meal and pondered over the construction. Now why would the owner bother to plaster over just a small bottom proportion? The building was on a small hill and the window above ground level so perhaps that entire wall was above ground level. She climbed onto the bed and peered out the dirty glass window. The ground directly below outside was out of sight so the window was higher and not directly on the ground as many cellar windows were.

In the whole prison, the only slight possibility of an escape route was the tiny hole in the corner where she'd seen the rat run out during the first night. She bent down and inspected it. Rather than round it was jagged where the plaster had broken off. When Dorothy reached down to feel inside cold air touched her hand.

She gave a tiny gasp, lay on the floor and peered into the hole. Light shone through a sort of tunnel from about fifteen inches away. That must be the width of the wall. She reached in and her fingers found a small stone that she pushed. It moved!

Time passed as Dorothy wiggled and moved the stone. She went and found the one knife she had been provided with. It was an ordinary blunt knife but useful to dig away around the stone. Her fingers became scratched and torn but finally she managed to drag the stone out of its surroundings. She smiled in triumph and was about to inspect inside the enlarged space when a sound made her body jump.

The door latch was moving. She stared in horror and did the only thing possible to cover the rock and hole. In one fast swish she yanked the blankets off the bed and bundled them in the corner over the stone, sat on the bed and grabbed a magazine.

She only just made it when the door flung open and the two men stood there. Their faces had no Balaclavas and they did not appear to care that she could recognise them. She shuddered at the thought of what this might mean.

'Rearranged the furniture, I see,' the leader said and smiled. He grabbed the chair from the kitchen and sat down.

The other man shut the door and stood leering at her. His face was a blotchy red from too much drink and a pot stomach hung out over his belt. The eyes, cruel and searching never left her, almost as if he was waiting to grab her just like in the nightmare.

'We probably won't need my friend's services,' the man, Dorothy was a sure it was Ruth's ex-husband, grinned. 'In the meantime...'

Dorothy shuddered as she saw the other creature purposely scratch himself in the groin and stare at her with that horrible fixed grin on his face.

'I'll bring you up to date, Dorothy,' the leader continued. 'Your husband must love you very much for he has decided to co-operate.'

Dorothy glared and her heart sank. This did not seem like Kevin.

'I'm afraid you're going to lose your jewellery.'

Dorothy made sure her facial expression did not change but her mind raced. She had no jewellery; at least nothing expensive.

'He is getting a small amount of money and your jewels from the safety deposit box at the bank…'

Dorothy nodded but also knew there was no such thing as a deposit box.

'Whether it is true or not, I don't know but your husband said the bank require a week's notice for access to the money and box.'

'It's true,' lied Dorothy. 'For our savings account we have to notify the bank seven days in advance for any withdrawal. I'm not sure about the box.'

Whiting, if that was who he was, shrugged. 'This means we'll need to keep you here for another week, Mrs. Robertson.' He emphasised the name but Dorothy remained impassive. He stood and walked into the kitchen. 'I see you've been careful with the food and still have some. Don't worry. We have come to replenish your stock. There's new bread, meat and milk. Aren't we kind?'

'You're just a bastard,' Dorothy hissed. 'We've done you no harm.'

Whiting glowered. 'With a traitor as a husband you've harmed everyone, Madam. You should hang your head in shame.'

Dorothy's indignation rose and she was about to make an angry retort but managed to stop herself. The two men were both leering at her and any provocation from herself could be all they needed to attack her. She wiped her hands on her skirt and just stared at Whiting but said nothing.

'You do have excellent control, Dorothy, I must admit,' Whiting smiled and the tension eased a little. He turned to Stanley. 'Get the provisions.'

Stanley brought in two boxes of groceries and placed them on the table, went out and returned with a couple more blankets and a sheet.

'It's getting colder,' he grunted and cast his watery eyes over Dorothy's body, again sending chills through her.

Whiting grinned. 'As I said; one week.' He chuckled. 'Of course, if things go wrong Stanley may be back earlier. I have to go to the city I'm afraid. Let's both hope your husband continues to co-operate otherwise my friend here may need to... shall we say... apply a little enforcement.'

Dorothy shivered.

The door was flung open, she got a glimpse of the bottom of a stairwell and they were gone. Tears rolled down her cheeks before she recollected her thoughts and settled down. The blankets tossed in the corner had not been mentioned so she was really no worse off than before the two men had arrived. Also, Kevin had been able to get a discrete message through. They had no jewellery or long-term money deposited, certainly nothing that required a week's notice. He was, therefore playing for time and wanted her to know that.

She blew her nose and felt a little better. After a hot cup of coffee with fresh milk and new bread she had regained most of her confidence and set about inspecting the hole in the wall.

As the day progressed she managed to dig out seven more stones. The building was ancient and she discovered only clay held the stones together in this section. She chipped back the plaster layer until there was a circular area of exposed stones about two feet in diameter. It appeared this was the corner of the building. Perhaps it had been undermined outside for the stones were not packed tightly together.

One massive stone, though, blocked her progress. She'd managed to extract the smaller stones around it and hide them under the bed. However, this large flat one was as solid as ever. For hours, Dorothy sweated and dug but to no avail. She stopped and realised it was twilight. The day was almost over and it was becoming chilly. She stopped, switched on the lights and small heater before she put her jacket and opened a can of soup.

As she sat sipping the soup and munching on a slice of bread she studied the hole. Perhaps she was going the wrong way. Until now she had dug all the stones out and brought them inside. Now what if she tried to push some out? If there was a slope outside they might roll away. With renewed enthusiasm she put her shoes on, lay back and kicked the large stone with full force. Nothing happened. She repeatedly kicked the object but it still didn't move. Annoyed at the lack of progress, she reached in and around the large stone. Her fingers touched smaller pebbles.

For hours, without even noticing the darkness and chilly temperatures, Dorothy worked on. Her fingers became scratched and nails torn. Blood trickled down her hands. She grimaced, put her leather gloves on and continued working. Finally she dug two more triangular stones out and another long flat one until utter exhaustion forced her to stop. She grabbed the little hand broom provided and swept up the debris, hid the new stones under the bed and stood up. Every bone in her body seemed to be aching from fatigue but the hole was bigger.

She gasped. Anyone walking in would see the gap. She grabbed the bed and heaved it along to that corner, rolled the stones beneath it and collapsed on the bed. Within moments she was asleep but her dreams were kind. She was home with Kevin, Cindy and the boys. Again it seemed so real that waking up made her almost burst into tears.

*

It was morning and freezing. The one bar heater that remained on all night hardly helped. After a rushed breakfast she set to work on the stone.

By around midday she had removed several smaller stones and used the broom handle to dig in parts unreachable with her hands. By pounding in the gap she found smaller stones could be pushed out. More light appeared and once she even heard several stones rumble away but still that big one eluded any effort to shift it.

It had to go! Further along the wall, the stones were sealed so close together they were like solid concrete and Dorothy conceded that the ancient craftsmen knew their job. It was, as she had originally thought, only a subsidence in the soil that had loosened this corner.

One more exhausting and frustrating day went by. Several smaller stones were removed and Dorothy could now see grass outside the hole but that horrible massive stone blocked the way. With it out of the way she could just about squeeze out. Perhaps tomorrow.

When it was dark again, she packed up, shifted the bed back to cover the hole and had a warm shower. As she stepped out for a towel she grinned. Without thinking she had a taken everything off and was now totally nude. God, she wished Kevin was here. Suddenly she leaped in fright. The door was rattling. She grabbed her clothes and frantically dressed without even wiping herself dry.

She only partially succeeded. Whiting stood holding a torch in the opened doorway and stared at her wet hair, wide eyes and still unbuttoned dress. 'Catch you unawares,' he chuckled. He placed a bottle of milk and loaf of bread on the floor.

'I'm away to the rendezvous. Wish me luck.'

As quickly as he arrived he was gone and the door latched. Like on the previous occasions, his visit left Dorothy completely demoralised. My God, that was close! What would have happened if he'd walked in two minutes earlier or, worse still, half an hour earlier when the hole didn't have the bed in front of it? She'd become too complacent.

She felt tired but the unexpected visit made her realise time was important. Rather than going to bed as she originally planned she pulled the bed away and continued to dig at the stones.

It was well after midnight when Dorothy rubbed her tired eyes and sat on the floor. She leaned back and gave *"Fort Knox"*, as she had nicknamed the stone, a gigantic kick. It wobbled! Dorothy stared and kicked again. Yes there was definite movement. With her adrenaline running and exhaustion forgotten she kicked and kicked until the impossible happened.

With a protesting groan *"Fort Knox"* gave way under Dorothy's constant pounding and rumbled away into the darkness. Cold air rushed in and beat against her legs while she just lay back on her arms and cried.

She remained inactive for only seconds before lying down and reaching in. Her head fitted easily and she realised her chin had touched frosty grass. Dorothy wriggled forward but her shoulders were too large. She slipped back inside and with renewed vigour started to chip away at the edges. The remaining stones there were quite small and with a new angle of attack she soon had three... four... and five out! The gap was almost wide enough when Dorothy shook herself and fluttered her eyes.

She had fallen asleep with her head in the hole. It was starting to get light outside so she must have been asleep several hours. She could see thick frost across the grass and her face felt frozen.

She crawled back, stretched her aching limbs and remembered the untimely visit from the night before. In a frantic rush she cleaned up the dirt and stones, shifted the bed over the corner and set about preparing, she was certain her last meal in that cell. She washed, gathered everything up and waited but nobody came. It appeared that the building was deserted so, with thumping heart, she continued her digging. When the hole seemed wide enough she gathered a grocery bag; packed it with food and clothes she would need and poked it through with the broom handle. Afterwards she squeezed in herself.

Her shoulders were too wide but Dorothy was not about to give up. She retreated inside and turned over so she was on her back. She pushed in, manipulated so her body was placed diagonally across the hole and heaved but her bulky coat hindered any progress. She wriggled back, stood up, removed the offending garment and tried again.

Sweat poured off her face as she pushed forward but she became wedged in with sharp sections of rock hindering progress. Her feet found the edge of the bed, which she used as a lever. With a grunt she pushed with all her might. Dust landed in her eyes, a sharp object scraped along one arm but she made progress. Suddenly the claustrophobic dank air felt cold and sweet. Wind was blowing against her face and her hair felt cold and damp. Grass! Her head was pushing against wet grass. She could smell it! That glorious smell of grass. Freedom! Her shoulders were outside; arms through and she could reach out to feel the stone wall.

The rest was easy. Her hips were a tight fit but nothing compared with her shoulders. She continued to slide on her back down the frosty bank and gave one final heave with her legs against the stone wall to free herself from that ghastly prison.

She lay panting for a second with scratched bleeding limbs, a ripped and dirty frock but she had escaped. She was free! It was a crisp winter's morning but a watery sun shone down and she could hear birds chirping in the nearby trees. The sound of those birds had never seemed quite so wonderful ever before.

*

With a feeling of sheer exhilaration, Dorothy rose, brushed herself down and gazed at the surroundings. The building wasn't a castle but an ancient, rambling manor and looked disused with the once fine gardens neglected and grazed by sheep. Windows appeared dark and unoccupied. Several were covered with sheets of iron. In the opposite direction, the land sloped away to a valley of oak and sycamore trees while stone walls encircled fields of sheep and cattle. Further back still, out of sight behind a hedgerow, was a road. Motor vehicles could be heard murmuring in the distance.

She crept forward to the building itself and grinned when she saw the hole she'd crawled out from. The wall had indeed been undercut by a small slip and the whole corner of the building seemed to be perched on a flimsy pile of rubble. Her stones couldn't even be seen amongst the other debris.

However, this was not the time to admire the scenery. Anybody walking around the house would see her straight away and her efforts would have been in vain. She pondered for a moment, grabbed her gear and walked quickly to the trees. Once there, she found a clump of dense shrubbery to crawl under, orientated herself and decide what to do next.

The trees circled behind the house so she could make her way to the rear without going back out onto the open. So far, the whole area looked completely desolate. She sneaked forward with her breath puffing out condensation. The trees circled behind several outbuildings, forlorn looking brick structures surrounded by stone fences.

She bent to almost a crawl and ran along behind one stone wall towards a barn before she stopped and studied it. There were two double doors at the front and a smaller opened door on the near side.

'Here goes,' she whispered to herself and dashed across to the building.

With adrenaline flowing, she crept inside the building and glanced around. It smelt of straw, soil and animals but, like the house, appeared unused.

'Yes!' she whispered in excitement.

*

The MG was parked right in front of her. Across from it was an empty space but tyre marks and oil stains showed where a second vehicle had been. That would be that black saloon of Whiting's, she guessed.

But her car was there and she could drive away. With senses on full alert, she approached the MG and peeped inside. It looked no different from when she'd been hijacked except the doors were locked and keys gone.

Dorothy felt up under the inside front mudguard. Yes, it was there! Kevin had conscientiously welded a tiny tobacco tin in one corner. Dorothy's fingers opened the lid and pulled out a wad of cotton wool. Everything was covered in mud but she had what she wanted. A spare key!

'Thank you Sweetheart,' she whispered and hugged him in her imagination.

Now came the dangerous part. She slipped around and opened the door. It rolled back on newly oiled hinges. Outside, the house looked ominously close but the grounds were still lifeless.

Dorothy climbed inside and inspected the interior in the dim light. It seemed perfect. Even to her purse was still in a basket hooked under the front passenger's seat.

She turned on the ignition, the usual red lights lit up and the gas gauge moved slowly up to half full. So far, so good.

'Okay, Girl, you're committed,' she said to herself and made one final check in the rear vision mirrors. Nothing!

She swallowed and pulled the starter button. The starter motor whirled and the engine caught. The sudden throaty roar made her jump in fright but there was no going back now. If anybody was around they would have heard. She engaged reverse, released the hand brake and roared out in a spin of wheels and screech of tyres. The sports car swung in a semi-circle and stopped while Dorothy engaged low gear.

Wheels spun and stones flung up as the car accelerated forward. She was up to third gear and doing fifty by the time the robust vehicle was out of the drive. Gears changed down and she gave a sigh of relief as the sports car swung onto the road. She had no idea where in the country she was but that horrible house was behind her.

But the escaping woman had been seen. Two heavily armed soldiers hiding in a woodshed glanced at each other as the car disappeared. 'Well, Mark, what do you reckon?' one asked.

'That is one brave lady,' Mark replied. 'My God, I was watching the house and didn't realise she was in the car until the engine roared and it came screaming out. It scared the shit out of me.' He grinned. 'What now, Gary? Do we follow her?'

'I'll radio in,' Gary replied. 'We came to rescue her and she did it all herself.'

'Yeah, but we've still got the bastards who did it to catch. Damn pity they had left before we arrived last night.'

Mark nodded. They'd been waiting all night but had been under orders to do nothing until the morning unless the kidnappers returned.

*

Dorothy drove for quarter of an hour before she came to an intersection with a road sign, The place mentioned to the left sign meant nothing but the right one said Norwich, a city about eighty miles north east of home. That's where she'd go!

Forty minutes later she pulled into the railway station in Norwich, By now, fatigue was catching up on her and she felt dirty and hungry. However, her first priority was to ring Kevin.

Nobody answered at home so she rang the newspaper. However, Kevin was out and a relieved Tom brought her up to date on the news, most of which was everyone's concern about herself. He promised to tell Kevin of her escape the moment he saw him and sounded so please to hear her voice Dorothy had trouble containing her sobs.

She found the station's rest room where she changed from her tatty clothes and was glad she had had the forethought to bring clean clothes with her. She was so hungry her stomach rumbled. She walked into the cafeteria and bought an enormous breakfast of bacon, eggs, toast, jam and a pot of tea. Half way through the meal she heard a polite cough and glanced up to see an army officer standing beside the table.

'Mrs. Dorothy Smithers?' he asked politely with an accent that wasn't a great deal different than Kevin's.

'Why yes, Major,' she replied after noticing the pips on his shoulders, 'But how do you know me?'

'Allow me to introduce myself. I am Major Andrew Denton, military attaché with the Australian High Commission in London. May I sit down?'

'Please do,' Dorothy said. 'Can I order you anything?'

'A cup of tea would be fine but keep eating. I'm sure you're hungry after your ordeal.'

Dorothy returned his smile and listened while the Major Denizen brought her up to date on everything that was happening. 'So if you'd like to make a detour you can meet your husband at two this afternoon,' he said.

'I'd like that,' Dorothy answered. 'Fancy, the whole time I was digging myself out, your men were sitting only a few yards away.'

'I apologise for the unnecessary distress,' the major replied. 'We wanted to catch the kidnappers in action. My men are still waiting there.'

'Good.' Dorothy pouted. 'God, I was scared!'

'But you came through with credit, Dorothy. I must congratulate you.'

'Why thank you, Major Denton. I appreciate that.' Dorothy beamed and took a sip of her tea.

*

Kevin was not nearly as happy as he sat in a train heading towards London. Even though he had been reassured everything was under control, he feared for Dorothy's life. The last few days had been sheer hell and the worse since before meeting her back in the war.

He glanced at the brief case beside his leg and sighed. It was filled with ten thousand pounds in unmarked notes. The notes were counterfeit but looked so real the only way they could be recognised would be to compare serial numbers. They also looked quite used so followed the kidnappers demand to a letter. He hoped Dorothy would be rescued before it was discovered that the notes weren't genuine.

Kevin felt physically ill as he watched the station signs until he came to the one he was looking out for. His heart pounded as the train chugged out and he walked to the end of the carriage. Now, all he had to do was wait for the train to stop at the next signal, climb off the train on the right hand side, leave the briefcase leaning against the signal pole and climb aboard again. He was assured the signal would not change until after he had boarded.

The train slowed and stopped. This was it! Kevin climbed down. His feet hit course gravel.

'Aye!' screamed a guard from two carriages back. 'You can't get off here. This ain't the station!'

Kevin grunted and walked briskly along up past the hissing engine to where the signal posts loomed. He placed the briefcase down and returned to the carriage to be met by an angry guard.

'Do you want to get yourself killed, Governor?' the man snapped. The Limited Express is due through on the other line and it'll be doing about eighty. You could have been sucked straight into it.'

'Sorry,' Kevin muttered. 'I thought I was at the station.'

When the signal fell and the train jerked forward, he caught the merest glimpse of the briefcase leaning against the pole.

*

Conrad Whiting smirked. Everything was all going well but if the fool thought his wife was going to be sitting at the next station cafeteria he was in for a surprise. He'd already decided this would only be the first of several more demands. After all, the man never confessed to being Timmy Robertson. Whiting shrugged. Perhaps he wasn't that traitor, after all. Not that it mattered. Smithers was a bloody colonial and deserved what he got and as for the wife, she should not be running a newspaper. That was a man's job, not some playgirl's toy to play with.

He placed his binoculars down and watched Kevin's train move away. It was only a quick step down the embankment across to the briefcase, and then back to a service tunnel he knew was there, and away. If all was well and the money was there, he'd telephone McKee and tell him to stay away from the woman. The plan was that if the man had not heard from him by midday he was to go and rough the snooty bitch up a little. Whiting grinned. He knew McKee would go further than just 'roughing up' and almost wished he was there for the action. Later he'd ring Smithers and say the bargain wasn't fulfilled because no confession had been made and he'd need another ten grand. It might even help to have the Smithers dame screaming in the background.

But that was later. Whiting glanced around and began to walk along the railway line. He reached the briefcase and could not resist a look inside. Yes, it was filled with ten and twenty pound notes as requested. He zipped it up and was about to walk back across to the service tunnel when he heard a footfall and froze in alarm.

Two soldiers and a civilian appeared out of the tunnel he was about to enter and two .303 rifles were aimed straight at him.

'You will not move!' one soldier barked above the city noises around. 'Hands away from your sides.'

Whiting's face drained of all colour. He clutched the briefcase and turned. Eighty yards down the track, a massive steam locomotive was thundering towards them on the second line. Whiting stared back at the soldiers, made a decision and ran. If he could get across the track...

*

He walked just five steps when the shot rang out, a bullet hit his right leg and he collapsed, screaming to the ground. The briefcase was dropped and forgotten as he attempted to stagger forward but fell sideways, just as the limited express screamed by in a rush of smoke and steam.

*

The last terrified shrieks were not even heard above the roar of one of the most powerful locomotives on the planet. By the time the driver realised something was wrong and applied the emergency brakes Lieutenant Conrad Whiting had already been dragged fifty yards under the second carriage. He was dead before he even realised both legs had been amputated.

*

Stanley grinned in anticipation as he drove the black saloon in behind the house. He didn't even notice the open door of the out building or the missing MG. The boss hadn't rung and he was about to have his way with that upper class bitch. He relished in anticipation of what he would do to her when he had her in his grasp.

He slammed the door and walked inside the deserted house, down the stairs and lifted the heavy latch on the door. It was a little after midday but the time didn't worry him as he contemplated whether how he would move in. One great slap across the face to get her scared. He liked them scared. No, he'd act friendly at first and get her distracted before the attack.

The door squeaked open and he walked in to find the room empty. 'It's no good hiding,' he growled forgetting his last decision.

He walked to the partition wall and searched around in disbelief. The woman had disappeared.

'The cow!' he snarled when he saw the hole in the corner. He hit his fist on the table in a fit of temper, swore and tore for the door. Perhaps she was not far away and he could catch her.

However, three steps later he skidded to a stop.

A man was standing half way down the stairs. 'Stanley McKee,' he said. 'I am Detective Sergeant Burk. You are under arrest for kidnapping, assault and stealing a motor vehicle. You have the right....'

'You bastard!' McKee and charged at the detective who stepped sideways and put a foot out.

McKee sprawled forward onto the stairs, his nose hit the banister and blood squirted everywhere. He shook his dazed head and glanced up.

'Handcuff him, constable,' Burke said in a quiet voice to the policeman standing by the door.

*

Kevin walked into the railway cafeteria but remembered he should not expect to find Dorothy there. Blackmailers very rarely released victims. He glanced around the crowded room, the queue at the counter, waitresses wiping down tables, people eating and meandering around. There was no sign of his wife.

His heart plummeted as he gazed at his watch. He was ten minutes early. Perhaps she could still come. Kevin wiped his chin and grabbed a tray. He didn't feel like eating but it gave him something to do rather than just stand there feeling self-conscious.

He placed a salmon sandwich on his tray and ordered a coffee when a voice beside him whispered. 'Make it two, Sweetheart.'

Kevin swung around and saw Dorothy smiling at him. She looked so beautiful in a new skirt and frilly cream blouse, her blonde hair was combed out and hung over her shoulders.

'Oh my God, Dorothy,' he whispered, placed the tray on the counter and swept her in his arms. 'You're here,' he wept, not caring if the whole room noticed. 'You're here!'

Their lips met and she wriggled in so close he could feel her soft body against him, her lips, that taste of lipstick.

'I was told not to expect to find you here,' he managed to get out between the kisses.

'Excuse me, Sir,' snapped an irate waitress. 'You're holding up the queue.'

Dorothy's twinkling blue eyes looked into his. 'Come on Sweetheart. We'd better find a table.'

While Kevin just remained frozen with a strange look of utter relief on his face, Dorothy paid for the food, placed the two coffees on the tray and led her husband to a tiny table in the corner where she placed everything down and again melted into his arms. The tears this time were hers as all reserve was dropped and true feelings rose in a crescendo.

All around, in typical British fashion, the other patrons ignored this uncouth behaviour of an adult couple frolicking in a public place.

*

CHAPTER FIFTEEN

November 12 1932
Dear Diary
Yes, I am back home with my love ones. Even Bertie and Timmy gave their mother a hug and Cindy was her usual delightful self when she welcomed me back.
It was a fast journey but Kevin managed to arrive at Kettingham in time to pick up Cindy after school. I'll never forget her look of surprise when she spied the MG waiting on the roadside and when I climbed out... Well, she does take after her Mum, I guess. (I've been told Canadians are more demonstrative than the British.) Of course, the surprise was not only Cindy's. It was only this evening we found out how it all happened and I wasn't the only one to have had a different experience.
Dorothy.

*

On Thursday the third of November when Dorothy was still a prisoner, across the ocean in Canada the situation was different. A red warning light flashed above the studio window of a radio station and recording studios on the sixth floor of a Toronto office block to indicate a live broadcast was in process. The announcer stubbed out a cigarette and glanced at the managing director of the company who smiled through the sound proof glass. The party was over and tonight the new high-powered transmitter was switched on.

'Good evening ladies and gentlemen,' he said into the massive desk microphone. 'Welcome to Station CJDT in Downtown Toronto coming to you with the new super power of 5000 watts and broadcasting seven nights a week into your living room.'

He banged three notes on a tiny chime bar and continued.

'Our program this evening includes Episode 27 of *Nurse Adams*. For those just receiving our new high-powered signal, this serial is written and produced right here in Downtown Toronto. For our new listeners, a summary of earlier episodes will be given at seven this evening. Right now, though, we begin today's transmission with supper music for your enjoyment.

The announcer signalled through the window, a technician brought the needle down on the latest big band recording and the red light went out to show the announcer's microphone was off air. 'Well Mrs. Hutchkins,' he asked, 'Are you impressed?'

'I am,' Amanda replied and smiled at the staff. It had taken months of effort but finally the *"O'Donnell and Williams Publishing Company"* became *"Hutchkins, O'Donnell and Williams Publishing and Broadcasting Company."* or *"HOW Broadcasting"* in a shortened version.

The business had been through difficult times since the big 1929 stock market crash and the *Weekly Dispatch* was one of the victims. Amanda and Samuel had sold off their remaining newspapers in the 1928 and their publishing company now devoted its time to book and magazine publications. By tying in with United States Companies they produced Canadian and British Empire versions of American books as well as original Canadian titles. It was only a recent suggestion of Samuel's that they purchase a small radio station and production studio in Toronto.

This new station with a high-powered transmitter and seven day broadcasting was the result. As well, the production studio now recorded six, fifteen-minute radio serials that were sold throughout Canada on huge 78 r.p.m. records which stations played and posted on to the next station in the network, almost like library books being distributed. It was an entirely new innovation and becoming popular with smaller stations without the finance to produce their own live serials. Samuel had been south of the border and had obtained the first selling rights to one of the new American broadcasting companies and within a month *Nurse Adams* and other serials would be broadcast from New York to San Francisco.

Now fifty-four, Amanda had grey flaking through the auburn hair but, especially in Samuel's eyes, was as slim and beautiful as ever. Their life together through tough times and the high rolling twenties had been cemented in heaven, as a friend had remarked at the ceremony to open the radio station's new transmitter earlier in the day. The change from a hundred watts to their present size made CJDT one of the most powerful stations in the city.

Amanda tucked her arm in Samuel's and stayed at the station for an hour as telephone calls came in from distant listeners. 'Another one from United States,' Diane, one of the telephone operators called out. 'We're being picked up loud and clear in Portland, Maine.'

Samuel grinned. 'Good put a blue pin on the wall map, Diane.' The map of eastern Canada and northeastern United States was dotted with coloured pins with the colours representing the signal strengths reported in. He turned to Amanda. 'Well, My Dear, shall we go home, relax and listen to the radio. The serials start at seven, I believe.'

'Yes, let's,' Amanda said and led her husband to the elevator. This new medium was the way of the future, she was sure.

*

Their evening, though, was not peaceful. Just before seven the telephone rang and Amanda answered.

'An urgent wireless telegraph has arrived for you from England, Madam,' said the operator after ascertaining it was Amanda speaking. 'Would you like it read over the telephone or delivered?'

'Read it please,' she replied and listened to the message Kevin had sent. She hung up and turned to Samuel with her expression grim. 'Dorothy's missing and it is assumed she has been kidnapped.'

'How did it happen?' Samuel asked in a stunned voice.

'She was travelling to Cambridge but never arrived. It happened yesterday and Kevin has notified the Australian military. That's all the message said.'

'That means his cover's blown,' Samuel whispered. 'It sounds serious.'

Amanda nodded and made an instant decision. 'I need to get to England even if it is to just to help Kevin.' She sighed. ' Why do they have to be so far away?'

'Are you sure, My Dear?' Samuel asked. He reached for the phone when Amanda gave a very definite nod. 'I'll see what I can do.'

He rang a business acquaintance and spoke for several moments before clicking the receiver down and asking the operator for another number. After two more calls he nodded, wrote some information down and hung up.

'If you can get to New York by seven tomorrow morning you can be in London by Sunday,' he said.

'Next Sunday,' Amanda grumbled. 'That's ages. Surely there is a faster steamship!'

'This Sunday, November the sixth,' Samuel corrected.

'That's impossible,' his wife snapped. 'No ship is that fast.'

'Not ship, My Dear,' Samuel added. 'Airship. The Graf Zeppelin to be precise. It takes two and a half days to cross the Atlantic. There were two cancellations and I got you a place.' He picked up the phone again. 'Now, we have to get you to New York. I'm sure there is a night express. I hope it hasn't left Toronto yet.'

*

It was a rush but by six in the morning, a cab dropped Amanda at the site of the gigantic German airship that was tied to poles and floating above a grass field. A small crowd was standing around and already passengers were passing through a small custom shed and walking up the steps to the passenger's compartment suspended under the sausage shaped gasbags. At one end of the airship, the four tails were painted with huge black swastikas that the German Republic had begun use in preference to the iron cross. It looked totally alien and, for no known reason, made Amanda shiver.

'Don't worry, Honey,' said an over painted woman who walked out of the customs line behind Amanda. 'The Germans are very efficient and capable. This will be my third trip in the Graf Zeppelin. Just think of it as a ship that travels above the water instead of through it.'

Amanda smiled nervously and exchanged small talk as she walked across the grass to the boarding ladder. It was a strange sensation to be entering a craft on the land that would take her out over the ocean. The passenger compartment even looked like a ship's deck with large windows with oval tops. The interior was similar to a first class railway carriage with sleeping cabins for the twenty passengers, as well as a dining room and day room.

'Can I help you with your luggage, Mrs. Hutchkins?' The crisply dressed first steward asked in accented English after sighting her ticket.

'Thank you,' Amanda replied and followed him to Cabin Six, a single berth cabin, again similar to one in a railway carriage or steamer.

After a quick sort of her gear she returned to a day room, sat in a cane chair and watched activities outside. There was the usual wait before the engines roared to life behind them and the door shut. Men could be seen unhitching guide ropes and the gigantic airship began to lift into the air. People and buildings grew smaller until they looked like models beneath them. Amanda had flown in an aeroplane but this was an entirely different experience. They were just sitting in space above the countryside far below. The throb of the motors increased and the land moved away behind. Buildings and suburbs were passed over until the land turned to ocean, the Atlantic Ocean. She was on her way!

*

It was noon on Monday when Kevin received a ring at his office.

'Mom,' he said when he recognised the voice. 'We have a clear line. Thanks for ringing but I'm afraid the news is bad' He is voice broke when he told of the kidnapper's telephone calls.

'Kevin, My Dear' interrupted Amanda, 'Can you free yourself from the newspaper for a few moments.'

'Sure Mom,' Kevin replied. 'But why?'

'I'm at the railway station. Can you pick me up? I'd walk but the luggage is a bit heavy.'

'Railway Station!' Kevin asked. 'In Toronto?'

'No,' Amanda gave a tiny laugh. 'Here in Kettingham and I'm tired out. I could get a cab, of course.'

'Here!' Kevin exclaimed, 'but how can you be?'

'Modern transport, Kevin,' Amanda replied.

*

That afternoon Amanda picked Cindy up from school and, for the first time since Dorothy's abduction, the family had a proper meal that night and Kevin had someone to relate his innermost feelings with. Amanda's presence lifted everyone's morale and this dynamic woman insisted on taking over all the household chores. Even a minor school problem Timmy had was dealt with when Amanda marched into the headmaster's office. She told the man quite bluntly, that if his only concern was a bit of unfinished homework when Timmy's mother was missing in suspicious circumstances, it spoke unfavourably of the English school system in general and Kettingham Grammar School in particular.

*

It was later in the day after Dorothy met Kevin at the station cafeteria that the pair pulled into the pavement outside Kettingham North Primary school about two minutes before the dismissal bell.

'My God, that was a fast trip. Lucky we were driving the MG and not the baby Austin,' Dorothy gasped referring to their other little car. 'It's going to be a surprise for Cindy.'

'You too,' said Kevin and leaned across to kiss Dorothy on the cheek.

'What do you mean?' she replied with a pout. 'Kevin, you're keeping something from me. What is it?'

'Patience My Dear.'

'Damn the patience, what is it?' Dorothy retorted.

'Nothing bad,' Kevin said but refused to say more.

Dorothy retorted but thought about the conversation, relaxed and squeezed her husband's leg. 'How did Cindy react?' she asked.

'She was pretty weepy,' Kevin confessed. 'The boys went all quiet but she just retreated into her bedroom with her teddy bear and cried and cried when she thought I wasn't watching.'

'Oh the poor dear,' Dorothy whispered. 'You know it was only by thinking about you and the children that I remained calm.'

'Did you think of anyone else?' Kevin asked with a mysterious look in his eyes.

'That's a strange question,' Dorothy replied. 'Sure, I thought of my childhood a lot. You know Mom and Daddy and the things I did when I was Cindy's age.'

The clanging school bell and chatting pupils who began pouring out of the school building interrupted their conversation.

'Wait!' said Kevin when Dorothy began to get out of the car. 'Let her find us.'

'Well, okay,' she replied doubtfully and sat down to gaze at the children dashing everywhere. 'My God, don't they all look the same?'

She noticed a girl about Cindy's size walking out holding an older lady's hand. She peered and rubbed her eyes. It was Cindy but who was she with? Oh My God it couldn't be, but it was!

'You old tease. Why didn't you say Mom was here?' She slapped Kevin on the leg and jumped out of the MG.

It was Cindy who saw her mother first. 'Mummy!' she screamed and left her grandmother to run full speed into her mother's arms. 'Mummy!' The youngster buried her head in Dorothy's shoulders. 'I was so scared.'

'Well, I'm back for ever, Sweetheart, and who is this with you?'

Cindy frowned at her mother. 'You know,' she said in a rush of words. 'It's Grandma. She flew here in an airship, Mummy, right across the Atlantic Ocean and she said...'

'Whoa!' said Dorothy. 'There's lots of time my pet. All the time in the world.' She kissed Cindy and turned to Amanda.

'Oh Mom,' she gasped. 'I never expected...'Again it was all hugs and kisses, questions and answers until Cindy interrupted.

'Look at our new car, Grandma,' she shouted and tugged on Amanda's skirt.

Amanda turned and saw Cindy's excited eyes. 'Wow!' she said. 'Do you think your Dad will let me have a ride in it?'

'Yeah, I think so,' Cindy responded. 'It's a four seater. We'll all fit in.'

'What about the boys,' Dorothy said.

'Oh them,' retorted Cindy with an indignant look. 'Let them walk home.'

Dorothy glanced down at her daughter's blue eyes and felt her own become moist. 'My Darling,' she cried and cuddled her daughter again, so tightly the youngster was almost smothered. 'I thought I might never see you again.'

Cindy looked up. 'But Daddy was here,' she said. 'I knew Daddy would find you.'

'Yes he was,' Dorothy said. 'Grandma, too. You hardly needed me.'

Cindy glowered at her mother, realised it was a joke, opened the MG's door and folded down the front seat. 'We get in the back, Grandma.' she directed in a very adult type voice.

*

That evening, everyone talked long and hard until Cindy fell asleep on the couch and the boys ambled off to bed. The subject of Dorothy's abduction was fully covered and conversation drifted onto other matters

'So what happened after Granddad died?' Dorothy asked. She hardly knew Amanda's father so the notification of his death six month's earlier did not mean a lot to Kevin or herself.

'In what way, Dear?' Amanda replied.

'Well, his lumber firm and other business interests. Did anything come to you?'

Amanda grunted 'A few personal items. His second wife had five children and four of them were males. They inherited everything. My half sister, Lillian got nothing either.' She shrugged. 'That's what usually happens, you know. I didn't need or want any of his money, anyhow. '

'Yes but your mother was crafty leaving everything to the female side of the family, wasn't she?'

'It was strange,' Amanda agreed. 'That will was drawn up just after I eloped with Jack. I think she was still annoyed with me at the time and that was the reason behind it. We became close again later but her untimely death came before she could alter it, I guess. At least she kept it out of my father's hands; otherwise it would have gone to my half brothers with everything else. Dear old Mom, she was a victim as much as I was. They were tough times for women.' She fixed her eyes on Dorothy. 'You almost never arrived in this world alive the day of the avalanche, Sweetheart. If your father hadn't found us we would have both perished.'

'But we didn't,' Dorothy said, 'and look at us now.'

'Yes,' Amanda replied. 'Overall we've been rather fortunate.'

'Me too,' Kevin interrupted and placed an arm round Dorothy's shoulders. She leaned against him, gazed into his eyes but said nothing.

*

A little before midnight, after coffee and just before they were all about to retire for the evening, the telephone rang. Kevin answered; listen for a few moments and hung up.

'That was Major Denton,' he said. 'Whiting is dead; killed by the express train only moments after I left the briefcase by the signal pole.' He said. 'It seems as though my cover is to remain intact after all. Stanley McKee was caught in your cellar just after noon and is under arrest.'

The two women both looked hushed and morbid at the news. Kevin frowned and glanced at them both. 'What's wrong,' he asked. 'Surely you aren't saddened by Whiting's death. He was a real sod of a man who could have continued to blackmail me.'

'No,' Dorothy replied. Her eyes were dilated and lips shook. 'McKee came back to rape me, I know that. He already fondled me when my MG was hijacked,' she continued. 'I didn't tell you that.'

'Forget the whole episode Dorothy,' Kevin whispered and pulled her into his arms. 'It's all over now and you're safe.' He kissed her tenderly and glanced over at his mother-in-law who continued to have a faraway expression on her face.

'What's wrong, Mom?' he asked.

'Nothing really,' Amanda answered. 'Memories, that's all. Jack, my first husband and Dorothy's father, was killed in a railway accident. When you mentioned this man all the memories came flooding back.'

Dorothy walked across to embrace her mother. 'I can't remember my real dad,' she said, 'but he seemed so alive to me when I sneak read your diary, Mom. I think you can feel proud to have had two wonderful men in your life. Samuel has been such a marvellous father to me.'

'I know Sweetheart,' Amanda stood up. 'I won't be a moment,' she added and left the room.

Dorothy glanced at Kevin but he only shrugged. Amanda returned with a blue cloth bound book in her hand. 'For some reason I brought my first diary with me. I guess it was something close to my heart.' She handed it to Dorothy. 'I want you to have it, Sweetheart. Read it again if you want to.'

Dorothy looked into her mother's eyes. 'I'd like that, Mom,' she said in a soft voice. 'I've kept a diary too so I'll keep yours with mine.' She laughed. 'I guess we're so much alike, aren't we?'

Amanda nodded. 'Yes,' she replied. 'I know I'm so proud of you both,' she glanced at Dorothy's husband. 'That includes you, Kevin and your family. Your boys have grown up so quickly and Cindy is a real darling.' She coughed and stood up. 'I'm off to bed. See you in the morning.'

'Night, Mom,' Dorothy and Kevin both said.

*

'Come upstairs. I have something to show you, ' Dorothy whispered after her mother had left. She took Kevin's hand and led him to their bedroom. 'Get into your pyjamas. I'll be back in a moment.'

A few moments later Kevin sat in bed when the door opened. Dorothy stood with the light behind her. She wore a satin, light turquoise negligee with a low front and material so transparent her body beneath could be seen as the light shone through from behind.

'I bought it just before I met you at the station,' she said. Her voice was husky. 'I want you, My Love.' She held out both hands so even her long slender fingers and red fingernails seemed to portray her love and desire.

Kevin tossed the blankets aside and grabbed her in his arms.

The thrashing bodies came together in an expression of their relief and love. Finally, they lay together on the messed up bed and held each other while Dorothy wept.

'I thought I'd never be back with you, Sweetheart,' she whispered. 'I was sure that horrible man would rape and murder me and I'd never see you again.'

Kevin patted her hair and held her close. 'I know,' he answered with his own voice charged with emotion. 'I never gave up hope but as the days turned into a week, then nine days I feared the worst.' He kissed her again. 'Dorothy I love you so much I could not have continued without you.'

'But you would have My Darling for Cindy and the boys.'

Dorothy stood up and slipped the negligee on again. 'Well it did the trick.' She smirked remade the bed and climbed in, 'If you wake me up in the middle of the night for another round, I'll scream.'

'No,' said Kevin and kissed her ear. 'Morning will do.'

*

Amanda stayed for two more weeks before returning home on a steamboat. She said the airship was okay if one was in a hurry but she preferred being on the ocean. Life in their household returned to normal and it wasn't until eight months later that the trial of Stanley McKee brought Dorothy's kidnapping to their attention again.

The main worry that Kevin's real identity would be discovered by the military because of publicity of the court case did not materialise. Perhaps the Australians had persuaded the British government to invoked the Secrecy Act. Kevin was contacted one last time with a brief telephone message that said the road had been sealed and he could continue his life as before.

Other aspects of the trial, though, were more nerve raking for Dorothy. McKee's defence lawyer maintained that his client was a victim of mistaken identity; he was at the house investigating hammering noises when the police arrived and arrested him. McKee himself, blatantly lied in his own defence and Dorothy was rigorously cross-examined about the day her MG was stopped.

'So I put it to you Mrs. Smithers,' the defence barrister stated in almost a sarcastic tone, 'that on the day in question, the men in the Balaclava and goggles who abducted you could not be recognised. Also, my client was not the man who accompanied Lieutenant Whiting when food was brought to the cellar where you were held prisoner.

Understandably, you were under acute distress and made a genuine mistake in your statement to the police.'

'That is incorrect,' Dorothy replied angrily.

She was about to elaborate but the attorney stopped her with a cutting, 'Thank you, Mrs. Smithers. That is all.'

The Crown Prosecutor, though, saw through this ploy and approached Dorothy sympathetically. 'We heard how your vehicle was stopped, Dorothy,' he said. 'However, I'm more interested in what the hijackers did.'

'I was injected with a hypodermic needle and woke up in the cellar,' Dorothy replied.

'But before that. Were you grabbed or slapped?'

'I was fondled,' Dorothy said very quietly. Her face was deadly pale.

'The men brushed against your body, you mean?'

'No,' Dorothy replied and fixed McKee with an icy glare. 'That man purposely put his hand inside my clothing while he was holding me. It was a deliberate action.'

She glanced over the jury and noted some sympathetic expressions on the men's faces. Being a very attractive woman was an advantage at that moment.

However, the defence lawyer continued his questions. 'Mrs. Smithers, how do you know it was the defendant who attacked you? You said yourself, the men were wearing Balaclava and motor goggles.'

'His build, mannerisms and voice,' Dorothy replied in a quiet confident voice. 'When he came into the cellar with Conrad Whiting later, I recognised him as the man who attacked me. There was not doubt in my mind, what so ever.'

'Yes! Yes!' the barrister replied with a wave of his hand. 'That is another piece of unsubstantiated evidence. Thank you, Mrs. Smithers.'

The trial continued for three more days and ended with two completely different scenarios that the Crown Prosecutor brought out in his summing up.

'Therefore, Gentlemen of the Jury, it comes down to whose story you believe. Is it that of an outstanding member of our society, a businesswoman and editor of a provincial newspaper; one of a very few in this country I might add. Or is it a man of no fixed abode and no known occupation with three previous convictions for assault and robbery. That is for you to decide, gentlemen.

I put it to you that the Crown has, beyond all reasonable doubt, proved Stanley Harold McKee, together with the late Lieutenant Conrad Whiting, purposely kidnapped Mrs. Dorothy Smithers and blackmailed her husband for financial gain.

Furthermore, I believe we have proved that if it wasn't for Dorothy Smithers' bravery and fortitude in managing to escape, the defendant would have been here on an additional charge today...' He paused and stared at the twelve men on the jury before continuing... 'That of rape or even murder. It was a particularly callous crime, Gentlemen and Stanley Harold McKee is guilty of all charges.'

*

The jury was out for five hours but came back with the verdict the Crown Prosecutor asked for. McKee was found guilty of kidnapping, blackmail, stealing a motor vehicle, breaking and entering as well as intimidation and sexual assault.

Dorothy grabbed Kevin's hand as the hushed courtroom listened when the judge began his deliberation. 'Stanley Harold McKee,' he began and peered down from the bench from under his white wig. 'I agree completely with the verdict the jury handed down to you.

Even though, as the Defence ascertained, you were not the major instigator of this crime you knew what was happening and participated without the slightest remorse. Throughout this trial you continued to show a complete lack of compassion and refused to acknowledge any participation in the offences. Your cowardly threats and assault on a brave woman were particularly odorous.'

The judge stopped and fixed his eyes on McKee who just stared at the wall without any sign of having heard. 'You have been found guilty on all charges... ' The judge went through each crime and pronounced a sentence. 'The sentences shall be held concurrently. It is the decision of this court, therefore, that you shall he incarcerated in one of His Majesty's Corrective Institutes for a total of fifteen years. Take him away.'

McKee, looking defiant and angry was led away. The criminal's eyes searched for Dorothy but she refused to return his gaze.

Instead, she nodded to Kevin and the pair walked out of the courthouse into a warm autumn morning where their MG was parked and waiting like an old friend. She smiled but still looked quite drained of emotion as Kevin drove them both away.

'I'm taking you to dinner My Dear,' he said and shook his head when she began to protest. 'No, the paper can do without us for a few more hours.'

Dorothy sighed. 'Yes Sweetheart,' she replied. 'Come to think of it, I am rather hungry.'

She took her hat off, tossed it on the back seat and undid the knot so her hair flowed freely over her shoulders before glancing at her husband as he changed down at next intersection. It was 1933 and the depression was almost over. She felt proud that the attractive man driving the car was her husband and father of their three growing children. Also, the assumed name of Smithers was still secure and they could continue to use it.

Their eyes met and they both smiled.

*

CHAPTER SIXTEEN

After the departure of Simon McDoyle, life improved for Nicole Tucker at *The Blue Mist Motel*. The clouds rolled in and a few local downpours helped the stream level to rise, late season campers arrived and an Auckland travel agent had booked in six busloads of overseas tourist right through March and the beginning of April. The units filled and Nicole was in the embarrassing but satisfying situation of having to turn people away. The days became busy so it was only at night she thought of Simon and missed him.

On these hot late evenings she would pick up the old blue diary and read Amanda's story. As it unfolded, Amanda became like a sister, not a far off long dead ancestor. Nicole felt she could grab the phone and call her up or write her a letter. Instead, she wrote long letters to her grandmother who would write back and fill in obscure parts or explain some of the early century words or customs.

February turned into March and the summer season drew to a close. Every night Nicole would read more from Amanda's diary until the year 1908 and the end was reached. The red covered diary, however, was different. The writing and style changed and she realised straight away there was a different author. Dorothy's story, though, was every bit as exciting as Amanda's but concluded three quarters of the way through with the last entries telling of the kidnapping and the follow up trial. Cindy was also mentioned in great detail.

Cindy!

Nicole frowned as she reread the last few pages for the third time. She gasped. That was Grandma so even without diaries, the lives of her ancestors could be followed. She could ask her grandmother the rest of the story. Nicole sighed. It was really only a dream, though. Grandma lived in Vancouver, Canada and the twelve hundred dollars airfare might as well be a million. Even with a successful end of season at the motel, the profits after paying mortgage and other expenses barely covered living expenses.

The bank had been quite generous in financing her to buy out Simon but the mortgage had to be repaid. Also, Whetu and Gina Makutu, a middle aged Maori couple who lived on a farmlet down the road had been hired to replace Simon and the girl he'd moved out with. Their wages had to be paid. Employing these two, though, had really been one of the best decisions she'd made. Whetu was a real handyman and caretaker while

Gina proved to be an excellent cook and had taken over cooking the guests' breakfasts.

Like many others in New Zealand, *The Blue Mist Motel* units were self-contained with their own kitchen and no restaurant was attached to the premises. However, breakfasts were cooked and taken to guests who ordered them the night before. In the busy times there were twenty or more to prepare each morning, Gina would arrive at six am and by the time Nicole walked into the motel kitchen half an hour later, the sausages, bacon and eggs would be sizzling away, ready for her to deliver to the units from seven.

When Simon was with her she did all the cooking herself and the day had started off very busy with the breakfasts, followed by guests arriving at the office to pay for accommodation and the usual cleaning of units and camp ground ablution blocks. In the afternoon there was a brief lull before guests would begin arriving for the next evening. Now Gina, Whetu and a part time lady did all the cleaning and Nicole could concentrate on the administration side. Except for the loss of companionship she was, therefore, now much better off without Simon.

*

Late one evening she wrote a long rambling and personal letter to her grandmother telling about the break-up and how lonely she really was. Afterwards, she reread the six-page document and felt annoyed with herself for being too emotional. It was times like this she missed her own parents. Grandma was her only living relative and she guessed the old lady who was over eighty would not be around much longer. Nicole placed the writing pad on the bedside table and glanced at the empty side of the double bed.

'You were a moody old bugger, Simon but I wish you were back here now.' She turned to the massive ginger cat curled up at her feet. 'No, Biscuit,' she whispered and picked him up in a big cuddle. 'I'm not angry with you. Only naughty old Simon but I don't know why I still think about him when I have a big fluffy pussy to look after me.'

*

Lunchtime at the motel was a time to relax after the hectic morning cleaning. Guests staying for another night were well away from the buildings, either walking the bush tracks or visiting the local beach while the others had left. Most empty units had been cleaned by now, ready for the next guests who began to arrive after four in the afternoon. Nicole shared the break with Gina and Whetu in the staff room. Whetu would place a massive mug of tea on the table and turn to the sports section of

The New Zealand Herald while the women chatted and munched sandwiches or other light food.

Afterwards, Nicole did administration work including reading the day's email on the computer. It was Tuesday and Nicole hummed a catchy tune overheard from the radio and sifted through the dozen or so messages. Amongst the inquiries and bookings one was headed *'Grandma.'* She gave a curious frown and wondered how her grandmother had found her email address. As far as had remembered she had not given it to her. Actually, she didn't even know her grandmother had a computer.

The message, when it appeared on the screen didn't really help solve her curiosity. *"Dear Nicole,"* it stated. *"I thought I'd try this new method to get back to you quickly, so drove out to B.C. University where this nice young man let me use a computer and found your address for me. I received your letter, Sweetheart. It was one from the heart, wasn't it? Expect a lumpy parcel in three days. Love Grandma. P.S. I hope this gets to you. I don't really trust these new contraptions."*

Nicole grinned and remembered her grandmother's dry humour. Fancy still driving at her age! The last time she'd seen the tall graceful white haired lady was eight years earlier at her mother's funeral. Grandma had probably aged since then. She printed off a copy and went to show Gina who was sorting the clean laundry.

'How old is your grandmother?' Gina asked after she'd read the message.

'Eighty-five, I think,' Nicole replied.

'That all?' retorted Gina. 'My grandmother lived to be ninety-five. Your's has got another ten years yet.'

'I hope so,' Nicole replied.

Gina stopped folding the sheet in her hand and looked over at Nicole. 'She's the only family you have left, Nicole?' she asked.

'Yes, Dad cleared out when I was at primary school. He's somewhere in Australia with a new wife and a couple of children. They'd be teenagers now. His letters stopped ten years ago and he never even contacted me for Mum's funeral.'

'What killed your Mum?' Gina's voice was compassionate.

'Breast cancer,' Nicole sighed. 'She was only fifty. God, I miss her sometimes.' She gave a tiny smile. 'Yet, from since I was about thirteen, all we did was yell and scream at each other. I was a real little witch but by the time I found out how ill Mum was, it was too late.'

Gina stepped across the room and placed an arm around her. 'You've been pretty good to Whetu and me,' she said quietly. 'You know the old man was pretty depressed about being on the dole and the farm not paying then you offered us both jobs. If you don't mind a couple of old grouches we'll be your family. Why don't you come down to the marae some time? You're well known and liked by my people, you know.'

Nicole blinked back tears. The local Maori community were a very close knit group who had been nothing but co-operative when she'd asked them not long after her arrival, if the motel guests could visit the waterfall on their property. They were so pleased she had approached them and told her the previous owner of the motel had just mumbled something about public lands belonging to everyone and there was constant friction between the groups.

'Thank you, Gina,' Nicole replied. 'I'll do that.' She squeezed the chubby figure in her arms. 'The motel is going well since Simon left, thanks mainly to Whetu and yourself. You are both more than just workers to me.'

Gina gave a laugh, patted Nicole's back and returned to her sheet folding. 'Come on Girl,' she said. 'There's still that mess in the women's showers to clean up.'

'Oh yes,' Nicole smiled. 'I'd forgotten.'

She grabbed the cleaning gear and wandered out into the afternoon sunshine. The fog from early morning had rolled away and the bush covered hills looked dark green and glistening. Far off, a bellbird whistled a melodious tune while, behind, the stream continued to chatter over rocks. It was so peaceful, Nicole's earlier hollow feelings disappeared and she began to hum the tune still in her mind from earlier in the day.

*

Six o'clock on the Friday evening was busy. Five families arrived simultaneously and Nicole was so busy dashing back and forth to the units showing guests the facilities, taking registrations and answering the phone that she never noticed the Toyota rental car pull into to parking area. A well-dressed, white haired lady stepped out and gazed around at the scenery. She slipped a bag on her arm, strolled into the administration block and sat down. A gentle smile covered her face.

'Can I help you, Madam,' Gina said from across the counter.

'No hurry,' came the slow reply 'I'd like to speak to Nicole when she is ready.'

Gina noted the soft accent, stared at the woman, frowned and slipped outside to where Nicole was returning up the drive.

'Your lumpy parcel has arrived,' she said without even a trace of a grin.

'Good,' Nicole replied. 'I never saw the courier arrive. Where is it?'

Gina nodded her head back towards the office. 'Inside,' she said.

Nicole swished a hand over her hair, strolled in the front door and gazed around for the parcel. Except for three or four people milling around, the room was empty.

'Well Sweetheart, you look well.' The voice, that seemed a hybrid of British and Canadian accents, spoke softly from behind her.

Nicole swung around 'Grandma?' she gasped in astonishment and realised it was indeed her grandmother, looking not one day older than when she'd last seen her eight years earlier.

The graceful lady stood and beamed at her granddaughter. 'Well aren't you going to welcome me?'

'Grandma!' Nicole cried out and seized the old lady.

'What are you doing here?' Nicole said and wiped tears of joy from her eyes.

'Well,' said Cindy. 'The family back in Vancouver are all well and don't need me around for a while and after your letter, I thought I may be able to help a little.'

'Oh Grandma,' Nicole said. 'I never imagined. Why didn't you tell me? I'd have picked you up at the airport. Come through to the flat.' She led her grandmother through to the living quarters and just stood gazing at her and smiling.

'Have I got a fly on my nose?' Cindy asked with a grin.

'Grandma, you look no older.'

'You do,' Cindy replied in her slight drawl. 'The chubby teenager has grown into a beautiful woman. I love your hair.'

'Oh Grandma,' Nicole flushed and tears appeared in her eyes again as she hugged Cindy. 'I'm so thrilled to see you but you should have told me, you know! '

'I did,' Cindy gave a wee chortle. 'Didn't you get my email?'

'I did but I expected something in a box.'

Cindy's eyes twinkled. 'I'm not about to be put in one yet,' she replied. 'If you aren't too busy I have a mountain of luggage in the car. Can't get used to the steering wheel on the passenger's side, though. This place is as bad as England.'

'Oh Grandma,' teased Nicole and slipped her arm through Cindy's. 'You should know all civilised countries drive on the left?'

Cindy Jervis proved to be one very active old lady. Not only did she insist on working a full day at the motel but also accompanied Nicole when she took guests on two-hour bush walks to see the falls. Often she outperformed many visitors twenty years younger than herself. It was only with Nicole's persuasion that she left a rock climb after snorting she could have done it but didn't want to embarrass Nicole by slowing her down.

On the second evening she produced the letter Nicole had written and asked her about Simon and the motel's financial problems.

'The bank's ripping you off, Sweetheart,' she said after seeing the mortgage document.

'I realise that, Grandma but it is a second mortgage and that's the going interest rate in this country at the moment. It was either that or sell up.'

'Why didn't you ask me, Nicole?' Cindy peered over her reading glasses at her granddaughter. 'Right from the time of my grandmother's mother, we have helped our family.'

'I didn't like to,' Nicole replied. 'I know Mum and you had some sort of disagreement and she came to New Zealand. You know I only really got to know you after Mum's death.'

'True. That wasn't your fault and I guess I secretly hoped Julie would come home, but that was not to be. I'll tell you about it one day. I guess we were both as stubborn as each other.' She smiled in a whimsical way and looked at her granddaughter. 'Well,' she continued. 'How about I give you a loan to pay back this three hundred thousand you owe on the second mortgage, three percent interest maturing when you get your inheritance.'

Nicole fixed her eyes on her grandmother with a puzzled expression. 'I can't do that, Grandma,' she whispered. 'The interest, for one thing, is way too low and I have no inheritance. I used the money poor Mum left to finance the initial part of this motel purchase and I needed a first mortgage as well. This second one was to buy Simon out.'

Cindy smiled. ' How much is the first mortgage, Nicole?'

'Two hundred thousand,' the younger woman replied.

'I see so you really need five hundred thousand, that's a bit less in Canadian dollars.' She frowned and gazed the ceiling a few seconds before looking back at Nicole. 'We might as well clear everything. I'll make the loan for five hundred and twenty thousand, New Zealand. That will give you a little capital for maintenance and emergencies.'

Nicole stared at her Grandmother and wondered if the elderly lady was joking but Cindy's face was held in a sort of determined smile.

'I can't accept that, Grandma,' Nicole said.

Her grandmother looked at her and spoke very quietly. 'I am a little like you, Nicole. Timmy has gone. There's Grace still and nephews, nieces, grandnephews and grandnieces scattered throughout Canada. However, I only had one child, your mother and she only had yourself so you are actually my closest living relative. Why shouldn't I help you out with a tiny bit of finance?' Her blue eyes twinkled. 'After all, I don't really need it now.'

Nicole nodded. 'I see what you mean, Grandma, but still feel guilty. Why don't we make it a partnership instead? It would be quite easy. The half I bought back from Simon could be sold to you.'

'No,' Cindy said. 'I know nothing about running a motel.' She took Nicole's hands in hers. 'I can afford it and it will tie you over until your inheritance comes through.'

Nicole frowned. 'I repeat there is no inheritance, Grandma. Everything I had is invested in this business.'

'But you have,' Cindy said. 'Have you Grandma Amanda's diary handy, Sweetheart? I can just about remember the page it is on.'

'Sure, Grandma,' Nicole replied and walked over to her desk, took the old book out of a drawer and handed it to Cindy who flicked through the front pages.

'Here it is,' she said after a couple of moments. 'Her mother's legacy from the year 1900 goes to the fifth generation, female descendant in the Year 2007 and that, Sweetheart, happens to be you.'

'What! ' Nicole replied and looked over her grandmother's shoulder at the page. 'I read that but didn't really take much notice. Surely it would have disappeared by now.'

'Oh, the old lumber firm's gone and even "O'Donnell and Williams Publishers" but the old lady had her head screwed on.' Cindy grinned. 'She wasn't that old really, much younger than myself when she was killed in that avalanche. Anyhow, just before I sent those diaries to you I asked my lawyer in Vancouver to trace the legacy and it's there all right, down in Bellingham, Washington State. The original law firm has long since gone but the records are on file, still being administered and interest gathered from dividends.' She retorted. 'The law firm that is the trustee now has made a small fortune administering it but there are still shares there returning dividends and this money has been reinvested.'

'How much?' Nicole asked.

Cindy shrugged, 'They would not say but I would imagine it would be a respectable amount.'

Nicole stared at her grandmother, 'But how do you know it comes in my direction?' she asked, 'There must be dozens of ancestors around the world.'

'Fifth generation, eldest female over twenty-one,' Cindy said. 'That's you, Sweetheart.'

'But Grandma!'

'Hush, Nicole, it will be yours but don't tell a soul, otherwise you'll suddenly find you have dozens of female cousins claiming they're the true heirs.'

'I see,' Nicole's head was in a spin. 'If that's true, I'll gladly accept your loan but at a sensible rate of interest.'

'No, Nicole,' Cindy replied in a firm voice. 'I don't need the money. My brother's family is doing okay so a significant proportion of my money will come to you anyway. In some ways, you'll only be paying interest to yourself. I like the motel, too,' she added. 'I'd say without that horrible mortgage hanging over you it should be making a profit in a year or so.'

'Yeah,' said Nicole. 'A keen business sense must in the genes.'

'Could be,' Cindy replied. 'Now how about a cup of coffee?'

*

Cindy was an astute businesswoman who visited three local banks and haggled about the exchange rate before making a decision on where to transfer her Canadian money. She followed that up by getting Nicole's bank to cancel a discharge fee on the two mortgages held over *The Blue Mist Motel* by offering to deposit quite a substantial amount of money into an account.

'Well, Sweetheart,' she said that evening to Nicole. 'How does it feel to own *The Blue Mist Motel* freehold?'

'I still owe you, Grandma,' Nicole said but Cindy only shrugged.

'We're family,' she said.

Nicole smiled and jumped up when she heard the kettle click off. 'What happened to your mother and Amanda, anyway? It's a pity the diaries stopped. She took down two mugs and poured out a drink for them both.

Cindy laughed. 'Mum was pretty busy looking after us and editing the *'Evening Herald'* in the thirties and her diary sort of fizzled out. As for my grandmother, I know she continued to write her diary even when I was living with her but I never managed to find the later copies. They could turn up somewhere, but after all this time, I doubt it.'

'Could you tell me about your life, Grandma?'

'Why not!' replied the elderly lady. 'Where would you like me to begin?'

'Where Dorothy's diary stopped. That was not long after that kidnapping court case.' She frowned. 'Did you ever hear what happened to that man?' She clicked her fingers in thought. 'What was his name, Stanley something?'

'Stanley McKee never came out of jail,' Cindy explained. 'He was one of the main organisers of a prison riot in the late thirties. They killed a guard and he was shot and killed when the army came in and took back control. A thoroughly nasty individual, that one.'

'I see,' Nicole replied. 'After reading those diaries everybody seems so real.'

'They were,' retorted Cindy. She reached over to sip from the coffee Nicole had placed in front of her. 'Those were happy days. Well, after Mum's kidnapping, that is. I was ten at the time but have vivid memories of everything. We became even more of a close knit family after that and everything went well until the war arrived.'

'Tell me about the war,' Nicole said. 'I know nothing about what happened.'

Cindy's eyes took on a far away look as she sipped the coffee. 'It was a hard and sad time, Nicole. Our family, like thousands of others, was changed forever by it.'

*

PART 3   CINDY 1941

CHAPTER SEVENTEEN

A hush settled over the Gothic styled university auditorium as students waited in long rows of wooden seats on the last day of the 1940-41 Academic Year. It was June and Europe was at war again, France under control of Nazi Germany and England one massive military camp waiting to repel an invasion.

Near the rear of the building jammed in a tight row of students, Cindy Smithers glanced at her companions. She knew what was coming but it still did not alter the realism of the situation. Cindy, now eighteen and almost in defiance to custom, wore no hat and had her hair cut in a modern style. Like the other students she had a feeling that this assembly was important.

Dressed in full academic robes, the vice chancellor looked a lonely figure on the rostrum as everyone settled into their seats after standing and singing the national anthem.

'Ladies and gentlemen,' the man began in a solemn voice, 'In these sad times when our country is fighting for its very survival, our institution cannot remain aloof. Already our student population is decimated by our young men enlisting so, it is with regret, I have to advise that, for the first time in its two hundred and twenty-seven year history, this university will not be holding academic classes after the summer vacation. Rest assured...' his voice continued on but Cindy had tuned out.

'Well, that's it,' whispered Grace McKenzie, one of her friends. 'What are you going to do, Cindy?'

'Help Mum on the paper.' Cindy replied 'However, I don't think we'll have any say in the matter. Even if we don't volunteer, we'll be called up to help.'

She gave a tiny shrug. Their family had already been affected. Timmy, who enlisted in 1939 was one left behind after 350 000 British and French soldiers were evacuated from Dunkirk a year earlier. Bertie was a pilot officer in the R.A.F. Eleven Group based south of London and had flown Spitfire fighter planes right through the Battle of Britain while Dad was a lieutenant in the Army Signal Corps.

For some reason unknown to Cindy, even though over forty he had volunteered straight after war was declared. She remembered it was one of the very few arguments he had had with Mum but her mother's pleads for him to stay home were ignored. It was almost as if he had to prove himself. She knew he had been a soldier on the Western Front in The Great War but neither Mum nor himself ever spoke of it. At this very moment he was at some secret location somewhere in southern England.

The 'Evening Herald' was still printing but wartime restrictions meant it was severely reduced in size. Mum wanted her to return and help on the paper as all the younger males had left to go into the armed services. These were desperate times.

'... All I can reiterate,' droned on the vice chancellor when Cindy's mind switched back to the speaker, 'is that your studies have not been in vain. When hostilities are over you will all be able to continue your courses. Meanwhile, this year's papers will be marked and results posted at the usual time.' He stood in silence for a moment and Cindy was certain his eyes touched hers as they circled the room. 'May God help all of you through these terrible days ahead. Thank you, Ladies and Gentlemen.'

There was a numbed silence as he walked off the stage. Finally, the student president spoke a few words and it was over, the summer vacation and one of the darkest seasons in British history had arrived.

'I'm heading home to Kettingham in a couple of hours. Would you like a ride?' Cindy said to Grace. They were friends from Kettingham Girls' Grammar School days and lived near to each other.

'How did you get the petrol?' Grace replied.

Cindy grinned. Like everything else petrol was rationed and the allocation for civilian use was almost zero. 'Dad anticipated the restrictions and had a tank installed under our garage back in 1938. There's not a lot there but enough for emergencies. Mum reckoned getting my gear home from varsity was one such occasion so insisted I full the MG up.'

*

A few hours later with Grace in the passenger seat, Cindy accelerated her car through the lines of military vehicles; double-decker London buses and tall black taxis that filled the roads. Their green sports car was one of the very few civilian vehicles around. The 1932 MG, still in perfect condition, had been an eighteenth birthday present after Bertie, Timmy and her parents insisted she accept it. Now, though, it usually remained parked in their Kettingham garage waiting for better times.

'I wish my parents were like yours,' Grace said. 'They give everything to my brothers and I get next to nothing.'

'You had a year at university.'

'Yes.' Grace shrugged. 'Only because I won a scholarship and even then Dad grumbled that it was a waste of time for girls and I'd be better off learning how to cook properly.' She turned her nose up. 'I hate cooking.'

'Life will change,' Cindy replied as she changed through the gears.

'Yeah, breeding Aryan children for the master race,' Grace grumbled. 'If the Jerries invade it's going to be sheer hell. There are already mass rapes in Paris.'

'They're only rumours and at least we aren't Jews. They're the ones in trouble. Anyhow, they have to beat the R.A.F. first. Their cranky old planes are no match for ours.'

'Except they have thousands of them,' Grace retorted. 'They've been building them for ten years while we sat on our bottoms crooning away about peace and doing nothing.'

'I know.' Cindy grimaced. Rumours were rife and all information strictly censored but the quick fall of France had stunned even the most optimistic of citizens.

*

Dorothy met Cindy at the back door after the MG drove into their Kettingham driveway. This was unusual and Cindy frowned at the anxious look and the two envelopes her mother held.

'What is it, Mum?' she asked.

'An OHMS letter from the government for you Dear,' Dorothy replied. Her lips were lips pale. 'Also there's a letter to officially state Timmy is missing in action while fighting with British forces in France.'

'You knew that would come, Mum,' Cindy said. 'He's not declared dead so could be a prisoner, you know.'

'I know, Dear,' Dorothy replied but her face showed no optimism.

Cindy ripped open her letter and read the contents. 'I've been accepted into the Women's Land Army, Mum.' she said in a matter-of-fact tone.

Dorothy nodded. 'That's everyone now, My Dear. Bertie, Timmy, your father had to go and volunteer and now you. It's not fair!'

Cindy realised her mother was quite distressed and placed an arm around the older woman's shoulder. 'I'll be okay, Mum,' she said. 'I'll be safer than you. As a Land Girl to help on a farm somewhere, I won't be fighting.'

'Oh Cindy,' Dorothy replied. Her eyes were moist. 'Your dad and I went through it all last time. I was your age when I came to England as a nurse and now my family has to repeat it all again. I wish I'd returned to Canada instead of staying here, then you'd all be really safe.'

'But Bertie and Timmy would still be in the war, Mum. Canadians are fighting with us. Bertie said there are Canadians everywhere in the air force.'

'I know,' Dorothy replied and attempted a smile. 'Land girl! Where are you going?'

'It doesn't say, Mum,' Dorothy replied and handed her mother the letter. 'I just have to report to the town hall next Tuesday at ten in the morning for orders.'

'They close the university and send you away to pull weeds,' snapped Dorothy. 'It would be a greater help to the country if they let you continue your studies.'

'I know, Mum but we can't do anything about it,' Cindy replied. 'If the Germans invade it will be worse for everyone, not just women.'

Dorothy nodded and helped Cindy inside with the cases. With the dark curtains and cardboard taped criss-cross over the windows to conform to blackout requirements, the house seemed eerie and empty, so different from the bright secure environment Cindy had grown to love throughout her life.

'It's awful, isn't it?' Dorothy whispered. 'It's so lonely now. I miss your father and the boys.' She glanced at her daughter. 'You too, My Dear, but you're here for a week. That's a blessing.' She glanced at her daughter. 'One good thing, I guess. With the Evening *Herald* only being published on alternate days, I have more free time. Come on, I'll get you a bite to eat. I've saved the rations and will have a roast meal tomorrow, just for you.'

'Thanks Mum,' Cindy replied but couldn't help feeling melancholy as she picked up the paper and glanced at the local news. Sometimes she wished she'd never grown up.

*

It was when Cindy climbed off the tiny three-carriage train in the town of Carlisle in north-western England only a few miles south of the Scottish border that the first pangs of homesickness arrived. She'd been living away from home for a year now but varsity life in London wasn't far from Kettingham and, anyhow, she had travelled home every second weekend.

Here, she was almost three hundred miles from home and dressed in the strange uniform they were expected to wear. The tight white collar and tie choked her neck but the dark green jersey was warm and the brown riding pants functional. She pulled her Boy Scout type hat down and glanced around. The station was the typical stone building with a platform and wooden trolleys to carry luggage on. Cindy grabbed a trolley and placed her suitcases on it. As usual, the crowd on the platform disappeared straight after the train departed, leaving Cindy alone with her trolley. Well, she was not quite alone. Grace was with her but her friend's face looked as uncertain as she felt.

'God, I'm glad you're here, Grace,' Cindy confessed in a quiet voice as she pushed the trolley to the end of the building and down a small ramp to where a battered taxi and a bus were parked.

Grace gave a slight grin. 'Yes, getting us both sent to the same farm was quite an accomplishment by your Mum. I'm sure that woman organising the rosters didn't like having to change her list around. You'd think it was chiselled out in stone.'

'I know,' Cindy retorted. 'All it required was swapping a couple of names around on a piece of paper. Nobody really knows anything about us. We're just names. That's why Mum got so annoyed.'

'Yeah, but it was only when she asked the woman the name of her superior the old girl decided to back down.'

'All aboard for Langholm, Hawick and points north,' interrupted a loud male voice. 'Excuse me young ladies, is that your destination?'

Cindy turned to face the man standing beside an ancient Bedford bus. 'Yes Sir, we're heading for Langholm,' she said. 'I'm sorry, I wasn't listening.'

'Aye, that's all right, Miss,' the driver said. 'Want your luggage put in the back?'

'Please,' Grace replied.

The two girls climbed aboard the half filled bus, found a seat and sat down. Except for an indignant look by a woman who looked at least ninety, everyone around completely ignored them. Cindy caught the woman's eye and smiled but the woman just stared coldly at her.

'Old Duck,' Grace whispered and added, 'No, we aren't Germans,' in a loud voice while looking directly at the woman. 'Are you?'

'I am not!' the woman managed to say through thin lips and glanced away.

'Grace, stop it!' Cindy hissed and poked her friend in the ribs. Grace was a bit of a character and could be outspoken at times. 'We have to live with these people.'

'But we've come to help them out,' Grace added and made sure the woman heard. 'They should be glad we're here, not treat us like dirt.'

Cindy sighed and wished she was home. This first encounter with a local did not improve that empty feeling in the pit of her stomach.

*

At the small village of Langholm, Cindy and Grace climbed off the bus and watched as it drove away. The streets around look deserted and the two girls had no idea where they were to go next. The instructions only said they'd be met by a Mr. Moffet who would take them on to his farm.

After twenty minutes an old truck rumbled to a stop beside them and a grizzled old man dressed in old-fashioned clothes, Wellington boots and flat cap, stuck his head out the window.

'Put your bags on the back,' he said between sniffs. 'You'll probably both fit into the front. If not, one of ya will need to sit at the back.'

Cindy glanced at Grace who just stared back, uncertain what to do.

'Are you Mr. Moffet?' she asked the man.

'Yeah,' sniffed the man. 'Hurry up. I haven't got all day.'

The girls nodded miserably and placed their suitcases amongst the bails of straw on the tray and slipped into the skinny cab. Cindy was in the middle and wiggled around to try to avoid being hit on the knees as the man double-declutched and changed gears. He peered out the window and said no more. There was no welcome, introductions; nothing, just them heading, they-knew-not-where to help their country in its time of need and a grizzled old farmer who didn't appear to want them, anyhow.

After only receiving snorts in response to her attempts to talk, Cindy lapsed into silence and gazed ahead. They moved from a valley of trees, grass fields and crops dotted with stone farmhouses through hedgerows that gave way to stone walls as the narrow road wound onwards. For another forty minutes the truck rattled on before they turned off into another even narrower road, this one little more than a lane.

Finally they turned into a cobblestone courtyard behind a grey stone house. The truck stopped and the man glanced at the two girls.

'Skinny aren't ya,' he commented. 'Sure you can handle the work?'

'We'll try,' Grace replied.

'Aye, well come inside. Edith would have stuck the kettle on for ya.'

Mrs. Moffet was a short plump woman with a leathery face and grey hair. Her eyes studied the girls but she had a tiny smile on her face and talked more than her husband.

'I'll show you girls your room, you can get out of your uniform and Mr. Moffet will explain your chores,' she said after they had finished their cup of tea.

She led them outside to a massive stone barn and down a narrow path to a small lean-to attached to the side wall. A door was pushed open to reveal a tiny room holding two beds and one small chest of drawers with a kerosene lamp sitting on top.

'We've only got electricity in the house,' she said. 'You've got the lamp.'

Grace gave Cindy a poke in the back and grimaced. The tiny window had a sack curtain that could be pulled across on a wire.

'You're the first girls to come here,' Mrs. Moffet said as if this was a reason for the austerity.

'Where's the bathroom?' Cindy asked.

'The long drop toilet is down the path. Careful, the door gets stuck if you shut it completely,' said the woman. 'There's a cold water sink just inside the side door of the barn. You can have a bath in the house once a week.' She glanced at Cindy. 'That's all the lads needed.'

Cindy nodded and shuddered. This was worse than she expected, far worse. It was awful!

'Don't worry,' Grace said when they were alone. 'At least we've got each other for company. Imagine if you were by yourself.'

Cindy bit on her lip. 'I need to go to the toilet,' she gasped. 'Can you stand guard outside while I go?'

Grace nodded and Cindy tore down to the little outhouse that held the long drop toilet, really was just a hole in the ground with a wooden toilet seat perched above it. Once inside, Cindy only just managed to hold the door shut behind her before her churning stomach reacted. Tears of frustration and loneliness rolled down her cheeks as she heaved and vomited into the hole.

No sooner had she come out when a white-faced Grace brushed past and was also ill. Cindy could hear the retching behind her.

Afterwards, the two girls gazed sheepishly at each other and Grace screwed her nose up. 'Great pair, aren't we?' she said.

Cindy nodded. 'It's awful,' she gasped. She did not know how she could survive in this dreary place.

*

The farm work was hard and time demanding but once a routine was established, not too difficult for the two Land Girls. They were up with the summer sun in the morning and were expected to have the ten cows milked by hand and the half dozen calves, hens and dogs feed before a seven o'clock breakfast.

The rest of the day was spent in the garden, weeding, picking tomatoes, fruit and vegetables. But their aching backs, chapped hands and sunburnt arms soon became hardened. By the end of July, life would have been almost pleasant if it wasn't for the farmer. The man merely grunted when they succeeded at doing something and made sarcastic innuendoes about their gender when they didn't.

Edith Moffet was better and the girls noticed her husband treated her much the same as themselves. There seemed to be no friends around and the only time the Moffets left the farm was for weekly market day and the Presbyterian Church service on Sunday morning. There was a mutter about being heathens when the girls denied an invitation to accompany them on the first Sunday but afterwards the matter wasn't discussed.

On the credit side, the two farm dogs, Blackie and Patches, were great companions and accompanied the girls for most of the day. Marmalade, a massive ginger cat, also took the girls under her wing and accompanied them at milking times for her saucer of warm milk. .

Two horses, however, caused the first major confrontation. One morning over breakfast Moffet gazed across the table at Cindy and Grace. 'That bottom field has to be ploughed and sown before winter. I want you two to do it,' he muttered

'How?' asked Cindy who was quite used to the man's blunt talking.

'Well, we're out of petrol and the government won't increase our ration even though we are an essential industry. You'll use the horses.'

Cindy screwed her nose up but said nothing. The gigantic draught horses, Bev and Gertie were used for numerous jobs around the farm, from pulling a grass cutter to hauling the containers of milk down the road to a small dairy factory. Until now, the girls had had little to do with the giant beasts as David Moffet was either using them himself or they were left in the far horse field to graze.

After breakfast the farmer showed the girls how to attach the plough, harness, reins and other equipment and led Bev and Gertie down to the meadow. He set the double plough, shouted at the horses and they trudged forward while the plough turned the soil over in a perfect double straight line.

At the end of the row he handed the reins to Cindy and said. 'Well, off you go.'

Cindy shook the reins and roared, 'Go Girls,' and the horses trudged off.

'Good. Expect to take a couple of days and keep the furrows straight ' retorted Moffet and wandered off.

As soon as the farmer disappeared the horses stopped. No matter what Cindy or Grace did they could not get the animals to move. The mares just whinnied and tossed their heads but refused to take a step. Yells or threats were useless and even offering them grass to eat didn't help.

For almost an hour the two girls tried until they were exhausted and frustrated. Finally it was Grace who stood with her hands on her hips and swore at the beasts.

'Bugger you both!' she stormed. 'Come on Cindy. I've had it. They won't work for us. I'm leaving.'

'Where?' Cindy muttered.

'Anywhere,' retorted Grace. 'I'm sick of it. We've worked our guts out and do we ever get any praise?' She rolled her eyes and answered her own question. 'No way! A grunt if we do well and a mouth of abuse if we don't and what does the old bugger do himself. Bloody nothing!'

'Let's try again,' encouraged Cindy.

'You can,' Grace snapped back and walked away. Cindy stared after her and shrugged. She was annoyed herself but Grace didn't help matters. She turned to the horses and almost pleaded. 'Come on Girls,' she said. 'Try it for me, will you?'

The horses retorted and frothed at the mouth and, perhaps because they were also tired of standing in one place, started moving. Cindy grabbed the reins and tried to operate the plough at the same time. She was moderately successful. She finished one line and even managed to turn the horses when Moffet came running across the field.

'Is this all you've done, Girl,' he snapped angrily, 'Look at the horses. They're covered in sweat. Jesus Girl, don't you know a bloody thing about farm animals? You're worse than bloody useless, I tell ya.'

Cindy stopped, flung the reins down and stared defiantly at the man. 'At least I know how to treat humans, Mr. Moffet.' she said quietly and walked away.

'You came back here, Girl,' growled the farmer. 'You've got these horses to wash down.'

'Do it yourself,' Cindy yelled back. 'I'm not your bloody slave.'

By now her hands were shaking and huge sobs shuddered through her body. Her walk broke into a run. She almost jumped a stone wall, raced into the barn and climbed the ladder up to the loft. Here she crawled into a far corner and lay down sobbing in complete misery.

For an hour she remained hidden there until she was found by Marmalade the cat who curled up beside her and began to wash itself. Somehow, the cat did for Cindy, what the humans on the farm didn't. The farm cat stayed with her. An hour later Grace persuaded Cindy to come down and go to the farmhouse for their evening meal.

Cindy carried Marmalade down the ladder and stoked the cat before putting it down. She glared at the farmer and his wife but refused to be drawn in any conversation. After the meal she excused herself and retreated to her bedroom.

*

'I hope you're proud of yourself,' Grace snapped at Moffet. 'Cindy and I spent half the day trying to work those horses. It's not our fault they're as stubborn as you are, Mr. Moffet. Our men are fighting for the very future of our country and it is not our bloody fault we're girls.'

She sniffed back tears and tore out behind Cindy.

Edith stared at the swinging kitchen door then back to her husband. 'I agree with them both, David,' she said. 'You should hear how useless some of the other Land Girls around the district are. These two really try, David and, between you and me, they're twice as good as the lads you employed before them. Just give them a little credit at times, will you?'

The old farmer's face looked angry until he noticed at his wife's concerned eyes. 'I guess I was a little hard, Edith,' he replied quietly and picked up a newspaper to read.

*

That night Cindy wrote home and set down everything that had happened on the farm, her frustrations and loneliness. No matter how hard she worked she received no praise or even a few words of kindness. She concluded by saying how she missed home and how much she loved her parents and family. The rural mail contractor would pick the letter up in the morning and her Mum would have it within a few days. That t made her feel a little better.

*

CHAPTER EIGHTEEN

'Poor Cindy,' Dorothy said to Kevin who was home on two days leave when the letter arrived. 'Why can't people be reasonable?'

'English stiff upper lip My Dear,' Kevin replied. 'Moffet sounds the type who wouldn't say thank you for a thousand quid if it was placed under his nose.'

'I've a good mind to drive up there and give the old sod a piece of my mind,' Dorothy retorted. 'If it wasn't so far, I would.'

Kevin grinned and tucked his arms around her. 'Perhaps that would be a good idea,' he whispered and kissed his wife on the neck. 'Don't you think Cindy would appreciate having the MG up there? It sounds so isolated she could get into town and...'

Dorothy stared at him. 'You're scheming, Kevin. What is it?'

'Well, we've got spare petrol in our underground tank, Cindy needs petrol for the tractor so she and Grace can plough the field...'

'But it's three hundred miles away,' interjected Dorothy. 'You'd burn more petrol getting there than you could provide them.'

Kevin shook his head. 'Not if I borrow a tanker trailer from stores back at base. They've got those little two wheeled ones they tow behind jeeps. Luckily, I fitted a tow bar to the MG years ago'

'But will they let you have one?' Dorothy asked.

'I am a captain now,' Kevin said. 'Motor vehicles and petrol are impossible to procure but these tanker trailers are just lined up in rows. They were originally going to be taken to France, but now...' He shrugged. 'I'll telephone stores and order one and we can pick it up tomorrow. On Monday you can head across to see Cindy, leave the MG and the trailer with her and take a train back. You'll probably only need one night away.'

Dorothy, though, was doubtful.

'Come on!' urged Kevin. 'Your mother flew right across the Atlantic when you needed help.'

Dorothy smiled. 'If you put it that way...'

*

Late on Monday afternoon the little green MG, minus the tanker trailer that had been left at a country inn five miles away where Dorothy had booked accommodation for the night, drove into the deserted courtyard behind Moffet's farmhouse. Dorothy climbed out, stretched her aching limbs and strolled around to the back veranda just as two dogs began to bark.

'Hush up, there!' a voice roared and Dorothy almost crashed into a grizzled looking old farmer coming around the corner of the building.

'We ain't got no petrol, Mrs.,' he said and glared at the visitor. 'If you want directions, you need to go back the way you came three miles to the last intersection and....'

'My you are an abrupt man, aren't you?' Dorothy retorted. 'I know exactly where I am Mr. Moffet and wish to speak to my daughter.'

Moffet stared at Dorothy then the MG before stoking his moustache. 'And you be?' he grumbled.

'Mrs. Dorothy Smithers, Cindy's mother. I'm delivering her car.'

'Her car?'

'Yes her father, Captain Kevin Smithers was fixing it for her, otherwise she would have brought it when she first came." Dorothy hadn't even told Cindy of Kevin's promotion.

The word 'Captain' seemed to stir something in Moffet's bones for he almost smiled. 'It's a MG, you say?'

Dorothy nodded.

'You'd better come in, Mrs. Smithers. Cindy and Grace are having tea.'

He stood back, allowed Dorothy past and even opened the kitchen door for her. 'Edith, a visitor's arrived,' he called. 'Have you any spare food in the pot?'

Cindy, who was sitting at a tiny wooden table eating with her back to the door, turned. She gasped and stared at her mother standing there.

'Mum!' she cried out. 'Mum. What are you doing here?'

She stood and rushed over to embrace her mother with so much excitement that her bulky riding trousers brushed the tablecloth and almost knocked everything to the floor. Even Moffet's scowl was ignored.

'Mrs. Smithers,' Grace screamed and jumped up to also hug Dorothy. 'Blimey, what a thrill.'

David and Edith Moffet stood back and watched the two girls embrace their visitor. After the welcome, Cindy introduced the Moffets to her mother.

'Goodness, you must be worn out,' Edith said. 'Sit down. There's plenty of food.' She smiled. 'Rationing doesn't affect us so much here in The Dales.'

'Why thank you,' Dorothy replied. She gave Cindy a grin that indicated she wasn't fooled by the Moffet's apparent friendliness one little bit. She refused an offer of a bed for the night. 'But I'll come back tomorrow to see the girls before I head home,' she added and again both Cindy and Grace's faces showed their relief. It was obvious they wanted to talk to her alone.

After the meal and small talk, David said he'd find place in the back stable where the car could be parked and Dorothy walked out with the two girls.

'Dad wanted me to deliver something to you but I thought it would be discrete to leave it out of sight' she said and told about the tanker load of petrol. 'I'll bring it up in the morning. There's a hose and hand pump on it,' she explained. 'Just run the hose into the tractor's tank and move the handle back and forth.'

'That will work out well,' Grace said. 'Tomorrow's market day and both the Moffets leave the farm about eight in the morning and don't return until mid afternoon.'

'We could get the tractor filled and ploughing started before they return,' Cindy continued. She grinned at her mother for a moment but her eyes clouded over and tears appeared. 'Oh Mum,' she said 'I'm wish I was home. It's not that the Moffets are really bad, they're just so cold and impersonal and we're just slaves to order around.'

Grace backed Cindy up and wasn't far from tears herself. 'That's true, Mrs. Smithers, Come and have a look at our bedroom, ' she said, ' It hasn't even got electricity.'

'Oh I will,' Dorothy replied with an expression that would have done her own mother justice, 'Unless things improve, I'll go and see the authorities. That's a promise.'

'Mum,' Cindy sniffed and wiped her tears with a handkerchief. 'Thank you for coming all this way.'

'I've news, too, My Dear,' Dorothy smiled. 'Your Dad's now Captain Kevin Smithers and I'm so proud of him.'

'He isn't!' gasped Cindy. Her eyes lit up. 'When?'

'He came home on leave on Friday with his new pips. He'd kept it a secret until then.'

'That sounds like Dad,' Cindy said.

She shut the MG's door and Dorothy followed her to the little outbuilding where the bedroom was while Grace grinned and followed on behind.

*

The next morning Dorothy waited until she saw the Moffets drive out in their truck then drove into the yard where Cindy and Grace were waiting. After much backing and directing, the tanker trailer was lined up by the tractor and petrol hand-pumped across.

'Right,' Cindy said and climbed on the old orange machine. She turned on the ignition and pulled the starter.

It whirled slowly but failed to start the engine. 'Damn!' Cindy swore.

'The battery's flat,' Dorothy said. 'We'll need to crank it.'

She walked around to the front where the crank handle was permanently attached. 'Pull the choke out, Cindy, and have the hand throttle about half open. When it fires, keep your foot on the accelerator and push in the choke.'

'Right, Mum.' Cindy grinned at Grace.

Dorothy turned the crank handle to the bottom, made sure it was connected and gave a pull. The engine clanged as the pistons moved but nothing else happened. She did it a second time then a third but still the engine did not catch. Her arms ached but she tried a fourth time. Grace tried a couple of times as well but to no avail.

'I'll clean the plugs,' Dorothy panted and wiped sweat off her brow.

She found a spark plug spanner in the toolbox and, after more grunting and straining, managed to undo all the plugs, clean them with a rag and tiny piece of sandpaper and replace them.

'I know nothing about setting the correct gap so hope they work,' she said. 'They were pretty dirty so I might have done the trick. Let's try it again, shall we?'

Grace, who had replaced Cindy in the driver's seat, set the controls and stared at Dorothy with her tongue held between her teeth in anticipation.

Dorothy placed both hands on the crank and yanked up; the engine clanked then there was a sudden chug and a cloud of black smoke puffed out the chimney. For several seconds it chugged before dying out.

'Here let me,' Cindy said and took the crank.

She wiped her sweaty hands on the longs she was wearing, gripped the handle and heaved.

The engine chugged, almost puttered out but caught again with a mighty roar as all four cylinders fired. Clouds of smoke puffed into the air and the engine screamed as Grace held the accelerator almost to the floor.

'Slacken off, Grace!' screamed Dorothy. 'Push the choke half in.'

Grace nodded and cheered as the motor slowed down to a steady rumble. 'What now?' she yelled.

'Put it in reverse and back up to the plough so we can hitch it on.'

'Me!' gasped Grace.

'Why not?' Dorothy replied.

There was a scream of gears until the girl remembered to depress the clutch. With the clutch held half in and engine screaming, the tractor moved back. It took another five minutes before the plough was joined on and the three set off out the barn and down the lane to the field where Grace stopped and jumped down. She was covered in perspiration but looked quite proud of herself.

'Mr. Moffet showed us how to lower the blades,' Cindy said and shifted the lever so the two 'V' shaped ploughs were at the height she had been shown.

*

The ploughs were old fashion ones, originally designed to be pulled by the horses and had a handle and controls at the back. They, therefore, needed to be operated by two people, a driver and the plough operator walking along behind.

'Your turn,' Grace said. 'I'll do the plough.'

Cindy climbed on the tractor, selected low gear in the 'H' shaped shift box and, when everyone was ready, let out the clutch. The engine immediately stalled. She'd forgotten to depress the accelerator.

'Damn!' she swore and had visions of having to crank the ancient tractor again. However, when she pulled the starter button, the engine fired straight away and roared into life. This time she had it correct and the tractor moved forward at a walking pace.

At the back, Dorothy and Grace both held the wooden handle and held the plough down. The two blades bit into the soil and curled the grass out and over.

'It's working!' screamed Grace and waved Cindy onwards.

The tractor moved in a reasonably straight line up the field next to the section Cindy had done earlier with the horses. The trouble came at the end of the field.

Cindy stopped, waited while the other two women raised the blades before shouting back. 'Where now, Mum?'

'Across to the middle of the field,' Dorothy shouted. 'Then head back.'

Cindy nodded and soon the tractor was in the centre of the field ready for the trip back. Solid grass stretched in front and there was no previous ploughed section to line up with. Cindy stared ahead, gritted her teeth and, after hearing Grace shout, set the tractor going. Again, it worked well with two rows of ploughed grass curling over so the soil was exposed.

At the end again, Cindy and Grace swapped places and continued. By lunchtime the field was three quarters done and Dorothy called a halt.

'Mum, look at yourself,' Cindy said.

Dorothy's street clothes were covered in dirt and soaked with perspiration under the armpits and down her back.

'You aren't too graceful yourself, my daughter,' she replied and grinned across at Grace. 'Neither of you are.'

'Yeah but look at the field, Mrs. Smithers,' Grace said. 'Not bad for a trio of city women, I'd say.'

'Bit crooked but not bad,' Dorothy muttered in a perfect imitation of David Moffet.

After lunch Dorothy said she'd get the girls started but would then have to leave. 'There's a taxi coming at one. Dad said the tanker can stay here and he'll pick it up when he's next on leave,' she said. 'Keep it locked so old David doesn't take your petrol. '

'We will,' Cindy promised.

When the taxi arrived Cindy and Grace both hugged Dorothy and watched the old square shaped Morris drive away.

'That's some Mum you have,' Grace said.

'Yes, just the very best,' Cindy replied. She had a lump in her throat but was determined not to cry again. 'Come on. Let's plough,' she said.

*

When the Moffets drove in at four that afternoon the two Land Girls had the field almost finished.

'Look at that, David,' Edith gasped. 'How did they get the tractor going?'

'Her mother helped,' Moffet replied. 'Look!'

Edith glanced in the bar and saw the petrol trailer. The farmer climbed out of his truck, strolled over to inspect it then continued out to the field and watched as Cindy and Grace ploughed another row.

Grace who was at the back saw him and waved. The girls completed another round and came to a stop by the farmer. He stood examining the field before glancing at the two girls.

'Not bad,' he grunted. 'Get it finished and Edith will get you some afternoon tea. Tomorrow I'll show you how to disc it.'

After he walked away Cindy grinned at her friend. 'Was that a compliment?' she said.

'Well, as close as old David can give one,' Grace replied. They were both filthy, exhausted and their hands were covered in blisters but for the first time since their arrival they felt proud of their achievements.

'Come on,' Cindy said. 'There's only about three rounds to go. Your turn to drive.'

*

As the farmer watched from the gate, the tractor started another journey up the field. He turned to his wife and grunted. 'Those girls mightn't be as strong as the lads we employed but they have spunk, I'll give them that much.'

'But where did Cindy's mother get the petrol from?' Edith asked with a worried look.

'Probably the army,' David Moffet's face cracked into a smile. 'But I'm not going to ask and don't you say a word to the neighbours, Edith.'

'No David,' she replied. 'That's a nice little sports car, Cindy's got too.'

'Yeah,' retorted the farmer. 'There's money in that family. I didn't think they were working class,'

He glanced out over the field and rolled himself a cigarette as the tractor made one last lap of the field. With the horses it would have taken at least two days to do that job. Perhaps he'd get the crop in on time after all.

*

Once the girls had won the respect from the Moffets, life became, though still lacking in personal warmth, more tolerable and the busy farm life left the world at war so far away it could have been on a different planet. Sure, restrictions and the crackling broadcasts over the oaken radio in the living room reminded Cindy it was there but it appeared the Germans were now fighting Russians in the east and attempts to invade Great Britain had been abandoned.

Every couple of weeks, Grace and she would take the MG to Carlisle or perhaps go to towns in the opposite direction and visit clothing stores or have a meal out together. In some ways though, they were glad to get back away from the uniforms, air raid shelters and reminders of the war.

Cindy's Dad turned up with a jeep one weekend to take the empty tanker trailer away. After he'd gone, two full jerrycans cans of petrol were left tucked in the back seat of the MG along with a tiny note. *"For you, Sweetheart. Don't give any to your boss. Love, Dad."*

Autumn moved to winter and with it, the cold weather. The cows and other animals were shifted into the huge stone barn. The cow bryers, as Moffet called them, were wooden compartments with partitions between each animal. The work now was difficult as the animals had to be feed in their bryers, excrement removed, straw changed and floors hosed down daily. There was no such thing as hot water and often the water supply was frozen so the hoses had to be thawed out before the cleaning could begin.

Ventilation in the building was almost non-existent so a permanent stink of animals premeditated the place. Both girls had painful chilblains on their hands. Darkness came early in these northern counties but with it, one improvement. Edith insisted that the girls be allowed to move into the spare downstairs bedroom in the house. This backed onto the living room, the heat from the fireplace took the chill off it and they had access to the bathroom with hot water. Moreover, there was electricity so, no more did they have to endure the stuffy stink of burning kerosene.

Slowly, too, the one weekly bath became two, then three until finally, Old David conceded they had plenty of water and with the wetback behind the fireplace feeding in hot water the girls could bathe whenever they wished. Every night, Cindy would strip out of her freezing damp farm clothes and wallow in the giant tin tub full of steaming water with a book in her hand to read. She had joined the library in Langholm and always had two or three books to read. Her main concern was to get to the bath before Grace and they often had playful fights over their turns. The Moffets never seemed to want the bathroom at night and the girls had this luxury to themselves.

After supper, even with the wind and snow howling outside, the four people would sit in front of the fire playing cards, reading or, in Edna's case, knitting endless scarves for the army boys. Cindy and Grace became fit and began to put on weight and they teased each other about their muscular arms and bodies. November turned to December and the news of Pearl Harbour and America's entry into the war. However, Cindy and Grace were more interested in the personal news that the authorities allowed them two weeks back at home for Christmas.

The girls loaded the MG full with luggage and presents and left the unusually demonstrative Moffets waving at them as Cindy drove out the snow-covered driveway. Grace waved out the side flap and wiped the windshield with red knitted gloves, a present from Edith.

'You know,' she said. 'I actually believe Old David and Edith were sad we weren't staying over Christmas.'

Cindy nodded. 'They took a while to get to know but it's not too bad there now, is it?'

'No,' agreed Grace with a whimsical look. 'Fancy, Old David even gave us a Christmas present. "Here, something to you both for helping us out," he retorted and even managed to smile. I wonder where they got the chocolates they gave us from. I haven't seen a chocolate since before the war.'

'They probably had the box from then,' Cindy replied. 'I'm going to share my half with Mum and Dad. I bet they haven't had a chocolate for years either.'

Grace nodded and turned to face her friend. 'Can I ask you a favour, Cindy,' she asked in a quiet voice.

'Of course,' Cindy replied.

'Can I stay with you if things don't work out at home?'

Cindy took her eyes off the slippery road for a second and saw her friend's intense gaze. 'Why, Grace?'

Grace bit on her lip. 'I never told you but my Mum remarried after Dad was killed in France and I don't really like my step-father.' She shivered. 'He gives me the creeps! I don't know why Mum married him. Our house isn't like yours.'

'How do you mean?' Cindy asked.

'I guess it's love or lack of it,' Grace blurted out. 'I don't think anybody cares about me. If I dropped dead tomorrow, nobody would even notice.'

'That's rubbish,' Cindy retorted. 'I would for one and I reckon the Moffets would, too, especially Edith.' She changed gears on a tight corner. 'As for staying at our place, of course you can if you wish. We've got stacks of room and Mum even invited you over for Christmas in her last letter. Remember, I did tell you.'

Grace smiled. 'Thanks Cindy. Isn't it funny? I hated the farm but now we're going away, it almost seems like leaving home. Of course, when your Mum came it made all the difference.'

'Yes, it did and Dad, too with that extra petrol.'

They slowed down for the village of Hawick and headed southeast towards home. The roads were filled with military vehicles but, except for buses, hardly any civilian vehicles were around. They stopped once, pumped petrol from a jerrycan into the tank and arrived at Kettingham at sunset; home at last.

*

However, the feeling of elation was dashed when Dorothy met Cindy at the door. Her face looked pinched and for the first time Cindy noticed her mother seemed strangely old and lacked the dynamic personality she normally had.

'Mum, what's wrong!' she said.

Dorothy grabbed her hands. 'It's Bertie,' she sobbed. 'I just received a letter from his squadron leader. He was shot down, Cindy. Over Kent, it was. They were attacking German bombers returning from a raid and...' She stopped as if she couldn't continue.

'Is he hurt, Mum?'

Dorothy looked into Cindy's eyes. 'He's dead, Sweetheart. Your brother never survived the crash.'

'Oh Mum,' Cindy cried and held her mother close. 'Does Dad know?'

'Yes, I telephoned him,' Dorothy replied. 'He'll be home tomorrow on four days leave and it was going to be such a happy occasion. I had other news.'

'What was that, Mum?'

Dorothy wiped her eyes and took a letter out of her pocket. 'This just arrived two days ago,' she whispered.

'Tell me,' Cindy replied.

'It's a letter from Timmy. He's alive and in a prison of war camp somewhere in Germany. The Red Cross sent the letter on.'

'Oh, my God,' Cindy exclaimed and opened the one page letter.

Dear Mum, Dad, Cindy and Bertie, it stated. *We are allowed to write one letter home for Christmas. I am alive and in...* At this point a black censor's ink blotted out the name of the camp. *I was caught north of Dunkirk and brought to Germany. It was hard at first but I have been in my present camp for over a year now and it isn't too bad."*

Another part was blacked out and Cindy muttered. 'Bloody Nazis'

We now get Red Cross parcels including cigarettes and chocolate bars, which we use almost like money. The guards are army officers and...

'Bastards,' Cindy swore at one more censored out part. 'I'm sure Timmy's letter isn't going to lose the war for them.'

I guess Cindy isn't a little girl any more. I love and miss you all. Perhaps I'll be home by next Christmas. You're always in my mind. Your loving son and brother, Timmy.'

The letter was dated 18 November 1941.

Cindy folded the letter and handed it back to her mother. 'Oh, Mum,' she cried. 'If it wasn't for Bertie, this would be such wonderful news. This bloody war!'

'I know Sweetheart,' Dorothy replied then turned to Grace standing a few steps back. 'Grace, please forgive me ignoring you. I hope Cindy persuaded you to stay with us over Christmas.'

'I'd be encroaching, Mrs. Smithers,' Grace replied. 'I'd better go home.'

'No,' Cindy snapped. 'You are staying, Grace. Isn't she, Mum?'

'Only if she calls me Dorothy or Mum,' Cindy's mother said. 'Mrs. Smithers makes me feel so old.'

'Thank you, Mum,' Grace answered. She smiled with relief. 'I would like to stay.'

Dorothy smiled. 'Come inside,' she continued. 'You both must be exhausted after the journey.' She looked at the muddy MG. 'The car go well?'

'Like new, Mum,' Cindy replied. 'I love that car.'

She walked inside and gasped. The whole interior was festooned with Christmas decorations; streamers, paper bells, candy canes, coloured lights, a corner Christmas tree with presents beneath; everything.

'Your Grandma sent them from Canada,' Dorothy said in a quiet voice. 'Aren't they lovely? We were going to have such a wonderful Christmas.'

'And we still will, Mum, ' Cindy added. 'Bertie would have wanted it that way.'

'I believe he would,' Dorothy said. 'You know, Mom even sent a Christmas cake?'

Cindy nodded. Even with the sad news she was home and all the security from childhood seemed to gather around her in a warm bundle.

'Mum,' she said. 'Can I just hold you for a moment again, please?' She turned. 'You too, Grace.'

'Of course Sweetheart,' Dorothy replied and put her arms out to include Grace in a massive bear hug of love and warmth.

Cindy was determined Christmas of 1941 was not going to be ruined by the terrible war around the world.

*

CHAPTER NINETEEN

Life back on the farm in the New Year took some adjusting to but the two girls appreciated being away from the bombed cities even though Cindy had to work through those pangs of homesickness again. Winter moved into spring and, with it, a whole new cycle of work on the farm. Days became longer and, except on the top hills, the snow melted and the animals were allowed outside to graze for themselves.

April flowers came out and the lanes around were covered in yellow primroses, Moffet's sheep began to lamb, two sows had piglets and the first calves were born. Cindy and Grace accompanied David around the hills of the farm and soon became experts at mothering ewes or bringing the orphan lambs back to the barn to be bottle-fed.

The weather was still chilly with a constant wind that managed to get through the thickest of clothes but the girls were happy and even David Moffet grudgingly admitted his Land Girls were the best workers he had ever had.

Millsfeild, a huge air force maintenance base had recently been opened on the low country, fifteen miles or so in a direct line east of Moffet's farm. Huge bombers and transport aircraft now lumbered in over the farm to be maintained in one of the areas of England most remote from enemy bombing.

The base, too, meant men and it wasn't long before the Land Girls in the district were well sort after for companionship. Canadians and officers from the United States Army Air Force mixed with the R.A.F. men and dozens of pilots from occupied European countries. Also of interest to Cindy were the number of women pilots around her own age who ferried in aircraft from around the country to be maintained.

Cindy and Grace tried to attend the dance on the base at least every second week and it was not long, much to David Moffet's annoyance, before they both had young men constantly around. The newly installed telephone on the farm rang constantly with males wanting to chat to Cindy or Grace.

'Bloody phone was meant to be for the farm, not a dating service,' Moffet growled but as long as the girls did their work, and they did, he didn't really mind.

This was also the time when Cindy had a major disagreement with Grace. Her friend was, as Edna summed it up, boy crazy and wanted to spend all her spare time down at the village. Cindy, though enjoying the atmosphere and company of the young men, was content to be on the farm reading or walking around the lanes in the spring sunshine with only the dogs for company.

The boys they were attracted to were quite different too, with Grace preferring the extroverted males who drank a lot and, especially with the Americans, had plenty of money to spend. After one or two unpleasant experiences, Cindy avoided these officers and gradually found there were also quiet young men as well as the noisy ones.

'No, I am not going to this week's dance,' Cindy told Grace one Saturday morning in May. 'I am, quite frankly, tired of drunken officers pouring their hands over me with only one idea in their minds and that is how quickly they can get their hands on my bra.'

'You,' retorted Grace. 'You'd freeze anyone before they could touch you. I bet you don't even let men kiss you. What makes you so special, anyway? Too bloody scared to show your feelings, I'd say.'

Cindy stared at her friend and replied softly. 'That was uncalled-for, Grace. Have I ever tried to stop you having fun?'

Grace blushed and nodded. 'I'm sorry, Cindy, I was being mean. It's just that with the war on, why shouldn't we have a bit of fun? We work bloody hard, you know.'

'I know,' Cindy replied. 'Look, there's a bit of petrol left in the MG. What say we go to the village after lunch? You can go to the pub and I'll visit the library. I want to change my books anyway. Afterwards, we'll have tea together and go to the dance. Okay!'

'You don't mind?' Grace replied. 'An afternoon at the library sounds dead boring to me.'

Cindy grinned. 'Of course not but I want to be back here by midnight. Is that fair?'

Grace laughed. 'Yes, Cindy, I guess having your steadying influence is good for me. Sorry I was so mean before. I guess I'm just jealous.'

Cindy frowned. 'What of?' she asked.

Grace laughed. 'Look in the mirror, my friend. With your looks and figure no wonder you attract the men. I have to work on it and as soon as you walk in a room the men start eyeing you up and down.'

Cindy smiled and swished her auburn hair back off her eyes. She hadn't really thought about it. The trouble, as she saw it, was that Grace was too enthusiastic and was inclined to flirt. However, she didn't have the heart to point this out to her friend. After all, neither of them would teenagers much longer. She would turn twenty at the end of the year. God, that sounded old.

*

The village library was really only a room attached to the side of the town hall but it had quite a good selection of fiction, magazines and reference books. Also the librarian was a progressive lady who had arranged three tables with chairs around them near the tall windows. In the afternoon from about two, the sun shone in and the dark little room became cheery and bright. Cindy enjoyed sitting at one these sunny tables with her nose deep in an historical novel, her mind transported hundreds of years back to the deep south of America or a Spanish estate where the women wore beautiful clothes and the men were dashing heroes.

Cindy was engrossed in her novel when she heard a scrape of furniture and glanced up to see an airman standing by the window. He turned slightly and Cindy gave an involuntary shudder. The left side of his face was puckered up in a gigantic scar from the chin to his eye.

'I'm sorry to disturb you,' he stated in a quiet voice. 'I'm afraid my face does affect people in this way.'

Cindy flushed. 'No,' she replied. 'I am the one who should apologise. It was so rude of me to react in such an unfair manner.' She smiled, looked the man directly in the eyes and tried to ignore his scars. 'What part of Canada are you from?'

'Toronto, Ontario,' he replied, 'but how did you know I was Canadian? Most English think I'm American.'

'My grandmother is a Canadian and I guess I can tell the difference. Do you come to the library often?'

'Whenever I want to have a break,' the man replied with a touch of sadness in his voice. 'I've always enjoyed libraries. And you?'

'Only a couple of times a month,' Cindy said. 'That's all I can manage.' She indicated across the table with an opened hand. 'Would you like a chair?'

'No, I disturbed you. I must head back.' He hesitated and Cindy smiled.

'No,' she added in a blunt manner. 'I don't think so Flight Lieutenant...'

'Jervis. Arthur Jervis.'

Cindy stood and held out her hand. 'Pleased to meet you Arthur,' she said and felt his firm grip. 'Cindy Smithers. I'm a local Land Girl.'

'Helping England?' Arthur smiled. If it wasn't for the scar, he'd be quite handsome. 'And what were you before? A school teacher?'

'No,' said Cindy. 'I was an university student but, Arthur, please sit down,' she repeated. She watched as he manoeuvred himself in an awkward manner and almost fell into the chair. He grinned and swung his legs under the table.

'I'm at the local hospital recuperating,' he explained. 'We were sent up here away from the bombs.'

'I see,' Cindy replied but didn't want to appear nosy so switched back to something they had in common; the library.'

The pair chatted for almost twenty minutes about the library, books and Canada before Arthur looked Cindy in the eyes. 'Thanks,' he said in a whisper.

'What for?' Cindy replied.

Arthur shrugged. 'For just talking and not making condescending comments about my injuries. Most people either look away, make an excuse to depart or gush and asked questions about why I am disfigured. You treated me as if nothing was wrong, like it was before my injury.'

'I see,' Cindy replied. 'I guess I was more interested in you being Canadian. 'She hesitated to gather her thoughts. 'Do you know the radio station CJDT in Toronto?'

'Sure,' Arthur replied. 'It's one of the top stations. Why?'

Cindy grinned. Her ploy to get Arthur's onto another topic worked. 'My grandparents own it, that's all,' she said.

'You're kidding!' Arthur said.

Their conversation continued until it was time for Cindy to meet Grace. 'I'm meeting my girlfriend at the Wooden Spoon Restaurant. Would you like to come, too?' She flushed at her own forwardness.

'I'm more or less a free agent,' Arthur said. 'If I'm not back for supper at five I miss out. They start to scream about eleven when they want to put the lights out so I'm free until then.' He coughed again. 'I would like to come but are you sure?'

'Arthur,' Cindy retorted. 'If I didn't want your company, I would not have asked.'

The Flight Lieutenant looked her in the eyes again. 'You are quite a blunt young lady, aren't you, Cindy? It must be your Canadian half.'

'Could be.'

*

They walked out the library together and along the narrow road to The Wooden Spoon where Grace looked all hot in the face as if she'd just arrived.

She smiled when Cindy introduced her new friend and, much to Cindy's relief, completely ignored Arthur's injuries, too. After an appetising home cooked meal, Cindy got Grace by herself in the Ladies' Room.

'You don't mind if I don't come to the dance,' she said. 'I'll still pick you up afterwards.'

Grace grinned. 'Got smitten have ya?' she replied. 'Poor bugger. He would have been a handsome hulk, too.'

'He still is,' Cindy said and her expression almost defied Grace to say otherwise.

'Oh Cindy,' Grace said and clasped her shoulder. 'Now don't you be late.' She finished powdering her nose and excused herself soon afterwards so Cindy was alone with Arthur.

'I have until midnight,' Cindy said, 'but if you need to be back by eleven?'

Arthur grinned. 'I'm sure I can twist Matron's arm. There's a cowboy movie down at The Regal. We only have one theatre in town but if you'd like to go...'

'I love cowboy movies,' Cindy said. It wasn't really true but that didn't matter. As they walked out of the restaurant her arm slipped into his and he smiled down at her. Cindy was quite tall herself but, at well over six feet, Arthur towered above her.

*

Love when it came to Cindy was intense. She could think of nobody except Arthur and met him every Saturday to do the things lovers do. They walked, talked and drove the MG to remote spots where kisses turned into heavy petting and Cindy knew she wanted Arthur; her body cried out for him but he seemed reluctant to respond. It was as if he was afraid. One afternoon while parked in a tiny viewpoint in the fell above Moffet's farm Cindy unhitched herself from Arthur's arm and stared at him.

'Don't you love me, Arthur?' she asked quite frankly.

He frowned and looked quite taken back. 'Cindy,' he said. 'I love you more than anything in this world.' He bit on his lip. 'You should know that.'

'Do you want to look at me?' Her eyes held back tears. 'I mean my body.'

Arthur froze. 'That's the trouble,' he whispered.

'What is?' she snapped.

'I'm afraid you might not want to see me,' he shuddered.

'Try me,' Cindy said.

Arthur nodded and almost gritted his teeth, then without another sound he undid his shirt and lifted it off. The whole left side of his body was a mass of scar tissue. It's a burn,' he said. 'They've put skin grafts on my face but haven't fixed this up yet.'

Cindy gazed at the horrible ruined flesh but did not flinch or look away. Instead, she took Arthur's hands and reached forward to kiss him.

'Can I ask you one question Arthur and get a truthful answer?'

The airman looked into her eyes and nodded. 'Yes,' he whispered.

'Your male organs. Are they burnt, too and is that why you're too scared to love me?'

Arthur suddenly smiled. 'No Cindy I'm fine down there. So much so, I have trouble stopping my urges when you are around. Do you want to know what happened?'

Cindy leaned across the seat of the MG and placed her head on his shoulder. 'Only if you want to tell me,' she replied.

'My Spitfire was shot up and heavily damaged,' Arthur said and stared out the windshield at the rolling hills below. 'I almost landed back at base it when an outside wheel must have hit a rut, the plane veered off to the left and the next thing I knew was that I was engulfed in flames..'

'So after almost two months you still think I just pity you? ' snapped Cindy.

'You are a beautiful woman, Cindy who could have any man you choose. I see the other men stare at you when we walk in a room.' He glanced away. 'So why do you stay with me?'

Cindy glared at Arthur's face. 'Look at me, Arthur,' she said and grabbed his face with both hands. She bent forward and kissed him on the lips. 'The answer is because I love you, you stupid man so stop feeling sorry for yourself.'

She swung around, pulled the starter button, and the MG roared into life. In a determined movement, Cindy reversed out of the parking area, changed into low and accelerated down the hill. 'We are going to the farm,' she said. 'There is something we are going to do this afternoon.' She glanced at him. 'You will not chicken out either.'

*

Ten minutes later they roared into the deserted farmyard. It was market day, Grace had gone into town with the Moffets so Cindy and Arthur were by themselves.

'Come on,' Cindy said and led Arthur along a lane that dissected the farm to the back field where the plateau sloped away into a vale with a rumbling brook at the bottom.

She took Arthur's hand and led him down the zigzag track to the brook that bubbled through the tiny pebbles and stones. A grove of trees above cut them from the world and even the sun was covered by the shady undergrowth.

At the bottom beneath a giant oak tree Cindy turned and placed Arthur's arms around her waist. She could smell his after shave and for suddenly felt all tingly inside in anticipation at what she intended to do.

'I come here often, 'she sighed. 'It's so peaceful even during the colder time of the year. It's my own special little place and I wanted to share it with you.'

She pulled Arthur's arms tighter around her, and felt his prickly chin rub her cheek. In a definite move, she next reached and placed his hands on her breasts.

He pulled her in close and their lips touched, but not the little good night peck given by a shy boy on a first date, this was a full kiss with open lips and Cindy responded. Her lips parted and without realising, tongues touched and the kiss became frantic.

The two lovers clung together until finally Arthur held Cindy back and she saw his eyes full of love and desire. Slowly he reached up and started to undo the tiny red buttons of her cardigan and slide the garment off. Because of the hot weather Cindy had no petticoat, only a bra beneath her white cotton blouse.

Arthur's hands groped at her blouse, the two topmost buttons were undone and he frantically lifted it over her head and tossed it into the grass. His eyes were huge as he stared at the bulge of her breasts barely covered by the brassiere.

Cindy flushed. No man had seen her in only an undergarment before. A little voice told her to stop but after encouraging Arthur to this point she could not back out now.

'Turn around,' Arthur almost choked and his sweaty hands undid the three little clasps of her bras and Cindy pulled the garment away. Her breasts felt strange, so tight and nipples tingly like her lips felt a few moments before.

Arthur turned her around again and stared at her full frontal figure, nude now from the waist up. Their eyes met and he reached forward and cupped her breasts with both hands. Cindy groaned and began to kiss him then, not knowing why; she shoved his head down into her breast. That scared face and body meant nothing, only the gentle kind and loving man over her was important. Her man! Her lover! Her life was complete.

*

CHAPTER TWENTY

It was also a fine summer's afternoon in Kettingham. At the *Evening Herald* Dorothy was having a final check of the day's paper before the late edition press run. Often after the early edition that went to rural areas and outlying villages they would stop the press and remake the front page if there was any important news. After a lull in the bombing since August of 1941, the latest news reported on a series of raids against London that morning with details added to the late edition as it came to hand. She heard a cough and glanced up to see Kevin standing there in full military uniform.

'Kevin!' she exclaimed and rushed into his arms. 'What are you doing here?' They had not seen each other for over a month.

They kissed and he held her out at arm's length and studied her. 'You look as beautiful as ever, My Dear.' He smiled but there was a serious look in the eyes.

'What's wrong, Kevin?' Dorothy asked.

Kevin shrugged. 'I have twenty-four hours leave. 'I've been posted to Egypt and possibly other Mediterranean areas. We leave in three days.'

'I see,' Dorothy replied.

This was always expected but like many war events, the thought had been put in the back of their minds. As a communications officer, much of the work was based permanently in England. Throughout the Battle of Britain, Kevin had operated in top-secret radar installations that, though out of the public eye, did as much to prevent a German invasion as the front line fighter squadrons. The long-range facilities could find German bomber formations gathering over northern France. Warnings were passed onto Fighter Command, aircraft scrambled and able to gain altitude before the enemy arrived over the coast.

Now, with no invasion anticipated, the war was in the Mediterranean. German and Italian armies had captured the Balkans but rumours were that if the enemy were beaten in North Africa, landings could be attempted in Europe, itself.

Dorothy sighed. 'Well, My Darling we're together tonight. Give me ten minutes and I'll be with you.'

*

Just as Dorothy gave Kevin a hug the air Sirens wailed.

'Blast!' Dorothy swore and looked around. 'Everyone down to the shelters,' she called but already staff were shutting down the press and heading downstairs where an air raid shelter had been constructed beneath the building.

The rumble of German bombers could be heard, loud and close. This was unusual. Though on one of the main flight paths to London, Kettingham had been largely spared from the bombing and the aircraft flew relatively high overhead. A raid in full daylight was also unusual.

'Come on, My Love,' Dorothy said to Kevin and took his hand.

The distinct rumbling of the Junkers Ju 88 could be heard after the air Siren died away. A new sound filled Dorothy's ears, a high-pitched scream. She gasped, turned and found Kevin's arms around her.

'Quick, under the table,' he yelled. He pushed his wife down then flung himself over her. He grabbed her so close she could feel his heart thumping against her body. Those were her very last thoughts as the building erupted in a blinding explosion.

*

It was nine at night but still daylight when the black Humber police car drove into Moffet's farmyard. A sergeant and constable climbed out and walked to the door that had already opened. Edith stood there looking worried. The police never came this far out unless something was seriously wrong.

'Yes, Sergeant?' she asked with her hands wringing a tea towel in her hand.

"Mrs. Edith Moffet?" he replied and the woman nodded. "I believe Miss Cindy Smithers works for you, Madam. May we speak to her, please?"

"Certainly Sergeant," Edith replied. "She is inside. Please come in."

Cindy was already standing in the corridor. Her face turned ghastly white. "I'm Cindy Smithers," she said. Her eyes were wide in terror.

The sergeant looked sympathetically at the young woman. "I have some bad news, I'm afraid, Miss Smithers." He stopped. "Would you like to sit down?"

"No," Cindy whispered. "Tell me, please."

"Both your parents were killed in an air raid at Kettingham just after two this afternoon." His eyes were filled with compassion.

'No!' Cindy gasped. 'It can't be!'

She turned and found Grace beside her and an arm tucked around her shoulders.

Edith was also in shock. 'Both of them, sergeant?' she gasped.

'I'm afraid so, Madam,' he answered. 'They were together at the newspaper office, which took a direct hit. The area was a victim of a mass bombing attack and over half the village was wiped out. We haven't the final numbers but believe over fifty people were killed in the raid.'

'No!' screamed Cindy and buried her in head in Grace's shoulder. 'No! It's a mean trick.' She stared at the policeman with tears streaming down her eyes. 'Tell me it's a lie.'

'I am afraid not, Miss Smithers. You have my deepest sympathy.'

'My mother?' gasped Grace who still held a shaking Cindy. 'I come from Kettingham, too.'

'We checked on that and found your mother was not one of the victims, Miss McKenzie,' the constable replied.

Cindy turned and, with shaking chin and tears still streaming down her face, fixed her eyes on the policemen. 'Thank you for personally coming to tell me,' she said in a valiant effort to stop herself breaking down again.

'That's the least we could do, Madam,' the man replied and glanced at Edith and David. 'Will Miss Smithers be all right with you?'

It was David who answered. 'Yes, Sergeant. We'll look after her.' He held out his hand. The policemen shook it and departed.

*

In the next few moments it was David Moffet who helped Cindy the most. He took her hand and led her into the front room where he poured and handed her a glass of wine.

'Sip it slowly, Cindy,' he said. 'I'll contact Arthur for you.'

After nodding to his wife he telephoned the hospital, talked for a few moments and hung up.

'I'm going to pick Arthur up,' he said quietly to Edith. 'Keep Cindy warm and don't let her outside. Understand.'

'I'll be okay,' sobbed Cindy and sat holding the wineglass.

*

It took over an hour but by ten fifteen the old truck rattled into the courtyard and Arthur ran across to meet a sobbing Cindy. He grabbed her and just held on tightly while huge sobs of anguish tore through her trembling body.

'I'm here for you, Cindy,' he said and kissed her forehead.

'Both of them, Arthur,' Cindy howled and tears once again flowed unabated down her face.

'Come inside,' Arthur led her inside, sat her on the couch and placed an arm around her.

'Thank you for coming for me,' he said to David.

The old farmer coughed and nodded. 'I knew she would want you at a time like this,' he muttered and glanced at his wife. 'Edith, perhaps a little to eat.'

*

Later that evening, Cindy took Arthur's hand. She led him outside and up the dark path to the old lean-to bedroom where Grace and herself had stayed when they had first arrived on the farm. She took a key from her pocket and unlocked the door.

Her arm went around Arthur and she whispered. 'You're all I have now, My Love.'

Arthur nodded and shut the door. Their love making a few moments later was desperate but every bit as passionate as the first time under the oak trees at the back of the farm. And somehow it helped. The love Arthur had for Cindy, together with the love and friendship from Grace and the Moffets helped her through that tragic evening.

*

When Cindy and Arthur arrived back in the kitchen over an hour later, the Moffets and Grace never questioned where they had been. Grace gave Cindy a knowledgeable smile and David invited Arthur to stay the night.

'I'd like that,' Arthur replied and watched as Cindy went and brought out a writing pad.

'I have to tell Grandma and Timmy,' she said. She gazed into Arthur's eyes. 'I know Timmy may never get the letter but I can try.'

David gazed at Cindy and stoked his moustache. 'How'd you like to ring your Grandma?' he asked.

Cindy glanced up at the man, usually so stern and uncompromising. Tears welled in her eyes. 'Do you mean it?' She saw he did, and kissed the grizzled old farmer on the cheek. 'Thank you. I have the number in my notebook. Mum said I might need it one day.' Her face went white again when she realised she'd mentioned her mother's name.

'It may take a while,' the farmer said and walked over to the phone. 'I want an emergency call to Canada,' he told the operator, gave the number, listened and hung up. 'They'll call back in about an hour,' he said.

It was ten past eleven when the phone rang. David answered, 'David Moffet speaking... Yes, that is correct. ... Yes, I'll hold the line.' He handed the phone receiver to Cindy. 'That was the Toronto operator They're ringing your grandmother's number right now.'

Cindy glanced at Arthur, then Grace and took the instrument with shaking hands.

'Good afternoon, Amanda Hutchkins speaking,' The voice could have been from across the road.

'Grandma this is Cindy in England...' She couldn't go on. Once more tears poured down her cheeks and choking sobs prevented her from speaking.

David took the phone and spoke. 'Mrs. Hutchkins, this is David Moffet speaking, the farmer employing Cindy. I am afraid there's some tragic news...' He continued and explained everything while Arthur held a sobbing Cindy in his arms.

A few seconds later David held the receiver to Cindy's ear. 'Listen Sweetheart,' Amanda's voice said. 'Are you there, Cindy?'

'Yes Grandma,.

'I want you to come over here to me as soon as you can. Understand.'

'But Grandma, I can't.'

'Yes you can.'

'But there's Arthur.'

David gently took the telephone from Cindy and explained in explicit detail who Arthur was before handing the receiver back.

'Cindy,' Amanda said. 'Do you love your young man?'

'Yes,' Cindy replied.

'David said he has burn injuries and needs more operations.'

'I can't leave him, Grandma.'

'Cindy, Leave it to me. I'll see what I can do and, Sweetheart, thank you for calling. Keep your chin up. Your Granddad and me are here to help and we both love you. I'll call back tomorrow. Can you give me Mr. Moffet's number?'

Cindy did so and hung up. 'Thank you David,' she said. That was the first time she'd called the farmer by his first name.

'That's what telephones are for,' he muttered but smiled at Cindy. 'I think we could do with another wine before bed. It's been a long and tragic evening.'

*

The letter to Timmy reached the Red Cross in Switzerland in three days and, when read by the censor, was stamped with a special stamp reserved for emergency mail. It crossed the border into Germany that night and because of the high regard both sides of the warring nations had for the organization, the stamp was respected and the letter allowed through without further censorship.

In Berlin, another Red Cross Inspector read the contents and immediately walked to a long grey filing cabinet and pulled open a steel drawer with *'English POW 1940 - France"* written in German on the front. There, neatly arranged in alphabetical order was a small card for every known British prisoner of war captured in France during 1940.

The next afternoon in a camp over a hundred and fifty kilometres to the south, a guard walked into the bare, bleak and crowded camp and up to Major John Kirton, the highest-ranking British officer imprisoned there. He handed him a pink envelope, saluted and left.

'Get me Private Smithers from Hut 39,' the major told his next in command. Even in a POW camp military discipline and order continued.

A few moments later a very thin man dressed in a clean but tatty khaki uniform appeared at the major's door. 'Private Timmy Smithers, Sir,' he said and stood at attention.

The major didn't know Timmy personally but realised that a letter dated only a few days earlier in England and counter stamped by the Swiss Red Cross must hold personal and probably bad news.

'A letter has arrived for you, Timmy,' he said using the private's first name. 'It's from England and came priority through the Red Cross. It may be bad news, Lad.'

'Yes, Sir,' Timmy replied and blinked rapidly, his only sign of emotion.

He took the pink envelope and stood looking at the neat writing.

'You can open it if you wish,' the officer said.

'Thank you, Sir. I think it's my sister's writing. She was always very neat.' He opened and read the three neat, completely uncensored pages and glanced up. 'If I wrote back would a letter get through,' he said. The only sign of tragic news was a faint quiver of his chin.

'Bad news, Timmy?' the major asked.

'Both my parents were killed in an air raid near London, Sir. Also my older brother Bertie was shot down and killed last year. He was a Spitfire pilot.' He glanced up. 'Cindy, my little sister wrote the letter.' He grimaced. 'It couldn't be much worse, Sir.'

'I see,' the major replied. 'I am sorry to hear that. You write the letter, Timmy and I'll see it gets to the Red Cross and back to England.'

'Thank you, Sir,' Timmy replied, saluted and marched out with the little pink envelope in his hand. It was only after he crossed the dusty compound that the tears began to flow.

*

Dorothy and Kevin were buried together in The Kettingham cemetery after a ceremony at the local cathedral. The building was full to overflowing and Kevin's regiment had an honour guard to carry both their coffins to the last resting place. Cindy with Arthur, Grace, David and Edna led the mourners to throw a pinch of soil in the opened graves before the closure.

The whole village was in mourning for these outstanding local citizens and the other villagers killed in the bombing raid. The tragedy was that the village had no military significance at all and the only explanation the government could offer was that it was a retaliatory bombing after heavy RAF bombings of German cities a week earlier. As well as the newspaper office, half the village was destroyed including the whole street where the Smithers lived. Just a pile of bricks and debris covered the whole area where Cindy's home once existed. All that now stood was the scorched but still standing oak tree.

'Can we go back to the farm and not stay the night as planned?' Cindy asked after seeing the devastation 'There's nothing here for me, now.'

'If you wish,' David replied and squeezed her gently on the arm. Cindy noticed softness in his eyes she had never seen before. 'You go with Arthur in the MG. Grace, Edna and I will follow in the truck.'

So they drove home the three hundred miles and arrived at three in the morning. Cindy kissed Arthur and walked around the back where Marmalade came up and meowed. Cindy picked the cat up, walked in the kitchen and poured out a saucer of milk. She found Arthur behind her, turned into his arms and just hung on tight while he stoked her hair but said nothing. He didn't need to say anything. His presence was all she wanted.

*

It took three weeks but when Amanda's efforts came through, everything happened at once. It began when three letters arrived in the mail, one each for Cindy and Grace and another for David. The girls' letters were quite brief and in effect told them their services as Land Girls were not required any longer and, as from the end of the month, they were civilians under no obligation to the government. A last paragraph thanked them for their services. The letter to David told him the same information but added that two more Land Girls had been allocated to his farm as from the new month.

'Just get 'em trained and they move on,' he muttered but his eyes were soft.

Cindy stared at Grace and shrugged. This was not what they wanted. There was nowhere else to go but somehow the two Moffets seemed strangely calm as if they knew more was to come.

It did on that very evening!

The telephone rang and David handed the receiver to Cindy. 'Millsfeild Airbase,' he muttered and Cindy smiled thinking it would be Arthur who had recently been released from hospital and had a temporary posting at the base. However, the call was quite formal.

'Good evening Miss Smithers,' said a female voice. 'Will you please hold the line for Squadron Leader Chelley.'

Cindy had never heard the name but said she would.

'Miss Smithers,' said a clipped upper class voice. 'I have received orders from London that you require priority transportation back home to Canada. Please report to the base at 0600 hours tomorrow with your luggage. All documentation will be here when you arrive.'

'Yes but...' Cindy interrupted and her mind whirled. Back home! Canada was never her home... but the squadron leader wasn't listening.

'Could you put Miss Grace McKenzie on the line, please.' he continued

Cindy stared wide-eyed at Grace, covered the phone with her hand, told her who it was and handed the receiver over. Grace frowned and spoke to Squadron Leader Chelley. Cindy watched her friend's face that seemed to be quite passive. Grace finally hung up and stared at Cindy.

'I've been offered a free ride to Canada as your escort,' she said in awe. 'The squadron leader said that due to your recent family bereavement it was best that you don't travel alone.'

'What?' Cindy gasped but had no more time to speak when the telephone rang again.

David answered and handed the receiver to Cindy. 'The boyfriend,' he said.

'Cindy,' Arthur sounded quite distressed. 'I've been posted back to the R.C.A.F. in Canada; back home in Toronto actually. I have to fly out tomorrow as second officer piloting a Catalina flying boat back there for repairs.' He coughed. 'I can't even get leave tonight to come and see you.'

'You aren't leaving at six in the morning, by any chance?' Cindy's heart raced and gave Grace a wink. Her friend shrugged and stared blankly at the Moffets who had condescending grins on their faces.

'I'll be there to see you,' Cindy said in an uncommitted voice to Arthur and rung off.

She turned to David and Edna. 'You knew, didn't you?' she accused and stared at them both with her wide blue eyes.

'Tell me what is going on,' Grace snapped.

'Cindy's grandmother phoned a couple of days back,' Edna confessed. 'We promised to say nothing as it wasn't all finalised. We didn't want you to be disappointed if everything fell through.'

'What is it?' Grace repeated in an angry voice. 'For God's sake will someone tell me what's happening!'

'Oh Grace,' Cindy said. 'By a merest coincident, Arthur will be second pilot in the plane we fly out on.'

Grace's face changed into a broad grin. 'I understand now,' she said and grabbed Cindy's hands. 'My God, when your grandmother says she's going to do something, she doesn't mean by half measures, does she?'

'That's Grandma,' Cindy said but suddenly felt quite flustered. 'But there's no time and what about the MG, all our gear? We've got miles too much and....'

'Whoa!' David replied. 'Slow down, Girl. We'll look after the car and any other gear. As you are not twenty-one yet, your grandmother, as your closest living relative has full responsibility for your welfare. She asked if we would be guardians of all your affairs in England, you know, your parents' estate, bank accounts and so forth and we agreed but only if you wanted it so.'

'... So just pack your bags with a few clothes,' added Edna.

Cindy smiled. 'Thank you,' she said and went and hugged both the Moffets. 'This will always be my second home. Without you help when Mum and Dad were killed I could not have coped.'

'... And you'll always be welcome back.' Edna wiped a tear out of her eye with the corner of her apron. 'Come on; we'll have some supper now. It'll be a busy day, tomorrow.'

*

CHAPTER TWENTY-ONE

After squeezing everything into the MG, including David and Edna who refused to be left behind, they left the farm for the last time and arrived at the airfield at quarter to six to find Arthur waiting at the guardhouse.

'I was told you were coming last night,' he said and jumped onto the running board beside Cindy who was driving. 'Now go up three lanes and turn left...'

They ended up beside a concrete hanger where a military policeman would not let the Moffets continue. There were hugs, tears and promises to write before the MG was unloaded and David reversed around, tooted and drove away. Cindy could not stop the tears when the little green car disappeared behind a building.

'We had that car from new,' she sniffed. 'Ten years it is. I wonder if I'll ever see it again.'

'You will, My Love,' he replied. 'I'm sure you will. Knowing David, he'll put it up on blocks in the barn and not let a soul near it.'

Cindy grinned and followed Arthur along to an office in the hanger where, as promised, Grace's and her own papers were waiting for them to sign in triplicate. Afterwards they walked out to the tarmac where the aircraft was waiting.

The Catalina was an amphibian with a long flat fuselage, high wings and two massive engines already being warmed up. A rear bubble had a machine gun poking ominously out and Cindy could see at another in the nose. Camouflage paint and blue RAF ringlets looked faded and dirty while the body was streaked in grime and oil stains. Several metal patches across the body still had undercoat paint covering them.

'I know the plane looks rather run down but it's quite a new model,' screamed Arthur in Cindy's ear above the engine noise. 'German fighters attacked it and those patches cover bullet holes. One engine was shot up and has been replaced. The manufacturers want to see how it survived such an attack so modifications can be made to new models, if necessary.'

The roaring engines switched off and the propellers swished to a stop. They could talk in an ordinary voice. 'We're heading to the northwest over Scotland and onto Reykjavik, Iceland for refuelling,' Arthur continued. 'That part will take about seven and a half hours. We have a night's stopover at the American base there and, tomorrow we travel down to Gander in Newfoundland. That's about a ten-hour flight, then onto Canada where we get off.' He grinned and gave Cindy a hug. 'Scared?'

Cindy looked at the massive aircraft but shook her head. 'No really,' she replied.

'Come and meet Graham and Basil, the chief pilot and navigator. They're the only other crewmen on this ferry flight. Normally there's a crew of seven with the gunners and so forth but we're keeping ourselves light.'

Graham Bromley was a R.C.A.F. Officer, one rank above Arthur. What was unusual, though, was his age. He looked to be well into his fifties. In contrast, Basil was younger than Cindy. He gave them a shy grin and buried his head back into the map he had stretched out on a table behind the pilots' seats.

'Welcome aboard, Girls,' Graham said with his Canadian accent quite noticeable. 'It'll be a noisy and rough ride but we'll get you there. These are slow but pretty dependable craft. This one was shot up, had one engine set on fire and it still made it back to base.'

Cindy gazed around, fascinated. Instruments were everywhere and the rest of the interior was filled with machine gun ammunition, supplies, handholds, square netting suspended from the walls and several steel seats bolted to the floor. Everything smelt of oil and grease and yellow or red warning signs were everywhere. It was a military machine designed for long sea patrols rather than luxury. It was Grace, though, who noticed a small stove in an alcove set out like a tiny kitchen.

'These Catalinas have a range of three thousand miles and can remain aloft for most of a day,' Arthur explained. 'The crews can get hungry. Now suitable clothes,' he said and handed Cindy a leather jacket, thick trousers, gloves and a helmet. 'Just put these over your other clothes. It'll get cold up there. Often ice begins to form on the bulkhead...'

He continued with instructions and showed the girls the emergency procedures, before directing them to seats and buckled them it. The hatch was closed, Graham chatted on the radio and the engines screamed. Cindy grinned at Grace's white face but she felt strangely confident, herself. Even the morning's illness was forgotten as she watched the pilots buckle themselves in, go through a safety check and taxi the Catalina along the runway ready to take off.

*

The Catalina shuddered, yet again, as another scrawl of rain lashed the fuselage. Scotland was behind and the dull choppy Northern Atlantic Ocean was five thousand feet below. Even from this height, white caps could be seen intersecting the dark water.

'How much longer?' Grace yelled at Basil.

The young navigator was used to her interruptions by now and his early shyness had gone.. 'Let me see,' he replied and glanced down to where he had just made a line across the map in front of him. He glanced at his watch. 'Just after eleven. The wind has slowed us down a little. I'd say a couple of hours at the most and we'll be there.'

'Thank God,' Cindy gasped. The journey had not been a happy one for her. Within the first half-hour she'd been airsick and her head now ached from the constant rumble of the motors and air pressure on her ears. She'd tried sucking barley sugar, swallowing with her nose held, but her ears remained blocked. Her stomach lurched again as the aircraft was buffeted and Grace who seemed embarrassing well, looked with concern at her friend. 'There's more than just airsickness, Cindy. I reckon you should see a doctor when we get to Iceland.'

'I will,' moaned Cindy and lay back in the uncomfortable seat with her head against the tiny pillow Arthur had provided earlier. This helped a bit. If only her vision would stop spinning it wouldn't be so bad. She shut her eyes but this did not help. Even in the blackness she could see flashes of blue and an occasional red.

'Oh hell,' she moaned, opened her eyes and reached out for another paper bag.

'Here, take a sip.'

Cindy looked up and saw Arthur holding a mug of steaming liquid in front of her. She responded with a weak smiled and sipped. It was hot lemon with only a tiny amount of sugar added.

'Thanks,' she said. The taste did help. 'I'm a bloody poor traveller aren't I?' She glanced up with wide eyes and folded the full bag over with shaking hands.

'I'll get rid of it,' he said and took the paper bag in his hands. 'You just stay where you are.'

'Better get back here,' interrupted Graham from the front. 'More rain is coming in.'

Arthur bent forward, kissed Cindy on the forehead and headed back to the co-pilot's seat. Cindy didn't understand but the motors appeared to change their tone and run a little smoother. Arthur could also be seen talking on the radio. Afterward, when he gave the passengers the thumbs up signal, Grace crawled forward and listened to his words and returned to Cindy.

'We'll be out of the storm soon.' she yelled. 'The weather over Reykjavik is clear with no wind.'

Cindy nodded and sipped the lemon drink again while her stomach heaved as the bulkhead before her eyes shuddered. In her whole life, she doubted if she'd felt so terrible.

But, the prediction was correct. Within minutes, the amphibian flew out of the cloudbank and a lazy sun bathed the amphibian in sunshine. The sea below changed from dark grey to blue and even the whitecaps seemed fewer. Graham cut back the throttles, tipped the nose of the craft down a little and the shuddering fuselage became steady. Cindy's ears popped and, with the pressure in her ears relieved, her vision stopped spinning and stomach settled a little. For the first time in hours she began to feel normal.

'It's not fair how healthy you are,' she grumbled at Grace who had taken a sandwich and begun to munch it.

*

Early in the afternoon, the Catalina flew low over the city of Reykjavik and landed at the massive American army air force base. A jeep roared onto the runway with a yellow sign that read *Follow Me Please* and led them through dozens of four engine bombers and transport aircraft, American and British, to a corner near one circular roofed hanger. Graham shut the engines off and the silence was like heaven. Cindy stared out at the activities outside, the wet tarmac showed it had been raining and little tractors with trailers appeared to be racing everywhere. She let Arthur give her a hand and staggered like an old lady when she reached the ground for the first time.

An hour later, after being given quarters in the woman's dormitory and having a shower Cindy was almost her old self again. Grace handed her a card. 'Hurry,' she said with her breath forming clouds of white condensation when she spoke. Even in mid afternoon the weather was chilly and far colder than the farm they left. 'You have an appointment with one of the base doctors in ten minutes. We have to find the base hospital.'

'I'm okay now,' protested Cindy. 'I was just airsick.'

'You go,' Grace replied firmly. 'God, Cindy, you can be so naive at times.'

'What do you mean?' snapped Cindy but Grace would say no more.

Thirty minutes later an air force doctor finished asking her a myriad of quite personal questions about breast soreness, her last period, whether she had itchy genitals and gave her a complete physical examination that left Cindy embarrassed and frustrated. This had never happened to her before.

'You are heading on to Gander in the morning, I believe,' the doctor continued after telling her she could redress and inviting her to sit on a chair next to the examination couch. For several moments he wrote copious notes on a clipboard before glancing up at her.

'Yes,' Cindy replied and her bottom lip quivered in apprehension. 'I'm sure it was just travel sickness, Doctor.'

'Well, there is no sign of any venereal disease.' he replied and stared at her from under searching eyes. 'I can prescribe a mild tonic for tomorrow's journey but would be hesitant to give you anything too powerful, considering your condition.'

'My condition!' Cindy replied and her forehead wrinkled up in anger at the way she was being treated. How dare he think she could have VD!

The doctor also frowned. 'Oh, I see,' he answered and gave a small professional smile. 'I don't know whether you will appreciate this news, Miss Smithers, but you are in your first trimester of pregnancy. However, I'm pleased to say that, except for this motion and morning illness it appears to be perfectly normal.'

'Oh my God!' gasped Cindy and thought back to Grace's innuendoes and comments. 'Am I?'

The doctor nodded and, for the first time, appeared friendly. 'Is that young flight lieutenant waiting outside the father?'

Cindy flushed bright red but nodded. 'Oh my God,' was all she could say again but the news was not bad. In fact she felt quite elated. She was pregnant with Arthur's child. It felt right, somehow. She smiled at the doctor. 'I didn't know,' she confessed, 'but I'm pleased.'

The doctor studied Cindy and handed two prescriptions. 'One is for the air travel and should be taken two hours before you leave. The other is an iron supplement. Don't worry, you are in perfect condition,' he said. 'You will need to see a doctor when you get to Canada. Good luck.'

He stood, shook Cindy's hand and held the door open for her. Cindy was almost in a daze as she went up the sterile, impersonal corridor and back to the crowded waiting room where both Arthur and Grace rushed across to meet her.

'How are you?' they both asked.

Cindy had a neutral look and squeezed Arthur's arm. 'You old bugger,' she said in a monotone. 'It's all your fault.'

'Why what have I done?' Arthur replied in a surprised voice.

'Got me in the family way,' Cindy spouted out. She was not sure whether to laugh or cry. It depended on Arthur's reaction.

'You don't mean!' he gasped as Grace grinned broadly from behind.

'Yes,' Cindy replied. 'I am about six weeks pregnant with your child, Arthur.' She waited for his reaction..

Arthur just stared and swallowed before he grabbed Cindy in an almighty hug and kissed her fully on the lips. He held her out with his arms and just stared at her before giving a sort of chuckle and hugging her again. 'Cindy!' he whispered. 'Oh, Cindy!'

'You don't mind?' she whispered.

'Mind!' the airman flustered. 'Cindy, why would I mind?' He kissed her again.

Cindy held on and, all of a sudden, felt so excited she just wanted to do something. Her eyes found Grace. 'You knew,' she spluttered.

'I guessed a week or so back,' Grace replied and managed to elbow Arthur out of the way so she could hug her friend, too. 'When you were so ill on the plane I became quite worried.'

'Thanks for getting me to see the doctor,' Cindy added. 'I honestly didn't suspect.'

'Well,' said Arthur. 'What shall we do to celebrate?'

'I'm going to bed early, tonight,' Cindy replied and poked Arthur on the arm, 'and without you, young man. I need my rest with that long flight tomorrow.'

*

The other patients stared at the young flight lieutenant with the scared face as he walked out. On each side of him with their arms tucked in his were two attractive young women, one quite tall, slim and with auburn hair; the other a cute blonde. Both were well proportioned with figures enhanced by the civilian clothes they wore.

'Hell pal!' retorted a muscular American air force sergeant who had just stepped aside to let them through. 'What's that Limey flight lieutenant got that I haven't?'

'Two gorgeous chicks, Sarge.' The corporal beside him replied. 'There's no justice in this war, is there?'

Grace overheard the whole conversation and poked Cindy who gazed at her with a twinkle in her eyes. Arthur appeared to be in a sort of trance as they walked out into the chilly afternoon air and headed for the station guardhouse and the countryside beyond. He reached out and grabbed Cindy's hand then decided it wasn't enough and placed an arm around her shoulders. She leaned her head against him, gazed up and smiled. The infant may have been conceived out of wedlock but it was the result of genuine and passionate love between them.

'I think so, too,' Arthur said as if he'd read Cindy's mind.

*

Their stay in Reykjavik grew into three days, as Graham wanted more maintenance done on the Catalina. Also, the long-range weather forecast predicted that the storm they flew through would disperse over the next forty-eight hours and this was followed by a high with tail winds.

Basil swallowed his shyness and asked Grace if she'd like to go out with him to see the local sights and she accepted. 'Better than mooching along behind you love birds,' she said when Cindy teased her about it.

*

So Cindy and Arthur had two days to relax in an entirely different culture. The American military presence was everywhere and Cindy noticed not altogether welcomed by the locals. On at least two occasions it was only when it was realised Arthur was a Canadian and herself, English, that surly looks turned into smiles. It was also Cindy's first trip out of Britain and she enjoyed trying to make herself understood and reading road signs and directions. The weather was cold and reminded Cindy they were in the far north of the world and winter wasn't too far away.

'You wait until you get to Canada,' Arthur said as Cindy changed some money to the local currency and bought a thick coat with a fur collar. 'It gets much colder there.'

Cindy looked up at him and snuggled in close. 'I'll have to get used to it then, won't I?'

They were walking along a main shopping street and Arthur suddenly stopped by a jeweller's shop.

'Why stop here?' Cindy asked.

'I want to buy you something,' he muttered. He took Cindy's hand and looked her in the eyes but became tongue-tied. 'I want to...' he stuttered.

'Go on,' Cindy encouraged with her eyes searching his face. It was funny but now she was in love, Arthur's scars did not even seem to be there. It was as if she always saw the good side of his face.

'I want to buy you an engagement ring but have only got Canadian dollars and English pounds.'

'Are you proposing?' Cindy whispered.

'Well, I guess I am,' Arthur stumbled. 'It's a bit late, I know...'

'No it isn't,' snapped Cindy.

'Will you, then?'

'Of course. You don't want an illegitimate child do you?' She reached up, placed her arms around his neck and kissed him softly on the lips. Afterwards she pushed the jeweller's door open and almost pulled him inside.

The shopkeeper spoke no English but smiled and nodded when Arthur produced a wad of Canadian dollars. Cindy stared at him and wondered how he had so much cash on him.

'You planned this, Arthur,' she accused.

'Yes,' he confessed. 'I was going to ask a while ago but with everything else happening I decided to wait and not take advantage of you so...'

'... You got me pregnant instead,' Cindy added but felt sorry when Arthur's face went red in embarrassment. She reached up, kissed him again and smiled at the shopkeeper who must have been totally confused about what was happening.

The man, however, was very astute and even produced a book written in Islenska, the local language, and English with the exchange rate between the kronur and the dollar. He took out several rings and wrote down the price on the paper but they were all too expensive. After several nods from the pair he chatted away and put his fingers to his lips, went out the back and returned with a ring with a tiny diamond set in an ornate golden casing. It looked expensive but when he wrote the price down it was cheaper than the others they'd been looking at.

'What's the catch?' Cindy asked Arthur.

'No catch, Ma'am,' said an English language voice behind them. They turned and saw an American major standing there grinning.

Arthur, who was still in uniform, snapped to attention and saluted.

'Relax Son,' the major said and gave a casual salute back. 'On your way home are you?' He looked at Arthur's scar then smiled at Cindy.

'Yes, Sir,' Arthur replied.

'Well, this gentleman here has a bargain as far as I can see. This ring was returned by a jilted airman so is second hand, more or less, and he's prepared to sell it to you at half price.'

'Arthur,' Cindy grabbed his hand. 'Can we afford it?'

Arthur smiled. 'It is the best here and the price...'

'I want it, Arthur,' Cindy replied.

So it was all done. The jeweller measured Cindy's finger and, through the American major, assured them it would be ready to pick up that afternoon, Arthur handed over the cash and Cindy thanked the major.

'Glad to help out allies, Ma'am,' the officer replied. 'Even if half the young women in England are ending up in North America.' He grinned, made a purchase of his own and left. Cindy tucked her arm in Arthur's and they walked out and along the crowded street.

'What would you have done if we never came to that jewellers, My Dear?' she asked later when they were having a coffee together in a quiet little cafe.

'Stayed a bachelor,' Arthur said and recoiled when she gave him quite a powerful slap on the arm. He grabbed her wrists, bend forward and deposit a kiss on her lips.

'My God,' Cindy said. 'I swear you're wearing more lipstick than me.' She took a handkerchief out and tenderly wiped his face. She then kissed him and put it back again, 'But I love you, Arthur.'

'I love you, too, Cindy,' Arthur whispered.

Somehow, that coffee in that little cafe tasted just right and the smell added to the romance in the air. They sat together for almost an hour just talking, looking into each other's eyes and glorifying in being in love in a land far away from the ravages of war.

At four, they picked up the ring that fitted perfectly. Cindy had a bet with Arthur on how long it would take Grace to notice it. Cindy's time of an hour won easily. Grace saw it within five minutes of meeting them again and retorted it was the least Arthur could do after getting her best friend pregnant. She was joking and Cindy knew that was so. Arthur, though, took her seriously and was about to make a lame excuse when Grace burst out laughing and kissed him on the cheek.

'Oh Arthur,' she said. 'Perhaps it was a good thing, otherwise I might have given Cindy a run for her money. True gentlemen like you are hard to find.'

'So how was your date?' Cindy interjected as she thought the present conversation had gone far enough.

'Oh he's all right for a cuddle,' Grace replied casually then added with a sly look. 'He was quite a hulk actually.'

Iceland was proving to be quite a romantic stop over.

*

CHAPTER TWENTY-TWO

It was dark with only a thin line of red in the east when the Catalina taxied out between the Reykjavik Airport blue runway lights that, in the morning fog, looked like remote candles vanishing into the swirling darkness ahead. It was as if the world finished at a point only yards in front of the aircraft.

Cindy grinned in nervous anticipation at Grace before switching her eyes out the front windshield over the pilots' shoulders. She'd been up since four thirty to take her travel sickness syrup but had not been able to sleep again afterwards so had made breakfast in the deserted kitchen for her companions.

The pilot eased the throttles forward and the heavily laden Catalina rolled forward down the runway before, with infinite slowness and engines roaring at almost maximum revolutions, it lifted off the runway. The landing wheels retracted into the hull as the ungainly aircraft headed south west towards Gander in Newfoundland, one thousand five hundred miles away, well within the aircraft's range but still a huge stretch of empty ocean.

'Isn't it beautiful?' Grace sighed and, indeed it was.

To the east, an orange sun was just appearing above the horizon and red clouds stretched away from either side while below, everything was covered in white fluffy clouds that looked solid enough to walk on. No land or ocean could be seen.

For half an hour the Catalina rose before the floor tipped horizontal and Graham eased the throttles back. Cindy shivered, did another button of her coat up and pulled the woollen scarf she was wearing up around her cheeks and nose. She gripped the seat and looked ahead. Her stomach, though, felt normal and even her racing pulse had settled down. Perhaps she would not get ill this time.

For hours the flying boat flew like a lonely albatross over the Atlantic. The sun rose slowly through the deep blue sky to become a ball of yellow while the clouds below continued to stretch from horizon to horizon. Grace undid a thermos and poured out five mugs of steaming coffee and handed them around.

'You look okay, Cindy,' she said. 'How are you?'

Cindy laughed. 'Apart from frozen toes and fingers, I'm fine,' she replied. 'The stuff the doctor prescribed seems to have worked and, of course, there's no storm today.'

She took the hot coffee, sipped it and relished the warm taste in her mouth. Afterwards she even accepted a sandwich and munched it slowly.

'Point of no return,' Basil called and explained when Grace queried him. 'It means we're now closer to Gander than Iceland so we can't turn back even if we wanted to.'

'I see,' Grace replied. 'So we're slap bang in the middle of nowhere?'

'You could put it that way,' Basil chuckled.

*

It was Cindy who, a few moments later, spied something moving from out of the cloud bank far below on the starboard side where she was sitting. She peered and, only when the black dot took a form, did she speak out.

'I think an aircraft is approaching,' she said. 'It's coming up fast from my side.'

The reaction was immediate. Graham turned his head, saw the object in question and yelled at Basil who, as well as being navigator, operated the radio. 'Call in and ask for a report of aircraft in the vicinity,' he said and frowned. 'I don't like it. No other transport would be flying at that angle towards us.'

'Could be an aircraft carrier patrol plane,' Arthur replied. He grabbed a pair of field glasses and focused on the incoming craft that grew larger by the second.

'Single engine float plane,' he said. 'Looks hostile.'

'No allied aircraft within fifty miles of us,' Basil reported. 'I'll try to raise the intruder.' He twisted the frequency dial and spoke rapidly into the microphone. 'Catalina PBY...' His voice continued but Cindy was more concerned with the approaching plane.

'Hang on!' Graham called. 'We're heading down to the clouds.'

The engines screamed and the nose of the aircraft tilted down but the lumbering flying boat was not built for speed. Within seconds Cindy could make out the shape of the pursuing craft. It was a low wing, single engine fighter plane with floats attached underneath. Even as she watched, the craft moved up and flew beside them,

The craft was now so close the pilot could be seen with his goggles turned towards them. Worse though, was the aircraft itself. It was grey with a black iron cross on the fuselage, and hideous swastika on the tail.

Grace swore!

'German,' muttered Graham. 'How could it get this far out?'

'I don't know,' replied Arthur. 'It's probably a spotter plane from a German raider or battleship. 'He turned to Basil. 'Report in and ask of any known German ships in the area.'

But Basil was already speaking over the radio and listening intently to a reply. 'There are no known enemy ships in the vicinity,' he replied with his face serious. 'Also no allied aircraft can be here for at least half an hour.'

'Bloody great!' Graham grunted. He pushed the throttles wider and increased the Catalina's angle of descent.

'Sit down and put on your safety harnesses,' Arthur screamed at Cindy above the howling crescendo of the engines. 'Keep an eye on the enemy!'

'It's behind us and turning up in a loop,' Cindy yelled. Unlike Grace next to her who was opened mouthed in terror, she felt unusually calm as she grabbed the field glasses from Arthur and looked out the side porthole. 'Yes, definitely turning and gaining height,' she reported.

'Put out a distress call,' Graham yelled. 'I think there's going to be trouble.'

Basil nodded and twisted the dial. 'Mayday! Mayday!' he called. 'PBY Catalina PJ437 being attacked by unknown enemy craft. Our position is...'

'It's lining up behind and above us,' Cindy yelled.

'On the floor between the seats,' Arthur screamed but could be hardly heard above the engine roar.

'What?' cried Grace who just stood in the centre of the aircraft gripping a hand strap suspended from the bulkhead.

'Get down!' shrieked Cindy and grabbed her friend's hand. Grace let go the strap and tumbled forward on top of Cindy between their two seats.

*

Without warning the cockpit was filled with screams of metal, the Catalina dipped down and Cindy found herself pushed further under the seats with Grace above her. The screaming motor was supplanted by a howling whine and a shrieking ping. A freezing gale roared through the cabin but before the she could react, it was replaced by hot oil impregnated air and choking black smoke.

Within seconds the human screams started, high pitched hysterical screaming from immediately above Cindy and deeper shrieks of another human in unbearable pain.

More choking smoke caused her to cough and splutter. Howling wind tried to tear her away but she found a strap to hold. The hysterical screams from above turned to sobs and whimpering.

The plane headed down at almost a seventy-degree angle and caused Cindy to slide sideways out from the seat. A knee was in her face and something was pouring over her, sticky warm stuff but it didn't smell like oil but of warm flesh. Blood! There was blood all over her face.

Cindy shook her head, her eyes stung but, with difficulty, she opened them. Everywhere was the screaming howling wind and still the human screams, over and over!

But through that hot smoke filled fog, Cindy heard a voice. Someone was calling her name. 'Cindy! Can you hear me! Cindy!' It was Arthur's voice. Even though he must have been yelling, his voice was hardly audible above the pandemonium.

She stretched out with her hands and tried to push a weight off her. Grace toppled forward. Her limbs moved so she was still alive.

'I'm here, Arthur,' Cindy cried while still trying to orientate herself.

'Thank God!' Arthur yelled. 'I have to control the plane, Cindy. Can you see how everyone is?'

Grace was still screaming hysterically and Cindy looked at her. The girl's right arm was hanging limp and blood was pouring out the top of her sleeve.

'Grace,' Cindy shouted. 'You're all right. Listen to me! You're okay.'

But still the other woman screamed, her eyes wide and mouth contorted in agony. She sucked in ready to scream again when Cindy shook her shoulders.

'Settle down Grace. I need help. Settle down!' But Grace was not capable of hearing.

In desperation Cindy slapped her friend across the face. It worked! Grace's screams stopped, her eyes focused on Cindy then she began crying, long pitiful cries that shook her whole body.

'Can you let me up?' Cindy cried. She realised the floor was not at such a steep angle. The Catalina must be coming out of the dive. Choking acid smoke was everywhere.

'Yes,' whimpered Grace and Cindy felt her friend's body lift off her.

She staggered to her feet and gazed around. Just outside, smoke was bellowing out of the starboard motor. She could see the propeller but it was barely moving. The Perspex machine gun bubble was ruptured and round holes cut diagonally across the cabin.

'Can you see the other plane?' yelled Arthur.

Cindy pulled herself across the passageway and was immediately buffeted by the howling smoke coming through the gap in the Perspex. Nothing could be seen in that direction. She managed to find a strap and pull herself up. It appeared that her limbs were working and she felt no pain. The cloudbank on the port side was rocketing towards them and the blue sky revolved around like they were in a roller coaster. But something was out there. Her eyes focused on a black shape. The enemy plane!

'I see it,' she screamed. 'It's well below us.' She gasped. 'It's gone! It went into the clouds. I'm sure it was travelling away from us.'

There was a bang and the whole aircraft shook. Cindy stared out the starboard side and saw that a whole sheet of the engine cowling above her was gone. It must have ripped off and hit the fuselage. Black smoke poured out of the engine on that side but there were no flames.

She turned and, really for the first time, examined the interior of the Catalina. Grace was now sitting in a seat weeping and Cindy could see why. Basil was slumped over his table with his head down, but there was no head, just a pulverised mass of flesh. Blood was everywhere but had stopped flowing. An arm hung in a grotesque angle down the man's side.

'We can't help Basil,' Cindy roared at Grace above the howl of the wind. 'He's dead.'

'Oh Cindy!' wailed Grace.

Cindy stared at her friend and saw the damaged arm was still bleeding. She grabbed a first aid box and took out a cotton roll, ripped off a large wad and placed it over Grace's wound.

'Hold it with your other hand,' she shouted and made her way forward.

Graham was slumped sideways with his head jammed by the windshield and vacant eyes staring nowhere. He looked perfectly sound until Cindy saw a small hole through his up turned chin. The pilot was also dead.

'Can you get him out and help me,' Arthur shouted. His arms were vibrating as he tried to maintain control of the aircraft.

'Come on, Grace!' bullied Cindy and forced the girl to stand. 'We need to help Arthur!'

Grace nodded.

'We're in the clouds,' Arthur yelled and pulled back on the controls. The Catalina levelled and with it, the screaming howl of the engine. 'I've cut the starboard motor,' he continued with his eyes finding Cindy. 'I think the fire is out but will you check, please.'

Cindy nodded and pushed past Grace so she could see. The air certainly had less smoke in it but was freezing. She wiped a porthole window and peered out. The exposed engine was still smoking but less so. The slowly revolving propeller looked buckled and made ominous scrapes as it turned but she could see no flames.

'Right!' Arthur replied after Cindy reported back. 'Now get Graham out, if you can.'

While Grace held wires and other loose objects back with her good arm, Cindy managed to drag the body of their captain onto the floor next to Basil. She wiped her brow and took off her helmet so she could hear more before climbing over into the pilot's seat.

'What now?' she yelled.

'Are you wounded?' Arthur asked when he saw her blood covered clothes.

'No. It's Grace's blood. She was hit in an arm.'

'I'll be okay,' Grace yelled from behind. 'You two keep the plane flying.'

Again, without warning, the light increased and Cindy realised they were through the clouds. Immediately below was the ocean, dark blue and stretching in every direction, so close the curling whitecaps seemed to be reaching up to grab the aircraft.

'Arthur!' she screamed.

'I know,' he replied and pulled back the controls so the front of the Catalina lifted a little. 'It was the only way to avoid the fighter. I thought it mightn't follow at this low altitude.' He grimaced. 'The trouble is, that with only one engine, I doubt if we can climb back up.'

'So what do we do?' yelled Cindy.

'Lighten the plane,' Arthur replied. 'Toss everything out you can.'

'You heard him,' Cindy replied to Grace and they strapped themselves to a roof mounted harness and forced the door open. She stared at the water below them and gasped as the freezing air tried to suck her out. But this was no time to be frightened.

'Hand me things!' she screamed at Grace. After all the loose material disappeared Cindy noticed the two machine guns. Without them the Catalina would be considerably lighter.

With Grace's help, not that her friend could do a lot with one damaged arm, she used a huge spanner to undo mounting bolts. It was hard work and one machine gun's mounting refused to budge. The other weapon though, was unbolted and dragged to the door. Cindy, praying her harness would hold her, sat down and pushed the heavy gun with her feet. It squeaked along the floor and toppled over the step of the door and was about to fall back in. Cindy leaned against the bulkhead and used both feet to push it out the door.

'We're still too heavy,' screamed Arthur.

Cindy stared around. There wasn't time to unbolt the seats and only small bits and pieces remained, except for two items. 'The bodies!' she exclaimed.

'You can't!' gasped Grace with tearful eyes wide in horror.

'We can and we will,' Cindy ordered. 'They aren't here any more, Grace. They're dead,' she continued in a more compassionate voice. 'If Basil and Graham were alive now, I'm sure they'd agree.'

It was sickening and difficult but Cindy managed to drag Basil's body to the door and push it out, again by holding on and pushing with her feet. The captain's body proved easier and almost slide out when the aircraft tipped a little. Finally, Cindy grabbed the door handle, managed to loop a rope around it and by using the rope like a pulley, pulled it shut.

*

The howling wind was immediately reduced with only the broken Perspex bubble continuing to howl. Cindy examined it and realised only a jagged part not much bigger than her hand was missing. She glanced around; found a blanket and jammed it over the gap. A piece of stray pipe wedged diagonally across the flat bottom section held it and the roar was reduced to a bearable noise level. Only high-pitched whistles from the bullet holes in the fuselage continued. Cindy made her way forward and returned to the pilot's seat. It was then that she realised her feet were freezing and hands were scratched and bleeding.

Arthur gave her a nod of encouragement and eased the throttle of the one remaining engine forward and pulled back the controls.

'Keep an eye on the temperature,' he yelled and tapped a dial. 'If it gets to the red, tell me'

'Right.' Cindy replied and watched the dial as Arthur persuaded the Catalina to slowly increase height.

When the Catalina re-entered the cloudbank the cabin temperature dropped but they were still increasing height. Finally they came out above the clouds into the sunshine.

'No aircraft around,' Grace shouted. 'There's nothing at all'

'Thank God,' Arthur murmured. 'Right, we'll head home.' He smiled optimistically but Cindy frowned. The enemy may have gone but they were not out of trouble, not by a long shot.

*

Now at a reasonable cruising altitude, the Catalina limped on with its one engine performing faultlessly. Arthur watched Cindy in the other seat as she stared at the temperature gauge and moved levers or controls when he asked. She had a tongue between her teeth in concentration and hair had fallen over her brow. When she swished it back and realised he was looking at her; the frown changed to a smile.

'You should be a pilot,' he praised. 'You have the tongue in exactly the right position.'

'Okay, I know I'm nervous,' she replied. 'What now?'

Arthur gave an encouraging smile. 'We're on automatic pilot. It will probably be better if I get into your seat. I'll try to raise Gander on the radio. Why don't you go and patch Grace up. I think she's in a bit of a mess.'

'Of course. I forgot.'

*

Cindy squeezed out of the gap between the seats and made her way back to where Grace had taken over the navigator's place. The girl looked quite ill as she stared at the blood over the table and the ruined navigation maps.

'Come on,' Cindy said. 'We'll patch the wound.'

'It's not so sore, now,' Grace replied. 'My whole arm's numb.' Her blue eyes stared at Cindy. 'It was hell, Cindy.' She quivered. 'And we aren't out of it yet.'

Cindy smiled and glanced out at the feathered starboard engine. All the portholes on that side were streaked in oil but she could make out the propeller swinging around in a lazy fashion. A streak of oil flowed out the back to replace the earlier smoke.

She turned her attention back to her friend. When the cotton wad was removed from Grace's wound, blood began to drip onto the floor. Cindy ignored it and helped Grace remove her coat and jersey. The other girl grimaced in pain and shivered in her blood soaked blouse as Cindy contemplated what to do next. A pair of scissors was required to cut away the bloody material.

Once the skin was exposed, Cindy noticed a tiny piece of metal deep in the raw bleeding flesh. 'The bullet is still there, Grace,' she said. 'It needs to come out.'

'Okay. Do it then.'

Cindy found a pair of tweezers and gently dug around the wound while Grace clutched the edge of the seat with her good hand and stared straight ahead to where Arthur was talking on the radio.

Cindy breathed in and decided to give no warning. She gritted her teeth, plunged the tweezers in and gripped the metal. Grace gasped and automatically pulled her arm back. This reaction helped and the tweezers came back with something between the claws. It wasn't a bullet at all but a jagged piece of metal that must have ricocheted in from the aircraft framework.

'It's out,' Cindy said and showed the splinter to an ashen-faced Grace.

She held a pressure pad over the bleeding arm for several moments before bandaging the whole upper arm.

'Thanks, Cindy,' Grace said. 'It feels better already.' She stood up and made her way to her luggage at the back, produced some clean clothes and, with Cindy's help managed to put something warm on.

'Christ it's cold!' She shivered as she slid her arms in a coat and Cindy wrapped a scarf around her neck.

'I know.' Cindy

Grace's hair hung down from under the leather flying helmet but the eyes were bright. 'We'd win no beauty contest, would we?' she muttered.

'Who cares,' Cindy replied. 'I'll see if I can get the stove going and get us something hot to eat and drink.'

The kitchen alcove was not on the damaged side of the Catalina so within a few moments, Cindy handed Arthur and Grace a steaming plate of baked beans and a mug of coffee.

'Thanks,' Arthur said. 'I'm in contact with Gander now and they're sending an escort out. All going well, we'll arrive in a little over four hours.' He stared at Cindy. 'How are you, My Sweet?'

'Cold,' said Cindy. 'Otherwise I'm fine. Grace is well, too.' She reached over and kissed Arthur on the lips. 'I still love you,' she added and moved away before he could respond.

It was an hour later when Grace yelled out in air force jargon, 'Two aircraft coming in four o'clock, low.'

Arthur grinned, reached up and clicked a switch. A voice came through the radio static.

'PBY PJ437. We have you in sight. Good to see you, Buddy! This is Lieutenant Jerry Hamilton, United States Navy speaking. What is your condition? Over!'

Arthur grinned and filed back a report.

'Roger, Arthur we'll give you an exterior examination in a couple of minutes. Out.'

Cindy found Grace's arm around her as they both squeezed in the co-pilot's seat and stared as the two dots took form and seconds later, two black United States Navy fighter planes came in on each side of them. They looked like Spitfires except for funny 'W' shaped wings and a white star and bars on the side instead of the R.A.F. ringlets Cindy was used to.

'They're F4U Corsairs from an American escort carrier,' Arthur explained. 'There's a convoy out there somewhere but they keep radio silence so the Jerry U-boats aren't warned.'

'Hang in there, Buddy,' cackled the radio. 'Some vapour is flowing from the killed engine but otherwise, you're looking good.'

Cindy could see one of the pilots waving and returned the wave.

'Are you Limeys always that good looking?' the radio cackled, Grace gave a giggle and waved frantically at the Corsair.

'Hold a moment,' a different voice said. 'Your starboard undercarriage looks shot up a little. Could you try to lower your undercarriage?'

'Roger!' Arthur replied and pulled a large lever on the console down. The aircraft gave a shudder and everyone heard a screech of metal. Two lights flashed red.

'Starboard undercarriage has not come down,' the radio cackled. 'Would suggest a water landing when you arrive. Over!'

'Damn,' Arthur swore and raised the wheels again.

'Why what's wrong with a sea landing!' Cindy asked.

'We're so full of holes we might get our feet wet. That's all.' He saw Cindy's expression and hastily continued. 'It's not dangerous, though, just nerve racking.'

'Good,' said Cindy. 'I was getting bored anyhow.'

*

The Corsairs stayed with them for ten minutes before reporting other aircraft would be along later and disappeared as quickly as they arrived. They were alone again but the world did not feel quite so empty now.

'Look,' said Cindy a few moments later and pointed through a gap in the clouds. Below them were ships, dozens of them sailing together with steaming funnels and long lines of white wake.

'The convoy,' Arthur said. 'Heading for England, no doubt. I bet that was what that Jerry plane that attacked us was looking for.'

Grace gasped. 'That aircraft carrier is down there somewhere. My God, how do the pilots find it?'

'We're quite high.' Arthur said 'Look!' He nodded to the port side where two more Corsairs with different numbers on their fuselages flew in beside them and the new pilots waved.

'Like old friends,' observed Cindy and waved back.

*

CHAPTER TWENTY-THREE

It was two in the morning, local time and Gander International airport, unlike its counterparts across the Atlantic, was a blaze of lights. Hundreds of B17 and Liberator bombers of the United States Army Air Force lined up on the taxiway and apron of the furthermost eastern North American staging point. Every minute, a mighty aircraft turned onto the main runway and rumbled forward, gained speed and roared into the night sky. No sooner had this happened when another accelerated forward, a third turned into the main runway and a forth moved forward on the taxi way. Ahead was the Atlantic and England.

In complete contrast, the tiny civilian terminal tucked in an insignificant corner was almost deserted. A pot-bellied stove blazed in the corner of what was really a tin shed but the heat did not lessen the tension present in the building.

'Is there any news?' the well dressed woman in her sixties asked a young air force officer who had just placed a telephone down.

He grimaced and looked sympathetically at the concerned face. 'The only news I have, Mrs. Hutchkins is that the Catalina is not in the air. It would have run out of fuel by now. I'm sorry.'

Amanda turned to her husband who was standing with his hand in hers and just stared at him with blue eyes. They'd received a telegram earlier in the week telling of Cindy's departure time and a follow-up one advised them of the delay in Iceland. Samuel and herself had flown into Gander two days earlier and, through a little arm twisting, had learned that the Catalina had left Iceland fifteen hours earlier.

'It's not fair, Sweetheart,' she said.

'The plane may have diverted or even landed on the ocean,' Samuel comforted. 'The weather report has been good so don't give up yet, Amanda.'

'No, I won't give up, Samuel but the waiting and not knowing is killing me inside. There is nothing we can do except wait.'

'Well, they're out there somewhere so it is no use waiting here. I think we should return to the hotel.'

Amanda bit on her lip and nodded. 'I guess so but I'm coming back first thing in the morning.' She turned to the Officer. 'Thank you, Flight Lieutenant,' she said. 'Sorry to have been such a nuisance.'

'That is all right, Ma'am,' he replied. 'If any news comes in, I'll phone the hotel.'

Amanda nodded, grabbed Samuel's hand and walked out to the background thunder of aircraft engines. Though also worried about his granddaughter, Samuel couldn't help grinning at his wife's determination. In all the years they'd been together she had been the same. The years had rolled by, hair had turned grey and faces become lined but inside they were no different.

She turned and glanced at him. 'I'm a silly old woman aren't I Sweetheart?' She sighed as they walked towards the main gate.

'No' replied Samuel and placed an arm around her shoulders. 'To tell you the truth, I was thinking exactly the opposite.'

*

Amanda gave a tiny smile and gazed ahead through the ocean of lights. Dorothy was gone, Cindy missing and she blamed herself. If she hadn't insisted her granddaughter come to Canada...

'Don't you dare blame yourself,' Samuel interrupted her thoughts.

Amanda glanced into his eyes. 'Mind reading again Sweetheart,' she replied and squeezed her arm tighter around his waist.

A few moments later they were in their little hotel room having a cup of coffee. Amanda stared at the liquid in her cup and sighed. 'It was going to be such a surprise meeting them here.' She glanced up. 'Remember the time I went all the way to England in that terrible airship to be with them when Dorothy was kidnapped. That was ten years ago now.'

'I do,' Samuel replied. 'I guess Cindy will be a bit bigger now.'

'Yes,' Amanda answered. 'She was ten then and really bright,' She glanced up with a far-away expression. 'Personality and ability. She's an adult now. God, time goes quickly.'

'You know what?' Samuel replied. 'I think she's like her grandmother and I bet right now she is somewhere safe, either on the mainland or on a ship somewhere in the Atlantic. It takes more than this to knock out our family.'

'Our family's stamina didn't help poor Dorothy,' Amanda whispered. 'And I couldn't even get over there for the funeral.'

'I know,' Samuel replied, 'but, My Dear, you tried and I'm sure Cindy appreciated that. Also she wasn't it totally alone. That farmer and his wife sounded to be real caring and there was Arthur and Gwen.'

'Grace,' corrected Amanda. 'I know. She probably doesn't need old relations like us any more, anyway.' She stood up and took her husband's hand. 'I'm going to bed, Sweetheart. Coming?'

*

'Land!' screamed Grace and poked Cindy in the ribs.

'Where? I can't see a thing except the mist over the ocean.'

They were two hours beyond the convoy, the carrier Corsairs had given their final good-byes and radio messages told them a Catalina was flying out from Newfoundland to escort them into a flying boat base in Onavista Bay, thirty miles east of Gander. This was one of several new bases that sprung up along the coastline for Canadian and American flying boats that patrolled the Atlantic looking for German U-boats and surface raiders. For that reason, the bases were often top secret and maintained radio silence with signals being diverted through Gander on the telephone. The base they were heading for was simply called Beaver Base 6 or BB6 for short. Where Base 1 to 5 were, or if they even existed, Arthur had not been told, nor had he been given the exact co-ordinances. They only knew they'd be met once the coast was reached.

'Land's there, I tell you,' Grace persisted.

Cindy gazed through the mist. The ocean below and the sky blended together in a dark grey haziness. She rubbed her eyes and concentrated until she finally saw a tiny black hill poking through the mist. 'I believe you're right,' she said and turned to Arthur.

He looked exhausted with red rings under his eyes. An afternoon shadow appeared over half his face. The burnt side with skin grafts remained free from any beard growth, so at these times, the scars became more noticeable. 'It should be there,' he answered, yawned, took off his goggles and rubbed his eyes. 'Would you like to try a little more navigation?'

'I will,' Grace replied and turned to the new map of coastal Newfoundland Arthur had pulled out earlier.

Both the women had become quite good at tracing their course. By taking into account speed and compass bearings they had traced a reasonably accurate line across the map. Their only mistake was that they had underestimated the time they'd see the coast by almost half an hour. Their fuel was low, but not dangerously so and Arthur had estimated they could fly for another hour before an emergency arose. It still was, though, a relief to see that far off hill rising out of the mist.

'Bare north west, ten degrees,' Grace directed and grinned at her efforts to speak like a professional.

'Yes Sir!' Arthur answered. Grace had become her old cheerful self again in the last couple of hours. The motion sickness syrup must have reached their limit for Cindy was feeling quite queasy. She never complained but her white face and tired eyes could not be hidden so easily.

*

At a lower than normal altitude, fuel was burnt at a faster than expected rate and, of course, their speed was cut by a third. But the one remaining engine performed well and only when Arthur increased altitude did the temperate gauge move into the red zone. At the moment, it was hovering only half way up the dial and well within normal operating limits. It was still cold in the cockpit but they'd all placed warm and dry clothes on and, together with the regular hot drinks and food, the ride was not too uncomfortable. After Cindy and Grace had plugged the bullet holes with cotton wool or rags soaked in oil, the whistling noises had almost stopped.

'Grace,' Cindy said and tapped her friend on the shoulder.

'What?' Grace swung around.

Cindy said nothing but pointed out the other porthole on the side away from where they'd all been gazing at the land.

'Yes!' Grace yelled and her eyes gazed excitedly at Cindy.

Outside, less than three plane lengths way, flew another Catalina; all camouflaged with blue ringlets and R.C.A.F. written in grey along the fuselage. The pilot was waving and Arthur acknowledged the signal.

Suddenly, the radio cackled into life. 'Welcome to Newfoundland,' the voice said. 'Follow me please, PBY PJ 432. Over.'

'Will do,' Arthur's curt reply did not reflect the grin across his face. 'Lead the way. Over!'

'You're a might shot up there, Buddy. Sure you can make a water landing. Over.'

'Have to,' Arthur replied. 'Undercarriage won't drop. Over.'

'We'll be with you all the way. Out!'

'Roger,' Arthur replied and turned to Cindy. 'Well, almost home,' he said.

Cindy eyes were glued on the Canadian Catalina as it took up a position above and parallel with them and waved at a hand in the machine gun bubble.

'Cheeky devil,' Grace retorted and pointed. The gunner had plastered a huge sign on the inside of the bubble that said. *'How about a date, Babe?'*

'Yes,' Arthur grunted. 'With two beautiful women on board, the message soon gets around.'

'I'm sure,' Cindy said and leaned over to kiss her partner on the cheek. 'But I don't need a date. Grace of course....'

'Yeah,' Grace said. 'I hear Canadians are friendly.'

Fifteen minutes later they flew up a narrow bay with steep hills rising on each side. A fishing boat was cruising along below like a black duck at the apex of two white lines of wake.

'Destination, five miles dead ahead,' the radio cackled. 'I'll let you go in first. On landing, steer to port and head towards the end of the sheds. You'll see a wind socket beside a ramp and flying boat cradle. Taxi right in before cutting your motor. You're expected. A boat will guide you. Best of luck. Over!'

'Buckle in ladies,' Arthur said and cut back the throttle.

Cindy could now see buildings on their left and several flying boats moored just off shore. A whisk of smoke curled up above the base. Dark green hills covered in mist formed a picture postcard backdrop to everything. The engine cut and water tore towards them.

Bang!

The hull hit, bounced and the nose went down. Spray streamed by the portholes. Arthur increased power slightly and the nose lifted again with a shudder.

Grace gasped.

They had landed.

'Don't tell anyone but I've never landed on water before,' Arthur shouted

The Catalina taxied in a semicircle and headed towards the buildings.

'Water's coming in!' hissed Grace.

'Okay,' Arthur replied without taking his eyes from the scene outside. 'As long as we keep moving we should be okay.'

And they were. The Catalina moved into the designated area to find a boat waiting with a man holding huge orange paddles up to direct them. Arthur cut the engine almost to an idle and the Catalina sank lower in the water with a list to starboard. The paddle directed him to cut the engine and Arthur pinched Cindy's arm and pointed to a switch. She nodded and clicked it up. After a couple of splutters there was silence! For the first time since leaving Iceland the roar of the engine was missing.

She smiled at Arthur and Grace. They'd made it.

*

Outside it was all activity. Lines were tied to the Catalina and it was towed into lapping water between a 'V' shaped dock of six poles, and tied firmly in. A giant winch cranked the cradle up a railway line until the whole flying boat was out of the water and held in place by the poles while lines of tyres prevented damage to the hull. There was a scrape and the hatch opened.

A grinning airman popped his head in. 'Welcome to Newfoundland, folks,' he said. 'You're just in time for supper.'

Cindy, Grace and Arthur climbed out without even getting their feet wet and gazed at the remote scenery around. A cold breeze cut right through Cindy's coat and jersey but she did not care. Except for the stopover in Iceland, she'd never been out of Britain before but she felt as if she was coming home. She slipped her hand into Arthur's as they made their way along a wooden jetty towards a building where the smell of cooking filled the air.

*

It was seven in the morning and still dark when the jeep pulled into the main gate at Gander Airport and the guard poked his head in the side.

'Is there a Miss Smithers from England here?' he asked.

'Yes,' replied Cindy in a curious voice.

'There's a message, Ma'am,' the guard said. 'You are to meet your grandmother at The Grand, that's a local hotel down the road a few yards.' He grinned. 'We were told to tell her the moment you arrived but you can deliver the news yourself, can't you?'

'Grandma. Here!' gasped Cindy.

'Been here for almost three days, Ma'am,' the guard replied. 'Been nagging hell out of us, if you don't mind me saying.'

'Grandma here at the base!' Cindy repeated. 'Oh my God!'

'I'll take you to the hotel,' the corporal driving the jeep said and glanced at Arthur. 'If that's okay, Sir.'

'Yes,' Arthur replied, 'That's fine, Corporal.'

*

Amanda awoke and shivered. Even with central heating it was quite cold in the pitch-dark room but something had awoken her. She yawned, clicked on the bedside light and smiled at Samuel snoring softly beside her.

What woke her? She frowned, climbed out of bed and pulled a dressing gown on. The noise that must have awoken her sounded again. It was a loud knock on the door.

Amanda was instantly alert. She'd said to be contacted whenever there was news. With her heart thumping wildly she turned on the main light and headed to the door. She undid the safety lock and opened it.

A woman stood in the corridor. She was young, slim and had long hair hanging down to her shoulders. Bright blue questioning eyes stared right at her. For a second, Amanda thought see was seeing a ghost and it was Dorothy standing there; the same shaped face, hairstyle but especially the eyes...

The woman spoke. 'Grandma,' she said with a quaint English accent. 'Remember me?'

Amanda stared and her eyes filled with tears. 'Cindy!' she cried. 'Is that you? Oh my God! Cindy!'

'Yes, Grandma. It's me!'

Amanda flung her arms around her granddaughter and burst into long sobs while Cindy just held.

'You look no different, Grandma,' she said when the older woman finally held her at arm's length and their eyes met.

'And you're a woman, Cindy. You look just like your mother except for your hair colour,' Amanda replied and blew her nose on a handkerchief she produced. 'You have my colouring there. Well mine used to be that colour before I went grey,' she added. 'Come in! I'll get Samuel.'

'I have two friends,' Cindy added in an almost shy voice.

'I know,' Amanda added. 'Arthur, your young man and Grace, isn't it? Bring them in.' She turned and yelled. 'Samuel. Get out here and meet your granddaughter.'

Cindy looked up and saw a tall, clean-shaven man with grey hair, stagger, half asleep into the room. When he caught her eyes he smiled and held his hands out. 'My God, I'd recognise you anywhere, Cindy. It couldn't be anyone else.'

*

Within seconds, Arthur and Grace were in the room and introductions made all around. Cindy noticed and appreciated that neither of her grandparents paid a slightest attention to Arthur's scared face and their only comments were how tired they all looked.

'We only had a few hours sleep at the flying boat base,' Cindy explained. 'We were awoken at some ungodly hour and told there was a jeep waiting to take us to Gander.'

'Nobody told us a thing,' Grace continued. 'We thought it would be to be interviewed by customs or something.'

'Look, sit down and tell us everything,' Amanda flustered and grabbed some cushions off the armchairs.

Samuel tapped her on the shoulder. 'You get dressed, My Dear, and I'll put the coffee on. There's no hurry.' He winked at Cindy. 'She takes a bit holding back at times,' he added with a slight chuckle.

'Sounds like her granddaughter, 'Arthur said and received a thump on the arm for his effort.

'Canada!' Grace sighed as she plunked herself in one of the armchairs.

'Well almost,' Samuel said. 'Newfoundland is an independent territory but it's close enough.'

Cindy just stood and gazed at the people around her and felt Arthur's arms around her waist.

'Your family,' he whispered in her ear. 'Everyone who loves you, My Dear.'

Tears rolled down Cindy's cheek as she wiggled back so she was closer to her lover. Suddenly she felt something entirely different. In her tummy she felt a little kick. She grabbed Arthur's hand and moved it slightly across above the kick. 'That's not me doing that,' she said softly and smiled at Arthur's reaction.

Yes it was her family. Her eyes caught Grace's intense gaze. 'You're family, too,' she said and the young blonde woman smiled.

*

'The Group Captain will see you now, Flight Lieutenant Jervis,' the W.A.F. officer looked up from her desk and avoided looking at Arthur's scars.

'Thank you, Pilot Officer,' he replied and stepped into the office of the highest-ranking R.C.A.F. officer at Gander Airport.

'Sit down Flight Lieutenant,' Group Captain LeQuesnie said in an abrupt voice after taking Arthur's salute. He took a dark blue folder out of his desk, opened it and withdrew several documents. 'Thank you for your report on your recent flight in with the Catalina. It was a close call, wasn't it?'

'Yes Sir,' Arthur replied. He was still standing at attention but sat down and relaxed a little when his superior indicated he should do so.

'A couple of points, Flight Lieutenant.' Group Captain LeQuesnie glanced up and gave a brief smile. 'You do have some scars. Are you still in pain?'

'No Sir,' Arthur replied. 'It feels okay.'

'I have a report here from your squadron leader in England,' He picked up the top document. 'According to this you chose to land your blazing Spitfire rather than bail out over a suburban area and cause possible civilian causalities.'

'Yes Sir.'

'Squadron Leader Jones recommended you for a Distinguished Flying Cross for bravery?' The group captain glanced up.

'I believe so, Sir,' Arthur replied.

Group Captain LeQuesnie stood and held out his hand. 'I have been notified it has been granted. Congratulations Flight Lieutenant.'

Arthur looked surprised but shook the other man's hand and listened as the officer continued to speak.

'A new posting has come through for you, too, Jervis.' The group captain took a second document out and handed it to him. 'You have been posted to the Pilots' Training School in Vancouver, British Columbia and put in charge of the initial training of new pilots.' He grinned. 'Harvard Trainers are different from Spitfires but you will remain in Canada.'

Arthur's head buzzed. This was unexpected. He had thought he'd be assigned to permanent ferry duties across the Atlantic. Vancouver was a long way away but....'

'One other thing,' the other officer said. 'It means you're promotion to squadron leader, as from today.'

'What?' stuttered Arthur forgetting to even add 'Sir'.

'Any questions, Squadron Leader?'

'Well just one, Sir,' Arthur's mind raced at all the news he'd just heard. 'Do they have married accommodation in Vancouver?'

'Why yes,' came the reply. 'I'll get you the form. You have two weeks leave and will report to the base in Vancouver on completion of your leave.' Group Captain LeQuesnie stood and saluted. 'All the best, Jervis,' he concluded. 'Look after that new wife of yours.'

Thank you Sir,' Arthur replied, picked up his orders and left the room.

'Well?' said Cindy a few moments later.

'I have two weeks leave,' Arthur said.

Cindy grabbed his arm,' And?' She stared into his eyes.

'Fancy living in Vancouver, British Columbia?'

'Sounds nice but keep going.'

Arthur grinned and blurted out everything else he had been told.

'My God!' Cindy gasped in excitement and flung her arms around him. 'That's wonderful. When can you put your new pip on?'

'Any time, I guess,' Arthur said. 'The group captain said my promotion was from today.'

'The D.F.C. too.' Cindy said. 'When do you get that?'

Arthur shrugged. 'They'll have a ceremony sometime, I guess but, come on, two weeks leave, Cindy. Think of it.' He grabbed her hand and they both headed back to the hotel to tell the others their news.

*

Cindy and Arthur were married two weeks later in a tiny suburban church near to where Amanda lived and the next day, took the Canadian Pacific Limited Express west to Vancouver and Arthur's new posting.

Amanda looked nostalgically as the train pulled out of the station and her mind travelled back to Cindy's mother's birth in the avalanche and the later accident that killed Jack.

'Trains just get me emotional,' she said as she walked back with Samuel and Grace to their Chrysler.

As they drove home, Grace who was sitting in the middle between Samuel and Amanda turned to the older woman. 'Are you sure you don't mind me boarding with you for a while?' she said. 'I can find an apartment, you know.'

Amanda grinned. 'Our house has felt empty for years now,' she replied. 'A young face around is what it needs.'

'And the job as secretary at CJDT,' Grace said. 'The radio stations here are so friendly. In England the BBC runs everything. Private companies aren't even allowed to operate and with the wartime restrictions...' She babbled on excitedly as Amanda caught Samuel's eye. Grace did talk a lot.

'Oh we have our restrictions, too,' Amanda said, 'but once the war is over it should free up a little.'

'Thanks Grandma,' Grace replied and reached forward to squeeze Amanda's arm. She'd been calling her that since the second day of their arrival.

*

Early the next year on a wet miserable day, Cindy gave birth to a baby daughter. Amanda insisted on being in town for the birth and had flown into Vancouver a week earlier. The infant was named Julie Dorothy, the first name because Arthur liked it and the second after her mother. Cindy didn't realise until Amanda pointed it out on a visit to the maternity home that the name Dorothy also came though from her own mother.

'She's the one who left that strange legacy,' she said. 'It's sad really but both Dorothys died in tragic circumstances. I hope your little girl has a better fate.'

'Oh Grandma,' Cindy replied. 'I'm not superstitious and anyhow, she's going to go by her first name.'

Amanda smiled at the tiny head poking out from the bassinet. 'Oh yes,' she said as if she'd just remembered something and dove into her purse. 'Two letters arrived at our place for you.'

She handed them to Cindy who noted the English stamps on the first one and opened it. 'The Moffets,' she said. 'I'd been wondering how they were.'

'The second letter was included with their one,' Amanda replied. 'Look at it Sweetheart.'

Cindy took the smaller, somewhat tatty envelope and gazed at the address. It was written to her maiden name, of course, and addressed care of the Moffet's. The stamps and cancellations were strange.

'German,' said Amanda. 'I almost opened it myself but that wouldn't have been fair, would it?'

Cindy's heart raced as she withdrew two small pages from the envelope. She read for a moment then fixed her grandmother with shiny eyes. 'It's from Timmy,' she said. 'He's alive and got my letter. Look!'

She handed the pages to her grandmother and Amanda read it through orally. The information was light and black censor's ink blocked out one paragraph but the news that Timmy was alive far succeeded anything actually written.

'Cindy,' Amanda said. 'I'm so thrilled. This is the best news I've had since you came to the door of our hotel.' She grimaced. 'Just before that, I thought our family had died out but now there's you, Timmy and baby Julie. It seems we're right for another generation, aren't we?'

'Yes,' Cindy chuckled and picked Julie up for a cuddle. 'Well Darling, with such a great daddy, Grandma, Granddad, and now Uncle Timmy, our family will certainly be around for a while.' She glanced up as Arthur, still in uniform, walked in the ward, 'And here's your Squadron Leader daddy right now.'

She smiled at her husband and reached up for the enormous bunch of flowers he held out to her. Yes, Grandma was correct. They were right for another generation, the war was all but won and, with luck, Julie could grow up in a more peaceful world here in Vancouver, the city her grandmother's grandmother and come to in her quest for freedom.

*

PART 4 NICOLE 2006

CHAPTER TWENTY-FOUR

'I don't really have a lot back in British Columbia now,' Cindy said in almost a sad manner when she finished her story. 'In Canada, we were away from the war and were thoroughly spoiled by my grandparents. Arthur had several operations but really carried his facial scars for the rest of his life. When he left the air force he went into Grandma's business. In 1950, I think it was, Grandma and Granddad retired and divided the companies they owned between Timmy and myself. The *HOW Broadcasting Company* was one of the first to introduce television in several Canadian cities and later became affiliated with CTV, the main opposition to the government run CBC.' She grinned. 'I still own a few shares in a handful of Canadian television stations.'

'A few?' Nicole asked. She realised her grandmother was liable to understate her worth.

'Well, when we amalgamated, part of the pay out was shares in CTV. They're there but I don't really take an interest now. It's all too big and impersonal.'

Grandma's share, Nicole found out later, consisted of a publishing house, radio stations and quite a large slice of the Canadian television network.

Cindy sipped from a mug of coffee and told of Timmy's return after the war. He and Grace had taken an immediate liking to each other, were married and had five children, three boys and two girls who had grown up and also had families. There were dozens of relations up in Canada, many about her own age.

'But they're Timmy's grandchildren,' Cindy said. 'I only had Julie and you're my only grandchild. Remember that, Nicole. With Timmy and Arthur both gone, you're my closest relation.' The old lady grinned. 'And one I am so proud of.'

'What happened to everyone else?' Nicole asked.

Cindy's face turned sad, 'Grandma Amanda lived to be ninety-two and died in mid 1970. Poor old Granddad lingered on until the end of the year; I don't think he wanted to live after Amanda died. Arthur left us three years later in 1973 and Timmy a decade ago. Grace is still in Vancouver and we see each other all the time.' She'd grinned. 'So that's it really, Nicole. The last thirty years have really rolled by and suddenly, here I am, a crotchety old woman visiting you here in New Zealand.'

'Oh Grandma,' Nicole replied. 'That is one thing you aren't.' She smiled, placed the two cloth covered diaries inside the china cabinet and stood back.

'A place of honour for my wonderful ancestors,' she said in a quiet voice. 'I wonder what they would be like if they were alive now."

'Like you, Dear,' Cindy replied. 'Probably just like you.'

*

The steep hillside one valley back behind *The Blue Mist Motel* had a long zigzag track from the summit to the valley below. This was intersected by three streams that tumbled down through thick fern and bush until they reached a small river in the valley. This, in turn, flowed through bush and later farmland until it reached the west coast of New Zealand. It was hard to believe in this remote area, that a million and a quarter people lived a hundred kilometres away in Auckland. Nicole walked down one of these streams to check out a possible shortcut between two stages of the zigzag. The area she was exploring contained a tiny but magnificent waterfall that could be of interest to tourists returning from the larger falls the zigzag led back from.

Crystal clear water tumbled over grey rocks worn smooth by countless years of friction, over the fall and into a deep pool four metres below. From there, the water swirled around, lost speed and bubbled on at a more sedate pace through the light green fern.

It was hot. Nicole slipped off her backpack, wriggled out of her jersey, hitched the pack on again and wiped her brow before stepping to the next rock. The descent became steep so she turned and let herself down backwards. One foot found an outcrop to support her weight and her fingers clasped a protruding tree root for support.

Wooden steps would need to be built in this area if tourists came through. Nicole let herself further down without worrying about the spray falling like continuous rain over her. She loved this country but knew it had to be respected. Often a beautiful sunny day at the motel could become dense fog up here within minutes when clouds descended.

She stopped and gazed at the view. The water here was a swirling mass of white as it tumbled into the pool below. A massive eight-centimetre dragonfly hovered nearby and zipped up and away over the top of the falls. Nicole turned and chuckled at two cheeky fantails, native New

Zealand birds, who twittered around looking for minute insects to eat. These tiny birds, the size of a sparrow, seemed completely undisturbed by her presence. In fact, they flew along near her as she began her final descent to the base of the fall.

Beneath the crashing water at the base, the deep pond filled a canyon between two cliffs. Nicole inspected the area and found that by stepping onto stones just beneath the surface, she could make her way along the edge of the pool to a shallow section ten metres downstream. It was slippery but the calm water at the edge only rose to her ankles. This was another area that would need a bridge or platform if tourists visited the site. Perhaps she could convince the District Council it was a viable track to build and maintain as an alternative to the longer one already under their care.

Nicole moved around the pool to where the canyon walls widened and the trees and ferns came down to the water's edge. Though still relatively steep, the going was now easier and would soon rejoin the main track. She glanced at her watch. It was four fifteen so there were a couple of hours of daylight left. Once she met the main track, the journey home would take less than an hour.

When she came to another small length of rapids tumbling down through a series of rocks she decided to make a short leap to a dry rectangular rock sticking out of the middle of the water.

*

It did not, though, turn out as she anticipated. The rock she landed on was unstable. When her foot came down, the rock moved and she was pitched her forward. The next few seconds played through her mind like a movie going in slow motion but she was powerless to stop herself. Rocks rushed up at her and she landed on her side. Unfortunately, her body still moved and the momentum carried her forward down the rocky slope. She gasped and shoved her right leg out in a vain attempt to break her fall. It slipped into a gap while the rest of her body continued forward.

Nicole heard a sharp crack and agony shot through her leg like a red-hot poker. She landed in a pool of water at the base of the rapids. The water cushioned her fall but saturated her. The backpack added insult to injury by propelling forward and crashing into the base of her head.

'Oh, shit!' she uttered and glanced down.

The bottom half of her leg just sort of flopped there at a ridiculous angle as bolts of excruciating pain shot through her body. She blinked tears and attempted to hobble to a standing position but collapsed down into the stream. Purple blotches blurred her vision and only with sheer determination did she managed to swing around on her good leg and collapse back on a curved rock just above water level.

'Bloody hell!' She shut her eyes and attempted to drive the agony from her mind. Perspiration rolled down her face and her hands trembled as shock set in.

Finally though, she used her arms to guide the broken leg around over a gap in the rock so it dangled down free of pressure. She lay gasping for breath before her vision cleared and she could form rational thoughts again. The backpack was still with her and in it was her cellphone brought for an emergency such as this.

It took another five minutes on manoeuvres before Nicole edged the phone out from the bottom of the backpack. It would be at the bottom! She pressed the preset number for home.

'Hello Grandma,' she gasped. 'I'm in trouble and need help...'

*

Cindy listened to her granddaughter intently and was about to ask a question when, without even a buzz, the line went dead.

'Damn!' she retorted and waited for Nicole to call back but nothing happened. Cindy put her reading glasses on and peered at the wall behind the telephone where the cellphone number was written. She punched it in but only heard ominous no connection beeps. She frowned and tried again. Something must have happened to Nicole's cellphone for nothing came through.

In spite of her age Cindy almost set off up the track herself but realised this was futile. Even if she found Nicole she would not have the strength to help her out. She cursed her old age and rang Triple One, the police emergency number in New Zealand. It was answered quite promptly and a calm voice assured her a rescue helicopter would be dispatched from Hamilton as soon as possible. Nicole had had the forethought to leave a map and details of her journey on the table so Cindy gave an accurate description of where her granddaughter would be.

Afterwards she rushed out to try to find Whetu or Gina but muttered in disgust when she remembered they were both away for the afternoon and weren't due back until evening. She walked down the drive looking for somebody who could help. However, the grounds were empty. It was late in the season and the few people booked for the night had not arrived. Cindy was about to ring a neighbour when she saw a movement in the far corner of the camping area. She peered beyond an ancient truck made into a motor home and saw a man's head.

'Hello there!' she cried and almost ran towards the man.

He was sitting on a small campstool behind an artist's easel. When Cindy approached, he stood and walked towards her.

'Can I help?' he said in a quiet cultured voice that seemed a complete contrast to his old clothes and scruffy beard. It had a calming affect on Cindy. 'You're the manageress aren't you?'

'My granddaughter is,' panted Cindy and explained what had happened. 'I have a map,' she said and handed Nicole's map to him. 'Keep it. I made a photocopy.'

'That's good thinking,' the man replied. A slow grin spread across his face. 'I'm John Leamy. What else did the police say?'

'Only that a rescue helicopter is coming,' Cindy repeated.

John stared up the valley. 'That fog is already covering the summit,' he said. 'Within ten minutes the whole upper valley will be in fog.' His eyes found Cindy's. 'I was waiting to draw it in my picture. Look Mrs. Jervis, I'll head up there and you wait for the 'copter. If they can't get closer it'll probably land here and the emergency crew will continue by foot. Okay?'

'Yes,' Cindy replied. 'Thank you. My God, I thought there was nobody around.'

John squeezed Cindy's arm and smiled. 'Don't worry. I'm sure your granddaughter is in no immediate danger. I have a reasonably good knowledge of the track and the streams.' He glanced at the map. 'I'll probably be quicker if I climb up from the bottom here.' He pointed a finger at the map.

*

Within two minutes John had packed some essentials in a backpack and, accompanied by a black Labrador dog, set off along the track that followed the river back up the valley. He could only remember Nicole as an attractive woman in her mid twenties who'd welcomed him to the camping ground five days earlier and had past the time of day with him a couple of times since.

'Come on, Jenny,' he said to his dog who followed him with her soft eyes. 'You can be a great help, I reckon.'

*

Back at the stream, Nicole had managed to manoeuvre herself into a sheltered alcove and pull her jacket on. There was no chance of her continuing, as the terrain was too stony and even the slightest jarring sent agonising pain through her whole body. She leaned back against the wall and tried, for the umpteenth time to coach life out of the cellphone. The annoying thing was that she didn't really know how much of the original message Grandma had heard. She was talking and had not realised the instrument's light had gone off. It was frustrating.

'Bugger!' she gasped and glanced at her watch. There was less than an hour to sunset and already the daylight had dimmed and the narrow strip of sky above the foliage overhead had turned from blue to white. Nicole leaned back, made herself as comfortable as possible and settled for a long wait. She shivered and cursed her wet clothes. The thought of spending the night was not at all comforting. It could get cold at night this late in the season and already misty rain was falling. She wriggled further back in the tiny alcove and found it became drier where a rocky outcrop sheltered her from the drizzle.

She must have dozed off for she suddenly jerked awake. The green foliage had turned to grey while the white water crashing through the rapids appeared almost fluorescent against the now black rocks. Moths had begun to fly and a distance a morepork began its mournful hoot.

Nicole lifted her buttocks to relieve cramped muscles but bumped her damaged leg in the process and gasped at the pain. It was cold and her whole body started shivering. Wet soggy clothes and jacket seemed to keep her cold rather than otherwise and beyond her tiny dry area, the misty rain was falling straight down. The clatter of the stream drowned out all other noises except for the distant bark of a dog.

Nicole listened. Yes, there was a bark of a dog.

'Hello!' she yelled. 'Is anybody there?'

Nobody answered. Nicole grimaced and was about to commit herself to spending the night where she was when she heard a rustle upstream. She cried out again and a distinct bark replied. There were more crashes of twigs and branches and now an ongoing dog's yelps.

Suddenly, there was a crash above her and a dog came bounding down the rocks beside the rapids. It was a very wet black Labrador who jumped across the stream in three bounds then proceeded to shake herself dry all over Nicole.

But Nicole didn't care. 'Hello Girl,' she said. 'What are you doing here?'

The dog looked at her and stood panting with her tongue out the side of an almost grinning mouth.

'I know you,' Nicole continued. 'You're the doggie from the camper van.'

She remembered, as usually they didn't allow dogs with campers but the man who'd booked in assured them his dog was well trained and wouldn't hurt or annoy anybody. This proved correct. The dog sat down beside Nicole as if she knew something was wrong and placed her head on her front paws for a few moments before standing up and cocking her ears.

'Is anyone there?' Nicole yelled and smiled when a male voice replied.

A few moments later torchlight shone above and a bearded face appeared. 'I found you at last, Miss Tucker,' a deep voice called out.

The man Nicole recognised as their camper, climbed down the side of the rapids and leaped across stepping-stones until he was beside her. 'John's the name,' he said.

'Nicole,' she replied. 'My God, am I glad to see you, John. Like an idiot, I broke my leg and then the cellphone packed up...' She looked at the new arrival thankfully.

'Yes,' he rumbled on in a slow voice. 'Your grandmother told me of your trouble.'

He opened his backpack and took out a thermos. 'Hot tea. That's all I had time to make. It's got milk and sugar added. I hope you like it.' He poured some in the metal mug that formed the top to the thermos and handed it to Nicole.

'Thank you.' She shivered. 'I'm freezing.' She sipped the hot sweet liquid and felt it warm her throat and body while John took more objects out of his pack.

'Get that wet jacket off and put this on.' He handed Nicole a massive tartan bush shirt and glanced away as she took her wet blouse off too and slipped into the warm gear. Her shivering stopped, she smiled and sipped the tea.

'How did you find me?' she asked.

'The map your grandmother gave me had the wrong stream marked,' John replied. 'Jenny and myself walked right up the one on the map until we came back to the track near the top. It was getting dark and I was going to give up and return when we came to this second stream and my dog took off down it yelping her head off. She's the one who found you.'

'Why, thank you Jenny,' Nicole said. She rubbed the dog's ears while Jenny frantically wagged her tail.

'I think we're stuck here for the night,' John commented after he'd examined Nicole's leg in the light of his torch. 'There's something else I have for you.'

He undid his backpack and unrolled a heavy waterproof sleeping bag that he unzipped and placed beside her. 'Now if you can move onto it and lie back I'll re-zip it and you'll soon get warm.'

'But what about yourself?' she replied.

John smiled. 'I'm not soaking wet with a broken leg,' he replied. 'The last thing you need at the moment is to get a dose of hypothermia...'

Nicole noted the empathy in his eyes and smiled in return. With his support, she moved onto the open sleeping bag which John zipped up so only her arms, shoulders and head were poking out.

'Thanks,' she whispered and leaned back with her head against the stone wall. She reached out and put an arm around Jenny who crouched beside the sleeping bag and looked set to stay there for the duration.

'I think you have found a friend,' John said. 'More tea?'

'No, I'm fine thanks,' Nicole replied.

John grunted, put the thermos to his lips and gulped down the last few mouthfuls of hot tea before stepping forward and rinsing the flask in the stream. 'You say the cellphone doesn't work?' he asked.

Nicole shook her head. 'It just stopped mid sentence. Whether it's the batteries or water inside I don't know.'

'I'll have a peep,' John replied. He placed his torch on a flat piece of the rock with the beam pointing upwards and opened the back of the instrument. A small amount of water poured out. 'Probably a short circuit,' he muttered almost to himself and took a handkerchief from his pocket. He dabbed the circuit board gently, took out the battery and fiddle around for ages before he gave a satisfied smile, reassembled everything and handed the instrument to Nicole.

She grinned when she realised it was working. 'I'll ring home,' she said. It only rang once before Cindy answered.

'Hi Grandma.' Nicole said. 'I'm okay. John and his dog found me...' She grinned at John and listened, answered a few questions and handed the phone to him. 'Grandma wants to talk to you,' she said.

He took the cellphone and talked for a few moments before handing up. 'Well, it's too foggy and dark for the helicopter now,' he said.

Nicole nodded. 'She told me a search party had just come back and a new search was planned at first light. Dear Grandma. She treats me like a little girl at times but her heart is in the right place. She sounded so thrilled to hear my voice.'

'You're lucky to have someone like her,' John replied with a slight trace of envy in his voice.

'Yes, I am,' Nicole replied. 'She's going back to Canada soon then there's only me.'

She sighed and stared down at the bubbling stream barely visible in the darkness. John leaned back against the cliff, flicked his eyes across her face but said nothing. For several moments the two remained quiet before he spoke again.

'I love the bush,' he murmured. 'Out here the worries of the world seem so trivial. It seems to put things in perspective, somehow.'

'Me too,' Nicole replied. Her body inside the sleeping bag had generated enough heat to make her quite comfortable so, as long as she didn't bump or try to move her damaged leg she could relax. 'Tell me. Why are you here?' She watched her companion's face change to a scowl. 'I'm sorry. I didn't mean to pry.'

'No,' John whispered. 'That's okay. I just needed time out from everything and everybody.' He scratched Jenny's ears and the Labrador glanced up and began to wag her tail. 'There's a song I used to listen to about old dogs being man's only loyal friend when you're down.' His voice trailed off.

Nicole studied her companion's face. The torchlight accentuated his beard, nose and heavy eyebrows but the far away look in his eyes made her feel sorry, somehow. John gave her the impression he was lonely rather than being a loaner as she had at first supposed. 'You haven't been by yourself for long, have you?' she prodded.

John shook his head and tucked his knees up between his arms. 'My wife, Claire, walked out on me. That was a year back,.' he said. He picked up a small pebble and looped it into the water. 'I guess it was my fault.' He stared into the darkness for a full minute before speaking. 'Anyhow, she had this affair with this other guy and got pregnant. I thought it was our child and was so thrilled as we have no children. Anyhow, one night we had a whopping row over some unimportant little thing and she confessed the child wasn't mine.'

'Oh, my God!'

'Yeah!' John shrugged. 'Anyhow, she left the next day and I haven't seen her since. I thought of contesting who the baby's father was but she pre-empt my arguments by getting the baby blood tested after it was born and, through her lawyer, sent me the details that proved I could not have fathered it.'

'The cow!' Nicole hissed. She turned her eyes back to her companion. 'Your wife makes my partner seem almost a saint....'

John just sort of blew out through his mouth and tossed another pebble into the stream and listened while Nicole told about Simon McDoyle walking out on her.

'Sounds typical,' John said when she'd finished 'It's all self nowadays and bugger anyone else.'

'So what happened to you next?' Nicole asked.

'I'm an art teacher in Auckland,' John said. 'Been there six years. I have a year's leave of absence and my job is held for me. At the moment I don't really want to go back. I'm just doing some painting and trying to work out where I'm going in life.'

'And why not?' Nicole said'

'Yeah, I guess,' John replied and gave a grin. 'I came to your camp intending to stay a couple of days and I've been here almost a week. There's some terrific scenery here and I sort of fell in love with the place.'

'I see,' replied Nicole and once again they both lapsed into silence.

John stood up, reached in his backpack, took out a battered lunch box and handed Nicole an apple. She smiled and munched into it without speaking. Somehow, John's story had saddened her. She glanced across at him sitting with his back against the cliff and wondered what sort of man he really was. So far, she was quite impressed but sitting here in the darkness with a bubbling stream tumbling by could make anyone seem great. She gave a tiny giggle and grinned when John looked across at her.

'Your leg okay?' he asked.

'Yes, as long as I don't put any pressure on it,' she replied. The intimate moment had been broken.

'I'd better turn the torch off,' John continued. There was a faint click and they plunged into darkness only punctuated by the stream and bush noises around.

Nicole leaned back and let her mind drift through the last few weeks, her grandmother's visit and news of the ancient legacy the lives of her ancestors and the motel without large mortgage overheads. Increasingly, though, her thoughts turned back to the man only a few metres away and his dog who had taken over a corner of her sleeping bag. She sighed and drifted asleep.

*

CHAPTER TWENTY-FIVE

Nicole's night was one of more and more agony. No sooner did she nod off to sleep when she'd bump her leg and jerk awake with pain so severe, tears would form in her eyes. It was as her whole body ached in sympathy with the broken limb. If it wasn't for her two companions she would have found the ordeal terrifying.

As it was, every time she awoke or lay there in a feverish state, John appeared to understand what she required. She woke once to find a small fire burning. He handed her a hot drink of tea and some painkillers. Another time he placed his rolled up coat behind her head and later he talked to her about every imaginable topic from current events to insect behaviour.

Later, Nicole woke to find the pain was almost gone, the fire was just a few glowing embers and John was snoring along from her. Even Jenny was fast asleep. With the man and the dog sharing the night with her, it seemed strangely peaceful with the stream chattering on and tiny mites flying above the faint glow of the rapids. Red eyes stared at her from high above and, after an initial fright, she relaxed. It was probably an opossum, one of the exotic animals that were now a pest in the New Zealand bush.

'Hello,' whispered John. 'Are you awake again?'

'I'm afraid so 'but those painkillers you gave me earlier seem to be working. As long as I don't try to move my leg, it's not too bad.'

'You're a brave young woman,' John continued and gave the embers a poke.

'I'm not that young,' Nicole chuckled. 'The years seem to be just rolling by.'

'It's worse after thirty,' John said.' I remember thinking one's life must be over by the time you get to that age but here I am, thirty two already...'

'That's not old.'

John laughed, 'Guess not...'

Their conversation continued until Nicole found her eyelids becoming heavy and she drifted asleep again.

Suddenly, it was light with whisks of mist covering the treetops. The cellphone rang and Jenny gave a surprised yelp.

'Hello Sweetheart,' Cindy's voice came through. 'The men here said you are not to try to move but should wait for the stretcher party. They'll be with you in about an hour.'

'Thanks Grandma,' Cindy replied. She chattered with her grandmother for a while and rang off.

'Time for breakfast,' John said and proceeded to take some bacon, eggs and a tiny frying pan from his backpack.

'For someone who only spent a couple of minutes getting ready, you are certainly well prepared,' Nicole said.

'I've taken lots of school outdoor education trips,' John replied. He tossed a little white cube on the fire embers. It immediately burst into flames. 'Fire starters,' he explained and added some wood to the fire. 'Usually the wood in the bush is too green to start burning until some heat is generated.'

'My God, you make me feel so ignorant,' Nicole replied. She wriggled into a sitting position and gasped in pain as her damaged leg scraped the rock. 'Thanks.'

John placed the frying pan on the fire and cracked open two eggs. They spat and sizzled when they hit the hot pan. A couple of rinds of bacon were added next and the smell was scrumptious. When he'd finished he glanced at Nicole.

'What for?' he asked quietly.

'Everything,' she replied. 'For coming in the first place, for giving me the sleeping bag, for having such a lovely dog and for talking through half the night with me.'

John nodded and used a spoon to splash some hot fat over the eggs. 'I enjoyed your company,' he replied. 'In fact, if it wasn't for your broken leg, I'd say it was one of the most fulfilling nights I've had in years.'

His eyes met hers and he smiled.

*

The journey out was easier than Nicole anticipated. Six people dressed in bright yellow coats arrived; she was strapped in a stretcher and carried out to the main track. There, a helicopter descended through the mist and fifteen minutes later it landed at Waikato Hospital in Hamilton, the city closest to her motel. Quiet voices talked to her, ceilings rushed by and she ended in a pale blue theatre gazing up at a shiny silver light. A man behind a surgical mask chatted away as he prepared a needle; her arm felt a prick and the world went blank.

She awoke to find herself in a hospital bed with her broken leg in plaster and placed in a counterweighted sling but best of all, there was no throbbing pain.

'Hello Sweetheart,' said that English Canadian voice she knew so well. 'I thought you were going to sleep through to the new year.'

Nicole turned her head and saw her grandmother sitting in a chair holding a book. 'Hi Grandma,' she smiled. 'Made a mess of myself, didn't I?'

'Possibly but I have a strange feeling some good is going to come out of it.'

Nicole frowned. 'How can a broken leg be good?' she asked.

'There's a man and a dog who drove me here who seems interested in sticking around.' She gave a tiny smile. 'Now, I wonder why.'

Nicole flushed, 'Grandma, don't you dare.'

'Dare what?'

This was getting nowhere but Nicole grinned when John walked in the ward and the conversation stopped. He coughed in embarrassment and stood at the end of her bed.

'How are you?' he said but before she could answer handed her a small parcel about the size of a slim chocolate box. 'I thought you might like this,' he muttered but avoided her eyes.

Nicole undid the wrapping and found a wooden picture frame. She pulled the frame out and turned it over. 'It's beautiful,' she gasped. 'Look Grandma.'

Cindy looked at the picture her Nicole was holding. It was a charcoal drawing of the motel and valley behind. Standing in front of the building was a woman in shorts and tank top with her hand against the veranda post and hair blowing in the wind. The face was smiling and easily recognisable. It could have been a photograph of herself.

'When did you do it?' Nicole's excited eyes turned to John.

'Oh, I had the scene drawn earlier,' John explained modestly. 'I just sketched you in, without the broken leg, of course.'

'Just sketched me in!' Nicole gasped. 'It's perfect. You've got real talent, John.' She held her arms up. 'Come here.'

John came and stood next to the bed. 'Closer,' Nicole said and when he was near she grabbed his head down and deposited a kiss on his whisker-covered cheek. 'Thank you,' she whispered.

John gave a grin, squeezed her arm and stepped back.

Cindy gave a tiny cough. 'See you later, Nicole,' she said and headed for the door. 'I've got a bit of business downtown.'

Nicole frowned then broke into a grin. Grandma was a crafty old lady. She turned back to the other visitor and suddenly burst into laughter. Poor John looked so self-conscious.

'Sit down and tell me about your art work,' she invited and waved to a chair. 'I think we talked about everything except that last night.'

John relaxed and deposited himself in the chair. He looked different somehow, sure he had a tidy shirt and walk shorts but there was something else.

'You trimmed your beard,' Nicole said. 'It does look nice.'

*

An hour later John walked out to the car park to find Cindy waiting by his camper van. 'Like it?' she said.

John screwed his nose up. 'What, Mrs. Jervis?' he asked.

'Oh, call me Cindy,' the elderly lady replied and walked behind the van. 'I picked it up in Hamilton. Took them a week to clear it. You'd think I had it filled with drugs or something.'

Sitting behind the van was vintage MG sports car. The chrome glistened and the black canopy looked brand new. John whistled in appreciation and examined the vehicle. It was in immaculate condition with genuine leather seats, a massive steering wheel and even running boards along the side.

'I though it would be better in New Zealand,' said Cindy. 'Being originally from England it is right hand drive. It's a 1932 model and has been in our family since new. I thought Nicole might like it.'

'It's great!' John exclaimed. 'But how did you get it here?'

'Drove it, of course,' retorted Cindy. 'I can't get used to driving on the left again after all these years but the traffic in Hamilton isn't too busy. I had it brought through from the ship in Auckland to the local customs. Like the number plate?'

John walked to the rear of the little car and glanced down. The personalised plate read 'N I 6 O L E'

'That's the closest I could get to Nicole's name.' Cindy grinned. 'I guess the 6 is close to a C. Think she'll like it?'

'She'll love it, Cindy,' he said. 'If she doesn't, you can always sell it to me.'

'Yes, I just might do that,' the elderly lady replied.

*

'Grandma,' yelled Nicole later that day when, equipped with a plastered leg and crutches she was released from hospital. 'It can't be!'

'Yes,' Cindy chortled. 'Your great grandparent's MG, Sweetheart. John hopes you won't like it.'

Nicole swung around and glared at the man pushing the hospital wheelchair she was sitting in but laughed when John explained. 'Sorry to disappoint you John,' she chuckled, 'but I love it.' Her eyes suddenly saw the front of the vehicle. 'Oh Grandma, the number plate!'

Cindy smiled. 'I had a new canopy made just last year and the motor was reconditioned three years back. By today's standards it's a slow little car but back in the war with petrol off the black market Arthur and I...' She stopped. 'Oh I'm beginning to ramble on, aren't I?'

'No Grandma,' Nicole interrupted, 'I want to hear everything about what you did in the car.'

'I can't tell you everything,' Cindy replied and gave John a wink. 'I wasn't a prim and proper old lady all my life, you know.'

'Grandma!' Cindy said. She stood up from the wheelchair and placed her arms, crutches and all, around her grandmother. 'I love you, Grandma,' she said and kissed Cindy on the cheek.

'Well, do you want to go for a spin?' Cindy asked. 'John can drive. I'll squeeze in the back. I'm sure it won't matter if we leave his camper van here for a while.'

*

A few moments later the vintage MG roared out of the hospital grounds and headed west towards home. The bearded driver and petite woman in the front passenger's seat looked just the part as they zoomed along the four-lane throughway past fast food restaurants. The elderly lady behind who urged them on, though, somehow looked more excited than the pair in the front.

'How about stopping at McDonald's or Burger King for a burger,' she shouted in John's ear. 'I'll shout.'

'Okay, Cindy,' John said. He changed down and turned into the next restaurant and acknowledged a wave from a couple of teenage girls. The tiny car with skinny wheels squeezed in between the modern streamlined Toyotas and Fords but didn't look out of place at all.

'Like vintage wine,' John remarked as he unwound himself from the driver's seat and walked around to help a struggling Nicole out her side. When he took her hand she gave it a squeeze and glanced fondly into his eyes.

*

Misty rain made *The Blue Mist Motel* an appropriate name when John made his way up to the office the next morning and found Gina muttering to Nicole behind the counter.

'Trouble?' he asked as he shut the blustery wind out the door.

Nicole looked up and smiled. 'Oh, just the usual stuff,' she replied. 'One of the units was left in a terrible state last night.' She shrugged. 'Usually I help Gina and Whetu with the cleaning but with my leg...

Grandma's offered to help but there's a bit of heavy work involved, you know, moving beds and so forth.'

'I'll help,' John replied.

'Will you?' Nicole asked with a look of relief in her eyes, 'but you're a guest.'

'...With lots of free time,' John interrupted. He turned to Gina. 'Point me in the right direction Gina.'

Before Nicole could protest, the Maori lady grinned and headed out with John following.

A voice behind made Nicole jump in fright. 'He's keen on you, Sweetheart,' Cindy said.

'Oh Grandma,' she replied. 'John's just a pleasant chap who would help anyone.'

'So he drew a picture of you and spent a whole day running around Hamilton while you were in hospital.' Cindy fixed Nicole with her blue eyes. 'Personally, I think he'd be good for you, Nicole. Reminds me of Arthur. Did I tell you we met in a library?'

'You did, Grandma.' Nicole swung her crutches out and made her way through to the kitchen. She felt an unfamiliar exhilaration inside; even with Simon in their earlier romantic days she could not remember the feeling, a sort of tingle of anticipation. 'Stupid woman!' she snapped to herself and grabbed some administration folders she had to check through.

*

John returned to the office, removed his oilskin coat and, on Nicole's invitation walked through to the kitchen. He reached for a cup of coffee waiting for him. 'What a mess,' he said. 'I reckon we should send them a bill for damages. Whetu replaced some of the carpet but a whole new section of wallpaper will need to be replaced. I washed it down the best I could.'

'Those sort never pay up,' Nicole said. 'All we do is blacklist them and refuse them accommodation if they ever come back. That's where the computers good. We also contact the other motels in our chain and tell them. There's quite a large data bank of undesirables.'

'But they looked okay,' John said. 'You know, new car and a couple of kids. I remember the woman looked quite snobby.'

'Often they're the worst,' Nicole added. 'The scruffy looking ones in a beat up car usually leave the units in perfect condition.' She stood and was about to manipulate herself around to take the breakfast dishes to the sink when John intercepted.

'Sit down,' he said. 'They told you at the hospital not to do much on the leg.'

Nicole smiled. 'But I can't...'

John stared at her and placed a finger on her lips. Their eyes met and he moved his hands down to her waist. She stood looking up at him and realised he was tall and smelt so masculine. She placed her crutches forward but found John in the way. His arms went around her back and he bent down.

Nicole ran a tongue over her lips. They tingled and herself reacting to the man in front of her. His eyes were a hazel colour and filled with compassion. Very tenderly he pulled her close into him. Her breasts rubbed against his chest and she turned her head up to find herself in a tiny embrace as he kissed her softly on the lips.

John flushed and stepped back a little. 'Sorry,' he muttered. 'I shouldn't have been so presumptuous.'

'It's okay,' said Nicole and gave him a light kiss back. 'Next time ask. Okay?'

John smiled. 'I'll remember,' he said and pulled her in close again so her head was tucked under his chin. They just clung together for a couple of precious moments before John squeezed her arms and again stood back. 'I was going to help with the dishes,' he stuttered in embarrassment.

'You were, weren't you?' Nicole replied. 'The dishwasher is full so I usually wash the extra ones by hand.'

She made her way to the sink and listened to the rain rattling against the windows. The sound seemed so friendly. She stared up at John who had turned on the sink taps, and placed one crutch aside so she could reach out to squeeze his hand.

'John,' she whispered. 'I changed my mind.'

'What about?' he answered with a curious expression across his eyes.

'You don't need to ask.' Her voice trembled. 'I liked what you did.'

John's whole face sort of lit up in a huge grin. He grabbed the plastic bottle of soap and squeezed far too much liquid in the sink water and began to whistle a little tune.

'You know,' he said as he gazed at the rain outside, 'When my wife left, I blamed all women. Somehow they all seemed self-centred and arrogant.' He turned to Nicole. 'But I was wrong. Do you know what I'm trying to say?'

'No,' Nicole teased as she wiped a dinner plate and smiled as John's arm went around her shoulder.

*

Over the next month Nicole and John just sort of drifted together and it seemed quite natural that his camper van remained in the grounds and he helped Whetu and Gina around the motel. He flatly refused any wages and only grudgingly accepted free rental for his van.

Every day Nicole found John beside her, working, chatting, and walking. Also he drove the vintage MG while she sat in the passenger's seat with a satisfied smirk on her face. Their petting also became more serious but John was the perfect gentleman and always stopped before full intimacy took place. This was a complete contrast to Nicole's previous partner who wanted everything almost from the first time they'd met. It was only when she took the initiative one dark rainy night that their lovemaking reached its natural climax, and it was love, Nicole was sure.

*

A week later when Cindy received a telephone call from Grace in Canada and declared she'd better head home.

'After all,' she said in reply to Nicole's protests. 'I've put it off twice. Poor old Grace's quite weak now and is distressed about something to do with her family. She's got so many grandchildren and in-laws; I guess it's only to be expected. Anyhow you've got John now, haven't you?'

'Yes, but that doesn't mean I want you to go.'

'Of course not,' Cindy said. 'I'll tell you one thing, though.'

'And what's that?'

'Invite John into the house with you. The poor man will freeze in that motor home if he stays there any longer with winter coming on.'

'Grandma!' Nicole said in mock horror. She pouted. 'Come to think of that, I just might do it.'

'And I hope you've taking precautions, Nicole,' the elderly lady warned with a stern expression. 'There's no excuse for unwanted pregnancies nowadays.'

'Yes Grandma,' Nicole said and changed back to their original topic. 'Remember this is your home now, too. Don't you forget it.'

'Thank you Sweetheart,' Cindy's eyes suddenly clouded over. 'I'm so glad I came to New Zealand and really got to know you. I grew up in England then moved to Canada and now, here in New Zealand I feel as much at home as anywhere. I guess it's people that are important, no matter where you are.'

Nicole reached forward and hugged the elderly lady who was her grandmother and nodded. It was going to be strange without her around.

*

Four days later Nicole and John drove up to Auckland in Nicole's station wagon and saw Cindy off on the flight to Vancouver. In the terminal building, just after booking her luggage in Cindy excused herself from her granddaughter and took John aside. Nicole could see her talking quite passionately with him but with the babble of voices in the crowded terminal she could not hear a word that was said.

'What was that all about?' she asked after they kissed Cindy good-bye and watched her go through the departure doors.

John grinned and gave her a hug. 'Don't worry your pretty little head about it.' He kissed her on the lips but refused to say any more.

'Meanie.' Nicole pouted but no matter how much she pleaded with him on the way home, John refused to divulge what was said.

'It was nothing bad,' was all he'd admit as they drove into the motel grounds. It was evening, the motel looked full and Gina gave them a thumbs up through the office as they parked their car next to the MG and walked inside.

The next day John parked his camper van in the security area, a fenced in enclosure where campers could be left over the off-season, and moved his few possessions into the house. Earlier, Nicole had rearranged her bedroom; thrown out everything that even vaguely reminded her of her previous partner and placed the picture John had given her in hospital in a prominent space across from the bed.

She'd also insisted that one condition of their new arrangement was that he went on the motel payroll. He agreed but only after a great deal of haggling and a little background persuasion from Gina. She told him not to be pig headed, he was bloody lucky to have a girl like Nicole and if he didn't treat her with respect he'd have her to answer to.

'That sounds like Gina,' Nicole said when John told her, 'She'd do it too. Perhaps you'd better slip away now, why you have the chance.'

'No,' John said and grabbed her in a massive bear hug and blew a floppy kiss on her neck. 'I think I'll stick around for a while. Jenny needs a good home.'

Nicole glanced at the Labrador sitting patiently at their feet and reached down to pat the dog's ears. 'Yes,' she sighed. 'Without Jenny we may not have even got to know each other.'

'True,' John answered. 'I was going to move out that next day, you know.'

Nicole reached up, grabbed his head and kissed him with a passion that left them both breathless. Meanwhile, Jenny gazed up with her big soft eyes and wagged her tail as if she approved of the new arrangement.

'Come here, dog,' shouted Gina from the kitchen. 'I've got a bone for ya and don't go drinking the saucer of milk. That's for Biscuit.'

*

CHAPTER TWENTY-SIX

After another torrid bout of sex where clothes, sheets, blankets and even pillows lay strewn over the floor of Nicole's bedroom, the two lovers lay gasping from exhilaration and exhaustion on the bare mattress. It was really a celebration, for that afternoon Nicole had her cast removed for the final time and her leg, though a little stiff, functioned well. With a session of physiotherapy, the doctor promised it would return to normal within a few weeks.

'My God,' she gasped as she found her shortie pyjamas and slid back into them while John remade the bed. 'I now know what Amanda felt like.'

'Amanda!' queried John. 'Who's she? Have I met her?'

Nicole crawled in the blankets and cuddled into her partner. 'It would be a bit hard,' she said and plunked a kiss on his lips. 'Amanda is Grandma's grandma. She's been dead for thirty years.'

'Then why?' John was curious.

Nicole grinned. 'Great Great Grandma Amanda wrote a diary, a very explicit diary. She was some lady. Want to see it?'

'Sure,' replied John.

He waited while Nicole slipped out of the room and returned with the two ancient diaries in her arms. 'Great Grandma wrote one too,' she said and lay down on the bed. She thumbed through Amanda's diary until she found the section about Capilano Canyon and showed it to John.

He switched on the bedside lamp and for several moments there was silence as he read the faded curly writing.

'Hell,' he said with a grin. 'She was some dynamic woman. You know, in those days women were told sex was something one endured from their husbands and advice was given on how to dissuade the male from performing the act too often.'

'How do you know?' Nicole giggled and sat up with her arms around her knees.

'Well, I took history at school as well as art and did a paper for my degree on the Victorian Era. They were so prim and proper yet quite hypocritical really. Just about every man of importance had a mistress.' He fingered through the diary and read other pieces before l glancing back at Nicole. 'Can I borrow it to read?' he asked.

'Sure,' Nicole said. 'Some parts are a bit hard to follow and that curly writing becomes illegible at times but she comes alive in there, John. You know, after I read some bits I felt as if I could grab the cellphone and ring her up.' She shrugged. 'Grandma gave the diaries to me. Often when I read them I thought they were written by her, actually, not her grandmother. The other one by Dorothy is good reading, too. She got killed in World War Two.'

*

Over the next couple of weeks John could be seen reading the diaries whenever he had a spare moment. Often he'd grin, refer parts to Nicole and at times even jot notes in a little notebook he always seemed to have in a pocket.

'I see where you got your energy from,' he said one evening after putting Dorothy's diary down.

Nicole glared at him. 'What do you mean, John?' she retorted and grabbed the offending document out of his hand so she could read it.

After a moment she handed it back with a grin. 'Trust you to find the sexy bits,' she added with a grunt. 'No wonder you can't keep you hands off me every night.'

'Me!' exclaimed John and deposited a smack on her bottom. Nicole gave a scream and ran out the room with the eager man in hot pursuit. He caught her and carried her kicking and protesting into the bathroom where he turned on the cold shower and held her head under for a few seconds.

'You rotter!' shrieked Nicole.

She managed to stand up with water streaming from her saturated hair. She cupped a handful of liquid from under the shower and flicked it at the laughing man. He grabbed her; swung her around and suddenly they were kissing passionately. The diary was forgotten. This was real life!

Their frolic was interrupted by the telephone ringing. Nicole grinned, ran and answered it.

'Hello, *Blue Mist Motel*,' she said and slapped John's hand when he attempted to tickle her.

'Hello Sweetheart, Grandma here. It's the middle of the night here but I have to talk to you.'

'Yes, Grandma,' Nicole said and waved for John to listen. She pressed the speaker button so her grandmother's voice could be heard.

'It's your legacy that's due out in the new year, Sweetheart. There's a hitch. That's why poor Grace was so distressed. '

Nicole rolled her eyes at John. 'What is it Grandma?'

'Well,' said Cindy with her voice loud and clear throughout the room. 'There is a discrepancy in the last will and testament of Dorothy O'Donnell. In those days everything was copied manually and one paragraph is slightly different in the second copy.'

'So what?' Nicole knew by the tone that her grandmother was worried.

'It makes a big difference, Sweetheart. Grace has a granddaughter who is filing a lawsuit claiming she should inherit the legacy. It makes me mad,' Cindy retorted. 'Betty has pots of money but is a spoilt little brat.' She paused. 'Always was, even when she was a child.'

'But how can she Grandma?'

'The part of the legacy telling who inherits is open for inspection but the rest is sealed to the family until after New Year's Day in 2007. My lawyer showed me the differences between two paragraphs in the text.'

Nicole frowned and continued to listen.

'I'll read you the two extracts,' Cindy said and a rustle of paper could be heard. 'The first said, "This inheritance shall be bequeathed to my daughter's eldest daughter's great great grand daughter; that being the eldest adult female descendant to the fifth generation (being the age of twenty one or over) on 1 January the year 2007...." '

'Okay,' Nicole said.

'But the second part at the end of the will said, "This inheritance bequeathed to my eldest granddaughter's eldest child's great grand daughter blar, blar... See the difference?'

'Not really,' Nicole replied and gave John a shrug.

'The word "child" can be interpreted as either a male or female, in other words Timmy's granddaughter who happens to be this Betty.'

'Oh I see but what about everything else in the legacy?'

'Only that one paragraph is different,' Cindy replied. 'Both pages were initialled at the bottom of the page and signed by Dorothy O'Donnell at the end. Anyhow, on that basis, Betty Hadfield is contesting the will down in Bellingham, Washington. She's got some hotshot lawyer and if it isn't defended, she'll win for sure.'

'But what can I do, Grandma?'

'Come out and defend it,' Cindy said very definitely. 'The court case is in October. I want you to come and stick up for your rights.'

Nicole screwed her nose up. 'But I don't really care, Grandma.'

'It's the principle,' Cindy snapped. 'Surely you can see that, Nicole?'

Nicole tried to argue her way out of making a commitment but her grandmother was adamant. 'Tell her, John,' she retorted. 'I know you're there.'

John spoke for the first time. 'I think the idea of the female line would mean it is your granddaughter who inherits,' he said. 'I'm no lawyer though and American courts are different than ours. I think Nicole should stick up for her rights.'

'Good,' snapped Cindy. 'Then come over. You too, John. I'll book you on the new fangled computer. You know, you don't even need tickets nowadays, just a number.   You can both stay with me. Make up for all the time I lived off you.'

'We can't expect that,' Nicole protested.

'Oh you can be obstinate at times, Nicole. Tell her John. Bye...' The line went dead.

'Grandma has spoken,' John said when Nicole glared at the telephone.

'She called me obstinate!'

'She has a point, though' John said.

'But to pay for our airfares. I'll cost two or three thousand dollars.'

'She wants to do it and, from what you said, she can afford it so let her.'

Nicole sighed. 'But the motel?'

'I doubt if October is a busy time. Gina and Whetu can easily manage. If you didn't go I reckon it would break your grandmother's heart.'

'Well,' said Nicole reluctantly, 'Only if you come too, John.'

John took Nicole's hands and gazed into her serious eyes. 'With you, Nicole, I'd go anywhere, even Bellingham in Washington State, U.S.A.' He kissed her, 'Cheer up. Even if we lose we'll be no worse off.'

'Except for an exorbitant lawyer's bill,' Nicole warned. 'Americans spend money like water on law suits and Grandma already said this Betty has plenty of it.'

'So you're just going to let this woman get away with it?'

'No, but...'

'You're just too nice,' John praised. 'In this world the nice people get walked over. '

He held Nicole in his arms and she snuggled in close. Her mind was a whirl of indecision. She glanced up. 'I'm glad I've got you, John,' she whispered. 'I really couldn't care a less about this stupid legacy but poor Grandma did sound upset.'

She bit on her bottom lip and appeared to come to a decision. Without saying any more she walked over to the telephone, found a number where it was written in the front of the telephone book and punched in Cindy's Vancouver number.

'Hello Grandma,' she said mere seconds later. 'Nicole here. John and I decided to accept your kind offer...'

*

Mid morning drizzle covered the landscape when the cab dropped Nicole and John off at the 1920s vintage house in New Westminster, a city that was part of Metropolitan Vancouver.

'We'll be fine,' John said, paid and tipped the driver with the unfamiliar Canadian money and picked the two bags off the pavement.

Nicole grinned and squinted through the rain at the skinny wooden house with a short path to the front door. 'Well, John, we're here. I hope Grandma gets as big a surprise as I did when she arrived at our place.'

It was September and three weeks before the pair were expected in Canada. However, once they'd made the decision to come they exchanged the tickets Cindy had sent for earlier ones.

'I'll take a case,' Nicole said and pulled one along on its tiny wheels as she walked up to the door and pressed a doorbell.

They waited for ages before a slight scrapping could be heard, the door opened. An elderly lady with white hair and square glasses peered out.

'Yes,' she said with a concerned look on her face.

Nicole glanced at John and the number beside the door. 'I'm sorry,' she apologised. 'We're looking for a Mrs. Cindy Jervis. Perhaps you could help and tell us where she lives.'

The old lady looked at Nicole and a slow smile spread over her face. 'You're Nicole, aren't you?' she said with a new warmth in her voice. 'Goodness, I should have recognised you with that Jervis nose. Come in! Come in! I'm Grace, Cindy's sister-in-law. We weren't expecting you until next month.'

'Grace?' Nicole said and shook the elderly lady's hand. 'Of course...' She gave John a grin and walked into the entrance hall. 'Where's Grandma?'

'Oh, she's in the kitchen,' Grace grinned and put her finger to her lips.

'Who was it, Grace?' Cindy's distinct voice came through the house.

'Someone making a collection,' Grace called back, wriggled her finger at the new arrivals and nodded up the corridor. 'She'll be thrilled,' she whispered.

Nicole and John sat the luggage down and tiptoed to an opened door behind Grace where the smell of cooking drifted through the air.

'I hope you didn't give them too much, Grace,' Cindy called out and Nicole saw her back in front of a long sink. A blender was buzzing and a tiny television blared away from a shelf above her.

Nicole tiptoed up until she was immediately behind her grandmother. She leaned forward and whispered, 'Pumpkin pie. You know we love pumpkin pie, Grandma.'

Cindy literally jumped several centimetres in the air in fright and swung around. 'My God, Nicole!' she gasped. 'Don't do that to me. I could have had a heart seizure. But how...'

"We decided to come early," Nicole said. "I hope you don't mind."

Cindy grabbed her granddaughter, then John and plastered them with kisses.

'You're both naughty,' she said a moment later as she wiped flour off her hands onto the flower patterned apron she wore. 'I'd have picked you up at the airport. We didn't expect you until next month... My God, you met Grace didn't you?' she flustered with her eyes filled with excitement.

'We thought we'd trick you,' John murmured.

Cindy just stared at them both and smiled. 'Well, you succeeded John. You know I just sent an email to you both this morning ...but you're both wet. Take off your coats and I'll show you your room.' Her eyes sparkled. 'You only need one room, don't you?' She reached up and switched the television off.

'Yes Grandma,' said Nicole. 'We only need one room.'

*

Chatting non-stop, Cindy led them up the narrow stairs to a large bright room at the front of the house. It smelt of new paint and varnish while brand new curtains, similar to ones Nicole had at home, bordered a tall window that overlooked the street. A brand new double bed and suite filled the room and one of John's sketches, given to Cindy when she left New Zealand, hung on the far wall. A computer sat on a desk in the corner.

'I refurbished it for you,' Cindy said modestly. 'Our old stuff needed replacing anyway. If you'd come last week the decorators would have still been here.'

Nicole just stared. 'It's beautiful, Grandma.' She placed an arm around John. 'It's just like home.'

Cindy nodded. 'I missed you both,' she whispered and once again hugged them before turning to Grace. 'Aren't they just how I told you?' she bragged.

'They are?' Grace replied with a tiny smile.

Nicole studied the elderly lady. Unlike her grandmother, Grace looked stooped and frail with wrinkled skin and a slight shake of a hand. Her eyes, though, were alive with a twinkle that lit up in reply to Nicole's gaze.

'Come on,' she said. 'The coffee percolator is on. I'm sure you're both famished.'

She toddled away and left the others. 'Grace lives with me now,' Cindy explained 'Her family wanted to put her in a home but I refused. With her granddaughter contesting the will and all that, I hope you don't mind.'

'Oh Grandma,' Nicole said. 'Of course not. It must be company for both of you.'

'Yes.' Cindy, sighed 'But not as good as having you two. By the way, there is your own bathroom across the hall. Freshen up and come downstairs when you're ready. You both must be exhausted after the plane journey.'

She also departed to leave Nicole and John alone. They stared at each other, grinned and slipped into each other's arms to kiss passionately. Nicole held her lover and surveyed the room. 'John,' she whispered. 'I never expected this, the new furniture, your picture, everything!'

'That's Cindy for you,' her partner replied. 'Expect the unexpected from her and you won't go wrong.'

'John,' Nicole said. 'Over a hundred years ago there was a Jack and Amanda in this very city. Doesn't it send a quiver up your back?'

John smiled. 'Yes,' he whispered and kissed her again, 'and I'm sure he loved Amanda just as I love you.'

Nicole smiled, took John's hand and walked over to the window. The rain pelted on the road below and several large cars swished by, all driving on the right, otherwise it could easily have been home.

'Coffee's on.' Cindy's voice drifted up the stairs. Yes, it was just like home.

*

Over the next few days Cindy and Grace too, delighted the New Zealand visitors with trips to the massive shopping malls and tourist attractions around Vancouver. Cindy whipped around in her brand new cherry red Toyota Camry at speeds which amazed Nicole and John as she accelerated onto freeways or weaved through bumper to bumper downtown traffic to find massive parking buildings to park in.

Of real interest to Nicole was Gastown; an area restored to its former glory with renovated period shops and cobblestone pavements. She almost expected to find Amanda's bookshop. It wasn't there, of course, but Cindy showed her where she thought it had been. The building had long since been replaced by a high rise of glass and concrete. Another delight was a trip to North Vancouver and the visit to Capilano Canyon. The swing bridge, a newer version of the one Amanda and Samuel visited, still spanned the canyon. Nicole shivered and grasped John's hand as they stared down at the dizzy depths below.

'My God!' she whispered. 'This makes the diary become even more alive. Amanda described it perfectly and that was a century ago.'

'I know,' Cindy replied in a hushed voice. 'Every time I come here I think of my grandmother and imagine her and Samuel. I'd never have had the nerve...' Her voice trailed off to be replaced by a faint grin before she turned back to Nicole. 'Would you like to see her grave, Sweetheart?'

Nicole glanced at her grandmother and nodded. She wasn't into visiting cemeteries herself but it was obviously important to her grandmother. Later that day they visited the cemetery and Cindy led Nicole and John straight to her ancestor's grave. Amanda and Samuel shared a double plot while a few metres away were the graves of Arthur and Timmy. In an even older cemetery closer to town, Cindy showed the pair Jack William's grave. Amongst the dilapidated and uncared-for sites around, his was shining and well maintained.

'I got it water blasted and cleaned up a few years back,' Cindy said in a sombre tone when Nicole remarked on its condition. 'That's the least I can do.'

Nicole bent forward and could make out the faded black letters without difficulty. *'Jack Amos Williams, Dearly Beloved Husband of Amanda and Father of Dorothy, Killed as the Result of a Railway Accident. 26 November 1905. Aged 31 Years. Taken From us Early but Forever in Our Hearts.'*

Nicole squeezed John's hand and reread the epitaph. 'I feel as if I knew him,' she said quietly. Somehow, that grave in particular touched her emotions and the memory of the man in Amanda's diary.

*

Nicole's fuzzy feeling of excitement at being in a new country and discovering her heritage there was shattered the very next morning after breakfast. Cindy and John had left early to visit some computer software shops John was interested in. It was another drizzly morning Vancouver was famous for and Nicole had decided to relax from the hassle and tussle since their arrival and spend the day with Grace.

The elderly lady's body had faded away but her mind was still crisp and alert. When Nicole got her talking about her life, it proved to be every bit as full and interesting as Cindy's.

'You know.' Grace said as she poured some milk over a bowl of breakfast food. 'You're so easy to talk to,' She glanced at her grand niece. 'Poor Cindy was devastated when her parents were killed and that trip across the Atlantic...' She gave a tiny smile. 'I was smitten on the navigator, you know! The poor man was killed when that German fighter tried to shoot us down. Here in Canada, Cindy's grandmother took me in and treated me like a daughter. I just sort of stayed with them and met Timmy when he came home in forty-five. God, he was a bag of bones. I felt so sorry for him.' She grinned. 'I was a bit of a flirt in those days, Nicole. Would you believe it?'

'And why not?' Nicole replied, 'After all you'd gone through.'

It was hard to imagine this little old lady was the Grace who worked with Cindy on that far off farm over sixty years ago.

*

'Has Mother been relating all those old stories again?' interrupted a loud stranger's voice that made Nicole jump in fright.

She turned to see a middle-aged woman standing by the door. For a second her heart raced and colour drained from her face. In that very first glance the woman looked like her mother standing there. The vision faded, though, when Nicole realised that though the visitor's facial features and hairstyle were similar, the woman was too short and dumpy to be her mother.

'Hello Dear,' Grace said in a neutral tone, 'Meet Nicole Tucker.' Her eyes shifted back to Nicole. 'This is Margaret, my daughter.' She blinked and added. 'Betty's mother.'

'Oh yes, Cindy's granddaughter,' Margaret said and held her hand out to shake. Unlike everyone else Nicole had met in Canada, there was no warmth in the greeting. The woman's eyes, indeed, looked quite hostile. She immediately turned away from Nicole and addressed Grace.

'Well, come on, Mother. Aren't you ready?'

Grace gave a wee quiver and Nicole noticed almost fear in the old lady's eyes. 'I'm sorry, Dear. I forgot. With Nicole here and all that...' Her voice trailed off.

'You know it's time to visit the hospital for your check up,' the woman said coldly. 'We had enough trouble getting you in.' She turned to Nicole. 'Mother's memory is fading, you know.'

'I never noticed,' Nicole replied in a soft voice. 'Grace seems very alert to me.'

'Sure,' the other woman replied. 'On all that old stuff maybe but ask her to remember about last week.' She talked about her mother in the third person as if she wasn't there.

Nicole glared at the visitor. On second study, her relation looked over made-up and a smelt of powder and perfume. The long fingernails were painted a bright red and ostentatious rings were worn on almost every finger. The woman wore an expensive business suit, gloves and hat but the clothes looked outdated, almost of 1970s vintage.

'I'm just coming, Dear,' Grace muttered and stood up. 'You'll be all right alone won't you Nicole?'

'Of course she will,' snapped Margaret. 'She's a grown woman, you know?'

Grace sucked on her lips and gave Nicole such a strange look of despair she realised this elderly lady was frightened of her daughter. Those few minutes told Nicole a lot about the situation and she took an immediate dislike to this overbearing cold relation.

Grace stood up and carried her half finished bowl of breakfast food over towards the sink. Whether it was her unsteady steps or the shaking hand that did it, Nicole never knew but just as Grace approached the sink, she dropped the bowl. Milk and food splashed down her frock and all over the floor tiles while the bowl shattered into a dozen pieces with a sharp twang.

'You stupid old woman!' snapped Margaret with anger in her voice. 'Look what you've done.'

Nicole stood and rushed to Grace's aid. She put an arm around the slim shoulders and found the frail body trembling and the eyes blinking back tears. Saliva ran out the corner of the shaking mouth.

The young woman swung and glared at Margaret. 'Don't you dare talk to my grand aunt in that manner,' she stated in a quite but firm voice. 'Anybody can see it was an accident.'

'Oh, come off it,' Margaret responded loudly. 'Who do you think you are anyway, coming over here to grab your bit of the family inheritance?'

'That has nothing to do with this situation,' Nicole replied. 'I repeat. You can treat your mother with respect or leave my grandmother's house.'

'Why, you young upstart!' Grace's daughter glowered and her eyes became wild. 'How dare you come here and talk to me in this fashion.'

'You're a bossy bit, aren't you?' Nicole snapped back with her own temper coming to the fore.

She was about to escort Grace back to the chair and clean up the mess when the other woman stepped forward, purposely removed a glove and slapped Nicole over the cheek. Her head snapped back but she immediately reacted.

'Get out!' she hissed and slapped the woman back across the face every bit as hard as the one she had received.

Margaret staggered sideways and held her hand up to her cheek. She glared at Nicole with pure hatred and, without any warning launched herself, screaming, at her.

Nicole found herself on the floor under a neurotic, scratching, slapping woman over twenty kilograms heavier than herself. A ringed finger slashed across her face and sharp pain followed by that sticky feeling of blood appeared. But Margaret hasn't about to stop. She dragged Nicole to her feet and heaved her against the wall.

'You damn foreigner!' she hissed and was about to lash out again when Nicole retaliated.

She was fit and, by now, extremely angry. In one deft movement she leaped back so quickly the kitchen table crashed sideways. She reached out and grabbed a soft flabby arm in front of her. Her grip was tight and in a second move she was beside the woman with her hand gripping a fat wrist. Seconds later, it was forced up the woman's back and screams of agony filled the room.

'Your welcome has gone,' Nicole hissed and frog marched the bawling, frustrated but now overpowered woman to the door.

Nicole opened the door with her free hand and flung Margaret out, so severely, the older woman landed on the pavement. With her dishevelled hair and crumpled skirt now wet from the damp ground, the woman looked quite pathetic.

'I will take my grand aunt to the doctor,' Nicole said in an angry whisper and slapped the front door shut before Margaret could utter a word.

She stood behind the closed door with her lungs heaving and willed herself to settle down. Finally she placed a handkerchief against her bloody face and walked back through to the kitchen where Grace was wiping the milk off the floor.

'Your daughter is a bitch,' Nicole said softly and knelt down to help her companion.

The old lady put her hands on Nicole's face and kissed her on the cheek. 'Thank you, My Darling,' she said in a tender voice and a smile of gratitude. 'Nobody except Cindy has ever gone against Margaret before. I think my eldest daughter has met her match.'

For almost the first time since she had met her, Nicole noticed that Grace's hand was steady and the frail body stood tall.

'You're so much like Cindy,' Grace added. 'I wish my family was the same.'

'Come on,' said Nicole tenderly. 'I'll get cleaned up and take you to your appointment. You know where to go, don't you?'

'Of course,' said Grace. 'Margaret thinks I'm senile but I'm not too bad, you know. How'd you like to drive my car?'

'I'd love that, Grace,' Nicole replied.

Twenty minutes later Nicole grinned to herself as she manoeuvred the black, fifteen year old Mercedes through the city traffic. She kept looking the wrong way and pulled left instead of right but did well and found somewhere to park at the hospital. Grace was with the doctor for almost an hour before a nurse brought her back and reported that the test results would be out in a few days.

'My old heart,' Grace explained. 'It decides to give a little flutter at times.'

Nicole smiled, thanked the nurse and escorted Grace out. 'John and Grandma will wonder where we are,' she said as she helped Grace into the Mercedes.

'Oh, Cindy will realise,' Grace said. 'Can we do one more thing before we go home, Nicole?' The voice sounded determined.

'Just name it,' Nicole replied.

'I want to visit my lawyer,' Grace said. 'There's a parking building near her office. If you turn right... '

*

Jessica Meikie, the lawyer knew Grace well and fitted her in between two appointments so there was only a small wait. 'I'll be okay, Dear,' Grace told Nicole and left her in the reception area.

'It's good to see you, Grace,' the lawyer said after the elderly woman was seated in a comfortable armchair, 'Who was your young companion today?'

Jessica specialised in elderly female clients and always began on a personal touch.

'That's my grandniece,' Grace stated proudly. 'She's the reason I'm here.'

'I see,' Jessica said and took Grace's file from the receptionist who had just brought it in.

'You know my daughter, Margaret?' Grace said and leaned forward in her chair.

'I certainly do,' Jessica frowned. Her dealings with that woman had not been friendly when the family had attempted to get power of attorney over Grace and stated she couldn't manage her own affairs. Between Cindy and herself, the move had been squashed and court action avoided. There was though, still considerable animosity in the family about it. Jessica sighed. This happened in families, especially when money was involved.

'Nicole stuck up to her,' Grace said. 'Threw her out of the house.'

Jessica said, 'Good on her. Margaret can be a forceful person.'

'Yes,' Grace said and her eyes met those of her lawyer, 'I want to change my will and I want it so tight that the Queen of England won't be able to revoke it.'

The lawyer smiled and took out a small recorder. 'Fire away. Tell me what you want and I'll get it put into legal language for you to read and sign.'

Grace spoke in a quiet determined voice for ten minutes before she smiled at the lawyer. 'I want the changes made as soon as possible, please, Jessica. I haven't even told Cindy but my poor old heart is not the best. My doctor told me today that unless I had immediate surgery, he could not guarantee I'd see the new year.'

'And when will you go in for it?' the lawyer asked.

'I'm not,' Grace whispered.

She stood up, shook hands and walked out to meet a young woman waiting in the reception area.

'We can go home now, Nicole,' she said. 'Everything is fixed.' She turned to Jessica. 'This is Nicole, my grandniece. I may have mentioned her in your office.'

The lawyer shook hands with the attractive woman and noticed the compassion in the blue eyes. They almost reflected the sparkle in her elderly client's own eyes.

'I'm pleased to meet you, Nicole,' she said.

*

CHAPTER TWENTY-SEVEN

To Nicole, Betty Hadfield looked a younger version of her mother. The dumpy dark haired woman barely acknowledged her presence in the courtroom as the lawyer for the plaintiff rambled on. For hours, it seemed he quoted from previous court cases and examined the wording of in Dorothy O'Donnell's will. Finally, the man sat down with a satisfied smirk on his face, spoke a few words to his client and the judge glanced at the young local lawyer Cindy had insisted Nicole employ.

'Would you care to make your opening statement for the defendant, Mr. Puleosi?' he asked

Anton Puleosi, stood, coughed and seemed quite overwhelmed by the expensive big city lawyer he was opposing. He spoke briefly then added, 'My Client, Miss Nicole Tucker would like to make an opening statement, Your Honour.'

The judge glanced at Anton and nodded. 'This is an unusual request at this stage of the hearing but I will allow it.' He switched his eyes across the defendant's bench. 'You may speak to the court, Miss Tucker.'

Nicole, dressed in a navy blue suit with her blonde hair allowed to hang free over her shoulders, stood and waited a few seconds for the faint bustle in the room to settle before starting to speak.

'I am not an American, Your Honour, but come from a small country of New Zealand, smaller in population than Washington State. In New Zealand, as in United States, we believe in justice. However, I am not prepared to employ expensive lawyers to defend this case.' She glanced across at the plaintiff's bench.

She paused as a murmur went through the room. 'My grandmother's, grandmother's mother, and I hope I have that right...' She smiled. '... wrote an unusual will a hundred and seven years ago. I believe her desires were quite explicit and do not believe the use of one different word in the legacy, changes the meaning of the content. If my distant cousin filing this complaint feels the desires of our common ancestor should be bypassed for monetary gains she has my sympathy.

Today as in 1899, I believe people are more important than cold hard cash. My defence will, through the diary of Amanda Hutchkins, Dorothy O'Donnell's daughter, show, I hope, the innermost feelings of these ladies, both liberals and born before their time.' She looked intently at the judge. 'They believed in freedom, Your Honour. Amanda gave up her family, her religion and her country for this freedom and, unbeknown to herself in 1898, her mother supported her. That will explain why the legacy was written as it was in the first place. By sheer luck, I guess, I happen to be the descendant Dorothy O'Donnell wanted to inherit, after five generations through the female line.

Dorothy O'Donnell died tragically in a 1900 railway avalanche and never knew her granddaughter was born in the same accident. If that young baby had not survived I, or Miss Hadfield for that matter, would not be standing here today.' She paused and glanced around the room before continuing. 'It would be a pity if one of Dorothy O'Donnell's last wishes was overturned by a court in the very state where she was a founding member and the freedom she strived for was lost.' Nicole caught the judge's eye. 'Thank you Your Honour,' she concluded.

There was complete silence in the room as the small crowd reflected on her statement. Nicole tucked her skirt under and sat down next to the lawyer.

'Thank you, Miss Tucker,' the judge replied. 'Like yourself, I hope justice will prevail.' He glanced at the plaintiffs. 'You may begin Miss Hadfield's case now....'

*

The trial had entered its third day when the plaintiff's main lawyer stood and waited for the courtroom to become silent. Nicole sat, as usual on the defendant's side and prepared herself for a gruelling time. It was their turn today. She had Amanda's diary with her and the pages they were about to read to the court already photocopied, ready distribute to the jury and plaintiff's lawyers.

It appeared as if the trial was in a balance with the final result hinged, as Nicole had expected, on what word in the two versions of the will, the jury believed reflected Dorothy O'Donnell's real wishes. Their defence was to make the thoughts of her descendants come alive so the declaration of a female line through every generation was, indeed, the wish of their common ancestor. She waited and glanced at the opposing lawyer who had been given permission to make a statement.

'Your Honour,' he stated. 'My client advised me this morning she wishes to withdraw all claims against the estate of the late Mrs. Dorothy O'Donnell.' He stopped as a rumble of hushed voices filled the room.

Nicole glanced at her own lawyer and the perplexed smile on his face.

'Is your lawyer's offer of withdrawal approved by yourself, Miss Hadfield?' the judge asked.

'Yes, Your Honour,' Betty Hadfield whispered with her eyes downcast.

'So be it,' the judge stated. 'The case is dismissed.'

He stood and left the room.

'What now?' asked Nicole.

'Go home,' Anton replied and smiled. 'The judge called me into his chambers just a few minutes ago and advised me this was about to happen. We can now make a claim for all expenses to be paid by the plaintiff.'

'But why after two days of intense arguing, have they withdrawn without us even presenting our case?' Nicole asked.

Anton rubbed his chin. 'All I know, is that Betty Hadfield rushed back to Vancouver last night and didn't return until an hour before the court was set to reconvene this morning. I was contacted half an hour ago and told of her decision to withdraw from the case.'

*

The mystery of the abrupt ending to the court case pricked Nicole's curiosity. She was sure her distant cousin was not motivated by a sudden pang of conscience. John, being very pragmatic, told her it didn't matter and to forget about everything and, surprisingly, Cindy was undemonstrative about the whole affair. In fact, Nicole noticed her grandmother seemed very withdrawn and was even worse after hearing that Nicole and John were to returning home in the first week of November.

'Of course you must go home,' she retorted when Nicole discussed it. 'Your busy season at the motel is coming up, the court case is over so there is no reason to stay.'

'Why don't you come back with us?' John asked. 'You're welcome, you know.'

Cindy gave a sad grin. 'No, I can't leave Grace. You know what her relatives are like. The others aren't much better than Margaret and Betty.' She shrugged. 'Why Timmy and Grace had such obnoxious children, I don't know. Perhaps they were spoiled as children.' She sighed. 'The kettle calling the pot black, isn't it?'

'What do you mean?' asked Nicole.

'Your mother and I had a similar problem, Sweetheart. The trouble was when they were all children; Grandma Amanda handed her companies over to Timmy and myself. We had money and were determined our children would not have the troubles we had in life. And they didn't. The last forty years have been prosperous but our children thought that was the norm and wanted something more. Your mother became a bit of a rebel and left for New Zealand and you saw how Margaret and Betty ended up.'

Nicole grimaced. 'Yes, I see. Perhaps I'd be the same if Mum had stayed in Vancouver.'

'Perhaps but I doubt it, somehow. Look, I'll try to get back out to New Zealand next year for a while. Okay?'

Nicole knew now what was wrong. Her grandmother was torn between wanting to remain with Grace and being with them.

'Okay,' she answered but she felt somehow empty inside. She glanced at John; he tucked his arms around her and squeezed her close in empathy with her feelings.

*

For some strange reason, Grace seemed totally immune to everything around. She barely mentioned the court case and chatted away with everyone. Even her frail body seemed, somehow to be more responsive. Her shaking hands still shook but only an insignificant amount, she began to eat more and became almost as energetic as Cindy. It was as if some gigantic burden had been lifted from her shoulders and life became fun again.

Margaret Hadfield returned one day but treated Nicole, Cindy and her mother with a new respect, indeed the new attitude was almost embarrassing as she gushed and fussed over her mother and even offered to take her home in the weekends.

But Cindy was not impressed. 'It has something to do with that court case,' she remarked. 'I'm not sure what it is but I'll find out.'

Nicole grinned at John. They had no doubt at all her grandmother would sort the family out.

*

It was still dark the next morning when Cindy tapped on Nicole and John's bedroom door. 'Sweetheart are you awake?' she whispered.

Nicole hadn't been but jerked up when she saw her grandmother standing in the shaft of light caused by the landing light. Cindy's concerned expression told her something was amiss.

'What is it Grandma?' she asked and rubbed sleep from her eyes.

'It's Grace,' Cindy said.

Nicole grabbed a dressing gown and slipped it on as she followed Cindy downstairs where nearly every light was turned on.

'She's gone, Sweetheart,' Cindy said in a sad voice.

Nicole glanced in the bedroom and realised what Cindy meant. Grace lay on her bed under the blankets with a tiny smile on her face but the eyes were glazed and lifeless.

'Oh, my God!' Nicole gasped. Her heart lurched at the sight.

'She was happy and just died a few moments ago,' Cindy said as she fought back tears. 'I heard her call my name and came in. She looked at me and said, "Thank you, Cindy. Ever since we met, you've looked after me. Tell Nicole I love her." Then she just sort of faded away.'

'Oh Grandma!' Nicole sobbed with tears rolling down her cheeks. She rushed from the room to where John was waiting to provide the comfort she needed.

*

Grace's funeral was large and impersonal with dozens of acquaintances attending as a mark of respect for the businesswoman she had been. The day passed by and it wasn't until the next morning when the relations, including Cindy, but not Nicole or any of the grandchildren, gathered in the lawyer's chambers.

Jessica Meikie took out copies of the document and distributed them to Cindy and Grace's children. 'Grace's will was changed only last month...' she started and began to explain the latest alterations.

'Betty's inheritance was subject to her withdrawing from the court case protesting the legacy of Dorothy O'Donnell. This she did so remains eligible for a tenth share of Grace's estate?'

Cindy watched Margaret's face turn ashen. 'That's why Betty withdrew in that court case,' she hissed. 'The little slut. She knew all along.'

'It was Grace's wish that Betty be told the contents of this legacy.'

Jessica's response was neutral but Cindy caught her eye for a second and an understanding flashed between the pair.

The lawyer continued talking. 'She was sworn to secrecy so cannot be blamed. Given the circumstances, she would have been foolish to continue the court case and possibly lose everything.' She coughed and turned to the amendment in the will. 'As you can read ladies and gentlemen, Grace changed the section of the will relating to the fifth share bequeathed to each of her children. Margaret has been left ten thousand dollars. The remainder of Margaret's original fifth of the estate has been split with one tenth going to Grace's granddaughter Betty and one tenth to her grandniece, Miss Nicole Tucker.' She glanced up as Margaret's face turned purple.

'I shall appeal...' Margaret leaned forward with her arms straight on the lawyer's desk and her voice now a high-pitched screech. Only on one of her brothers' insistence, did she sit again. She turned to Cindy. 'It's your fault. You set it up with that slut of a granddaughter of yours. I know...' she hissed.

'Cindy knew nothing about it, nor did Nicole,' Jessica responded in a quiet voice that cut through the room far more successfully than

Margaret Hadfield's outburst. 'In fact, I asked Grace if she wanted to reconsider before she signed the final document.'

'Oh I'm sure you did,' Margaret muttered sarcastically and stared tight-lipped at the wall.

'Grace thought this might happen,' Jessica continued. 'She made a statement in front of a high court judge, Judge Michael Steedman actually, that the will was changed entirely as the result of her own decision without any outside persuasion or influence by a third party. Also, two doctors signed an affidavit stating she was of sound mind when she made the decision to change her will.'

She reached into her drawer and extracted the high court document and medical certificates, which she slid across the desk. Margaret face contorted into that of utter contempt before she caught her brothers' and sister's gaze and it changed to humiliation. She staggered to her feet like a drunk, grabbed her handbag and stalked out.

'The bitch,' she hissed as she disappeared out the door.

Her three brothers and younger sister glanced at each other with differing emotions but did not seem over worried. After all, they were not directly affected. Cindy, though, could not stop the small grin from appearing on her face. So that was why Grace was so contented over the last few days! It all fitted together like a gigantic jigsaw puzzle.

*

'Well, Sweetheart, you're a millionaire now,' Cindy told Nicole that evening. 'Your part is worth about one and a quarter million Canadian dollars.

Nicole just looked flabbergasted. 'But I don't want it,' she replied.

'I guess not,' Cindy answered. 'You gave Grace her pride back, Sweetheart. It was what she wanted. I found out from Jessica that Grace knew she only had weeks to live and refused a heart operation that may have prolonged her life for a while. She never told me but I knew something was about to happen. That bribe to Betty to withdraw from the trial was great stuff.' She stopped and took her granddaughter's two hands. 'So accept it graciously Sweetheart. It was what Grace wanted.'

'I agree,' John added. 'You really impressed her Dear.'

Nicole turned to John. 'You watch it,' she said in a stern voice.

'Why, what have I done?' John screwed his eyebrows up.

'Well, you could be just chasing me for my money, now couldn't you?' she said.

'Women!' John exclaimed. He reached up from the chair he was in and grabbed Nicole, purposely flipped her over his knee and inflicted a sharp slap on her bottom.

'John, stop it!' Nicole screamed as she lay, kicking without making a slightest impression on her partner's hold. 'It's not fair males are so strong,' she muttered when he finally allowed her to stand.

Cindy discretely withdrew from the room and thought about when she used to be so much in love and acted in the same way. 'You'd be proud of your granddaughter, Arthur,' she whispered as she gazed out the window at the streetlights shining in the evening mist

*

The next morning while Nicole was having a bath, Cindy sat at the breakfast table slowly stirring her coffee while her mind was deep in thought.

'Out with it, Cindy,' John whispered.

Cindy glanced up. 'Will you be scrupulously honest with me, John?' she asked.

'I will.'

'With Grace gone, there's nobody here for me now. If I returned with Nicole and yourself and built or bought a little cottage near the motel, would I be a burden to you both? Nicole, I know, would not let on even if I was, so I want you to tell me how you both really feel. Is this old lady an interfering old pain in the butt?'

John looked at Cindy and grinned. 'You know, we were talking about this very thing at some ungodly hour in the middle of the night.'

Cindy grimaced and John noticed, for perhaps the first time that her hands shook and eyes were downcast.

'I have no close relations, you know,' he continued, 'and you probably realise what a cot case I was when I first met you and Nicole. I love your granddaughter, Cindy, more than anything in this world but without you, I doubt if I'd have even got to know her so I owe you, don't I?'

'That's the trouble,' Cindy whispered. 'I don't want to be around just because you feel duty bound to...'

John interrupted. 'I'll tell you what happened last night,' he said. 'We agreed that if you refused to come back home with us next week, we'd sell the motel and stay here. I'm sure with Nicole's ancestry, it wouldn't be hard for us both to get permanent residency.'

'Is that true, or are you only being kind?'

'What do you think?' John answered and bent over to kiss Cindy gently on the lips.

Cindy stood and peered into his eyes. 'Well, if I going home with you next week, I'd better get onto my lawyer, the bank manager, the travel agent ... My God there's so much to do.' She grinned at John. 'I bet you didn't tell me everything that happened last night, either.'

She smiled when he had the grace to turn red.

*

When the Air New Zealand Boeing 777 landed at Auckland International Airport and the three weary travellers walked out of customs, the first thing they noticed were Gina and Whetu standing there with wide grins on their faces.

'I thought you might be with them,' Gina said as she hugged Cindy. 'The motel seemed so empty without you all. You too, John,' she added. 'Whetu can hardly keep up with all the odd jobs.'

'Yeah,' her husband grumbled. 'Nagging bloody women everywhere and now I've got two more.'

'But love every minute of it,' Nicole said and placed a big sloppy kiss on his cheek. 'God, it'll be good to get back to the motel and into the bush.'

'Oh yes,' Whetu added as he picked up a couple of their bags. 'They've started the new track down to that little waterfall and rapids where you had your fall. It should be finished by Christmas.'

Nicole's eyes sparkled as she nodded and linked arms with John and Cindy. It was good to be home.

*

CHAPTER TWENTY-EIGHT

'Karl Golding,' the American lawyer introduced himself and shook hands with Nicole, John and Cindy. 'Thank you for being prepared to meet me at such short notice. I was in New Zealand on other business and thought it was a good chance to get the legacy cleared up.'

'You're not from *"Smith, Smith and Golding* the Bellingham Lawyers from 1900 are you?' Cindy asked.

Karl smiled. 'James Golding was my ancestor, yes. The company, though, has changed many times over the last century and is now part of *LawNorwest*, the firm I represent. Our head office is in Seattle where I am based.'

The clean-cut and immaculately dressed man in his thirties accepted a cup of coffee and sat in the motel living room. He extracted a pile of documents from his brief case.

'You already know you are the sole beneficiary of Mrs. Dorothy O'Donnell's legacy, Ms. Tucker,' he began. 'I'll skip down to the main contents that were unsealed on your permission after this year began three months back.'

It was now April 2007 and a very successful summer season at the motel was almost over. 'I am afraid the shares your ancestor bought are mainly valueless. She bought into railroad and steamship companies that, at that time were the top companies,' the lawyer began.

He glanced at Nicole who nodded.

'Dorothy left a small amount of cash in a savings account. Now let me see,' Karl turned over a page. 'Yes here it is. $547 was in the account. This was quite a considerable amount in those days. This however, is more or less wiped out by a section of Amanda's last will that requests that this money be used to repay an outstanding debt to her father's estate. This matures this year, as well,' Karl said and flicked through the pages of a second document. 'This was to purchase a printing press and cost $415.19 plus interest at the rate of two percent over the last hundred and seven years. The original account paid one and seven eighths percent interest so the two transactions more or less wipe each other out.' He glanced up. 'Amanda's request is not binding and can be refused if you wish.'

'I remember reading about that in Amanda's diary,' Nicole replied. 'No let it stand.' She stood and reached for the lawyer's empty coffee mug. 'More coffee, Mr. Golding?'

'Yes, please,' the man replied, gave a slight smile and turned the document's page. 'This next section is of more interest to you, I'm sure,' he continued. 'Dorothy O'Donnell left you twenty thousand acres of recently milled land in northern Washington State.'

'Recently milled?' John asked.

'Yes.' The lawyer said. 'They cut out all the mature lumber and left the small trees to grow. I drove out to inspect it only last week. The land recently milled in 1900 is now covered in century old fir trees worth a considerable amount of money.'

'So my grandmother had her head screwed on?' Cindy chortled.

'It appears so,' Karl smiled. 'There has already been a milling rights offer made to the estate from a Japanese lumber company' He slid a piece of paper over to Nicole and her eyebrows shot up at the amount offered.

'Look!' she whispered to John.

'I believe we can get more if we tender it out,' Karl added. 'They're trying to rip you off.'

'Are they indeed?' Nicole responded, 'and is your firm prepared to work on our behalf in this matter, Mr. Golding.'

'Certainly,' he replied. 'After all, we've been associated with your family over a hundred years. I'm sure we can continue to provide an excellent service.'

So the legacy was revealed and Nicole was pleased at the outcome. With the inheritance from Grace's estate she was already a rich woman so this was really like froth on a mug of beer.

'Oh, one other thing, I almost forgot,' Karl said as he was about to leave in his rental car. 'He leaned his satchel on the car seat and took out an old, very thick book. It had a faded black cover and was held shut by a tarnished brass clamp.

'A family bible?' Nicole asked.

'No,' said Karl. 'This was included in the sealed package we opened. It's a diary.'

Nicole reached out with a slight tremble of her hands. She clipped back the clamp and opened the musty cover.

'My God!' she gasped and read the faded writing.

'What is it Sweetheart?' Cindy asked.

'Dorothy O'Donnell's diary,' Nicole replied in astonishment as she turned the first brittle page and ran a finger over text. 'This one starts in 1869. Listen to this.' She began to read the first entry.

Wednesday, June 12 in the Year of Our Lord, 1869.

Mamma has given me this diary for my sixteenth birthday and told me it is my access to immortality and I believe it will be so. My life is at a crossroads, for next week Father, Mamma, my two sisters, three brothers and myself shall be leaving Ireland forever. Father has purchased, sight unseen, a patch of land in Oregon. Mamma said he is crazy but we all know what Father is like, don't we?"...

Nicole shut the old cover and glanced up.

'Well, lots more reading there, Nicole,' John said and placed his arms around her.

She leaned back, rubbed her head into his chin and waved as the American lawyer drove out the gate. Up the valley, dark rain clouds were hovering around the hill tops while close by, the builders had arrived, late as usual to continue on the villa Cindy was having built across the lawn from *The Blue Mist Motel* administration block.

'I hope they replaced those ghastly red bricks with the white ones I wanted,' Cindy retorted and went to speak to the foreman.

John turned to Nicole. 'Fancy a walk up the new track to your waterfall?' he asked.

'Yes,' whispered Nicole. 'I'll just put this diary inside.'

'Another forty years of ancestors,' he said.

'Yeah but right now I'm more interested to see if they completed that viewing platform where I slipped and broke my leg. Come on,' she said. 'I'll get our jackets.'

She broke into a run with John dashing after her. She was too fast for her partner. With her hair streaming out and bare feet pounding onto the concrete path she reached the building three metres in front of him, rushed inside and stood puffing for breath as he bounded in, grabbed her waist and turned her into his arms. She gazed lovingly into his eyes and cuddled close while he stroked her hair.

*

EPILOGUE

The new blocks of the *Blue Mist Motor Lodge* filled the space where the driveway curved back towards the old administration block but, on Nicole's insistence, only a few trees had been removed. The 'L' shaped accommodation block, built with white bricks to match Cindy's villa, was two storied with every unit opening either to a balcony or private courtyard. Adjacent to this block was a new administration block, conference room and restaurant all opening out to a landscaped swimming pool that could be made completely indoors by the use of a sliding roof panels.

After the traditional blessing and Maori welcome led by members of Gina and Whetu's marae and songs from the local high school cultural group the guests moved into the trapezium shaped foyer leading to the conference room. Chairs had been arranged in a semicircle so guests faced a large curtain four metres high and six wide that filled the area between two double doors leading into the main auditorium.

The mayor of Waikato District stood behind a rostrum and introduced the Minister of Tourism, a deep-set man in his fifties who had the task of dedicating the new works and officially opening the buildings.

'…and finally Ladies and Gentlemen,' the minister concluded after making the usual speech politicians reel off with abundance every day, 'I have one final task to perform before officially declaring the *Blue Mist Motor Lodge* open for business. That is to unveil a fine painting which Mr. John Leamy, partner in this joint venture, has spent many long hours producing. I think it is fitting that John and Nicole help me unveil this work.'

John, looking awkward in his dinner suit, stood and glanced down at his partner sitting so calm and self-assured beside him in a long evening gown worn off the shoulders, a modest diamond necklace with matching earrings and elbow length white gloves.

'Come on Dear,' he said in a modest but proud voice and grabbed her hand.

Nicole smiled and followed him up to the front. They both shook hands with the minister and smiled politely to acknowledge the round of applause.

There was a golden tassel hanging down on each side of the curtain. While the minister took one, John insisted Nicole take the other. The two pulled together and the curtain rolled silently back to reveal the scene behind.

The painting depicted three young women and a girl. One woman dressed in 1900 style long white dress and holding a parasol, stood full sized to the left of the scene. The centre depicted a nurse in World War One style nurse's uniform with her arm around a girl around ten dressed in 1930s vintage attire. To the right, a tumbling stream and waterfall surrounded by native trees and ferns included a massive flat rock with a young woman, dressed in tank top and shorts, leaning back on her hands so her blonde hair touched the rock behind. Her head gazed, as if deep in thought over the waterfall. If one studied the background carefully, it could be seen that the foliage varied from left to right with Canadian firs behind the lady with the parasol, English oaks as a background to the nurse and finally a typical New Zealand bush scene.

The audience gasped at the colour and quality of the painting before switching their eyes to Nicole. She was obviously the subject of the modern woman in the scene. A murmur of approval rippled through the crowd, followed by spontaneous applause.

'It's a perfect likeness,' gasped a woman in the front row and began clapping wildly. Soon the whole foyer echoed her as everyone rose to their feet to continue the applause.

'This painting, showing young women separated by a century of time reflects the theme of this convention centre,' continued the minister, 'I am privileged to declare *the Blue Mist Motor Lodge and Conference Centre* now officially open.'

*

When the applause finally died down and everyone was seated, a middle aged woman whispered to the elderly lady beside her. 'I know the young lady on the rock is Ms. Tucker but can I be bold enough to ask if you are the subject of other lady portrayed so delicately in that 1900s gown, Mrs. Jervis. She looks so much like you, it is uncanny.'

'No, I am the little girl and the nurse is my mother.' Cindy smiled at her companion. 'That is my grandmother portrayed there. Her name was Amanda.'

Meanwhile, the minister pulled a third little tassel. Beneath the painting, a small thirty centimetre high curtain slid across to reveal the name of the block in golden Olde English Style lettering.

"Fir, Oak and Fern Conference Centre" was written on the plaque.

The End

Visit the author's web site at http://www.hifiction.com